Jean-Luc Na....,

Published:

Jeremy Ahearne, *Michel de Certeau*
Peter Burke, *The French Historical Revolution: The Annales School 1929–1989*
Michael Caesar, *Umberto Eco*
M.J. Cain, *Fodor*
Filipe Carreira da Silva, *G.H. Mead*
Rosemary Cowan, *Cornel West*
George Crowder, *Isaiah Berlin*
Gareth Dale, *Karl Polanyi*
Oliver Davis, *Rancière*
Maximilian de Gaynesford, *John McDowell*
Reidar Andreas Due, *Deleuze*
Eric Dunning, *Norbert Elias*
Matthew Elton, *Daniel Dennett*
Chris Fleming, *Rene Girard*
Edward Fullbrook and Kate Fullbrook, *Simone de Beauvoir*
Andrew Gamble, *Hayek*
Neil Gascoigne, *Richard Rorty*
Nigel Gibson, *Fanon*
Graeme Gilloch, *Walter Benjamin*
Karen Green, *Dummett*
Espen Hammer, *Stanley Cavell*
Christina Howells, *Derrida*
Fred Inglis, *Clifford Geertz*
Simon Jarvis, *Adorno*
Sarah Kay, *Žižek*
S.K. Keltner, *Kristeva*
Valerie Kennedy, *Edward Said*
Chandran Kukathas and Philip Pettit, *Rawls*
Moya Lloyd, *Judith Butler*
James McGilvray, *Chomsky*
Lois McNay, *Foucault*
Dermot Moran, *Edmund Husserl*
Michael Moriarty, *Roland Barthes*
Stephen Morton, *Gayatri Spivak*
Harold W. Noonan, *Frege*
James O'Shea, *Wilfrid Sellars*
William Outhwaite, *Habermas, 2nd Edition*
Kari Palonen, *Quentin Skinner*
Herman Paul, *Hayden White*
Ed Pluth, *Badiou*
John Preston, *Feyerabend*
Chris Rojek, *Stuart Hall*
William Scheuerman, *Morgenthau*
Severin Schroeder, *Wittgenstein*
Susan Sellers, *Hélène Cixous*
Wes Sharrock and Rupert Read, *Kuhn*
David Silverman, *Harvey Sacks*
Dennis Smith, *Zygmunt Bauman*
James Smith, *Terry Eagleton*
Nicholas H. Smith, *Charles Taylor*
Felix Stalder, *Manuel Castells*
Geoffrey Stokes, *Popper*
Georgia Warnke, *Gadamer*
James Williams, *Lyotard*
Jonathan Wolff, *Robert Nozick*

Jean-Luc Nancy

Marie-Eve Morin

polity

First published in 2012 by Polity Press

Polity Press
65 Bridge Street
Cambridge CB2 1UR, UK

Polity Press
350 Main Street
Malden, MA 02148, USA

ISBN-13: 978-0-7456-5240-5
ISBN-13: 978-0-7456-5241-2(pb)

A catalogue record for this book is available from the British Library.

Typeset in 10.5 on 12 pt Palatino
by Toppan Best-set Premedia Limited
Printed and bound in Great Britain by the MPG Books Group

The publisher has used its best endeavours to ensure that the URLs for external websites referred to in this book are correct and active at the time of going to press. However, the publisher has no responsibility for the websites and can make no guarantee that a site will remain live or that the content is or will remain appropriate.

For further information on Polity, visit our website: www.politybooks.com

To C. S.

Contents

Acknowledgments

First, I would like to thank Emma Hutchinson and her assistant David Winters at Polity Press for their support and, most importantly, for their trust. I am much indebted to several family members and friends who have encouraged and supported me throughout the year and a half I was involved in carrying out this project. I am thankful to Chris John Mueller and Pieter Meurs, whose initial encouragements were essential in persuading me to take on this project. I am also grateful to the chair of my department, Bruce Hunter, who, at a time when my workload was especially heavy, encouraged me to teach a seminar on Nancy's work. It was in this seminar, held at the University of Alberta during the fall of 2010, that I gained the assurance that not only could I explain Nancy's philosophy to students, but also that they would find Nancy's thought as powerful and transformative as I do. This experience would not have been successful were it not for the exceptional students who took part in that seminar, in particular Daniel Erin, Michael Peterson, Miranda Pilipchuk, Yasemin Sari, Evan Stait, and Hande Tuna. A great many of the explanations in this book were developed in response to their questions. Steven Sych was the first student to read Nancy's work with me. His relentless questioning and his unwillingness to accept anything short of a clear explanation supported by a clear argument challenged me to think more thoroughly about many issues. I also wish to acknowledge the financial support of the Faculty of Arts at the University of Alberta and the research assistants who worked for me by helping me survey the secondary literature on Nancy, commenting on earlier drafts, and proofreading the final version of the manuscript: again, Miranda, Yasemin, Evan, and Hande, as well as Jessica Moore, Kristin Rodier, and Rachel Loewen Walker. Finally, I am indebted to Jean-Luc Nancy himself for the way in which he has interrupted, interpellated, and inspired my own thinking for so many years. This book is an attempt to share that gift with others.

.

List of Abbreviations

A	*L'Adoration. Déconstruction du christianisme, 2*
BP	*Birth to Presence*
BSP	*Being Singular Plural*
BWBT	"The Being-With of Being-There"
C	*Corpus*
CC	"The Confronted Community"
Com	"The Compearance"
CW	*The Creation of the World* or *Globalization*
D	*Dis-Enclosure: The Deconstruction of Christianity*
EF	*The Experience of Freedom*
ES	*Ego Sum*
FT	*A Finite Thinking*
GI	*The Ground of the Image*
GT	*The Gravity of Thought*
IC	*The Inoperative Community*
IRS	*L'"il y a" du rapport sexuel*
M	*The Muses*
NM	"The Nazi Myth" (with Philippe Lacoue-Labarthe)
NMT	*Noli Me Tangere: On the Raising of the Body*
OBC	"Of Being-in-Common"
OT	Jacques Derrida, *On Touching – Jean-Luc Nancy*
RP	*Retreating the Political* (with Philippe Lacoue-Labarthe)
SV	"Sharing Voices"
SW	*The Sense of the World*
TD	*The Truth of Democracy*

Introduction

Approaching Nancy's corpus

Jean-Luc Nancy's work spans almost four decades and includes more than fifty authored or co-authored books in French and hundreds of contributions to journals, collected works, and art catalogues. But the breadth of Nancy's work is not best captured by the sheer number of books. Nancy has written on major thinkers in the history of European philosophy, such as Descartes, Kant, Schelling, Hegel, Nietzsche, Marx, and Heidegger, and has engaged contemporary French thinkers such as Lacan, Bataille, Blanchot, and Derrida. He has written on topics as diverse as psychoanalysis, globalization, hermeneutics, community, Nazism, resurrection, Christian painting, German Romanticism, techno music, modern dance, and film. The diversity of Nancy's corpus obviously represents a challenge for any book that pretends to provide a comprehensive introduction to his thinking. Nancy's work is certainly not systematic and neither are the majority of his books. Some of them are collections of essays loosely connected around one theme (e.g. *A Finite Thinking*, or *Dis-Enclosure*) and even the more straightforward books rarely present a linear development from axioms to arguments to conclusions but rather a plurality of sections that circle around a central idea (emblematic here is *Being Singular Plural*) and are often supplemented by fragmentary notes (for example, the fragments at the end of *The Experience of Freedom* or of *L'Adoration*). Yet, if Nancy's work challenges the modern idea of systematicity, it nevertheless adheres to a certain conceptual regularity in which all the pieces and fragments cohere or at least "play" together. What holds the fragments of Nancy's thinking together is the thought of the "singular plural" or of "being-with." This central ontological insight informs Nancy's way of approaching the world, the body, politics, art, etc. In a sense, the "singular plural" furnishes the "axiom" of Nancy's thought, from which everything else follows. Yet it is also this "axiom" that undermines all attempts at finding any "wholeness" or "systematicity" in his thought. Cursorily said, the singular plural means that there are singularities whose identity or selfhood can only be found in their "relation" to other singularities: what exists finds itself in being exposed to or being in contact with other singularities in such a way that nothing exists or makes sense on its own. Nancy's description of the "play" between what exists can be applied here to his own work:

> By itself, articulation is only a juncture, or more exactly the play of the juncture: what takes place where different pieces touch each other without fusing together, where they slide, pivot, or tumble over one another, one at the limit of the other without the mutual *play* – which always remains, at the same time, a play *between* them – ever forming into the substance or the higher power of a Whole. Here, the *totality is itself the play* of the articulations. (IC 76)

Nancy's ideas make sense but this sense arises more from moving across sentences than from the internal signification of any one particular sentence taken in isolation.

This gives us some hints as to how (or as to how not) to approach Nancy's work. As Deleuze said in his lectures on Kant, "the important thing is not above all to understand, but to take on the rhythm of a given man, a given writer, a given philosopher." Of course, we want to *understand* what Nancy is saying but the point is that this can be better done by following the rhythm of the text rather than by getting bogged down by every detail and trying to fully grasp each line before moving to the next. Nancy's writing is not linear. His sentences and propositions do not build on each other according to some sort of geometric or syllogistic method. Rather, his books or his essays tend to be circular, each section presenting the "same" point, reiterated each time from a different perspective, with a different emphasis or in relation to a different thinker, in such a way that each section sheds a bit more light on the issue in question. We can take *Being Singular Plural*, which in a sense could be seen as Nancy's treatise on ontology, as emblematic in this regard. In the "Preface" to the book, Nancy explicitly says that the traditional form of the treatise is not adequate for an ontology of the singular plural. He warns the reader:

> The first and principal essay of this book, which gives it its title [i.e. the twelve sections making up "Of Being Singular Plural"], was not composed in an altogether sequential manner, but rather in a discontinuous way, taking up over and over again the same few themes. To a certain extent, then, the sections can be read in any order. And there are repetitions here and there. (BSP xv, trans. mod.)

The reader should therefore not expect to understand each individual step as she or he proceeds through Nancy's text. It feels rather as if one were jumping midway into a circle: the beginning only becomes intelligible at the end or indeed after many times around. This is also a consequence of the "singular plural": there is no single, independent truth that could be immediately identified as the beginning. But my wager is that if one keeps reading, Nancy's thought has the power to transform our way of seeing the world and our understanding of what it means to exist with others in the world.

A second comment concerns not so much the structure of Nancy's book as his writing style. Nancy can be situated in the tradition of deconstruction that started with Derrida. Yet, for those who have read Derrida, Nancy's style is bound to strike them as diametrically opposed to that of deconstruction. Derrida's style has been qualified as abstruse and opaque, not only because of his play on French words or expressions, but also because it is essentially aporetic. Derrida shies away from any straightforward, affirmative use of "traditional" concepts. Instead, we find repeated uses of undecidable phrases such as "X without X" ("community without community" – a phrase borrowed from Blanchot) or "X, if there is such a thing" (justice, if there is such a thing), and definitions of central concepts often take the contradictory form of a "both x and not x" or "neither x nor not x."[1] This, of course, can be explained by what Derrida is trying to do. Essentially, we can say that deconstruction is a way of dealing with conceptual systems, a way of engaging with systems by pushing them to their limits so as to reveal their internal tensions, their blind spots. Deconstruction begins from the observation that our conceptual thinking, our conceptual grid, as well as the very intelligibility of our language and our values,

constitute a "total" system, that is, a system that also determines
its own "outside": the other, the irrational, the ineffable, etc. One
cannot undermine the primacy of the system by simply positioning
oneself outside it, for example, by valorizing madness to undermine reason. No rational person listens to what the self-declared
madman has to say. The problem therefore becomes: how is one to
work against the system from within without being rejected as a
madman or being forced to conform ultimately to the internal constraints of the system? This position on the margin of the system
(both inside and outside, neither inside nor outside) allows one to
point to instabilities and show how our conceptual systems (and
this is true of specific philosophical systems, like Husserlian phenomenology for instance, but also of our basic western ethical
categories) are always already deconstructing themselves. What
Derrida tries to show in his texts is that our conceptual oppositions
are not as rigorous as the system leads us to believe. To do this, he
takes a specific opposition that is central to a specific "system" (e.g.
the opposition between indication and expression in Husserl or,
more generally, the opposition between philosophy and literature
or between law and justice) and asks: what exactly is the deciding
factor that allows us to discriminate between the two terms? In
other words, he tries to find the exact point where something flips
from being x to being y. This tipping point or systematic hinge is
the indispensable mechanism of all systems of conceptual opposition. As the decisive criterion that separates one from the other, this
zero point of difference makes the system possible, yet it itself
remains outside of the system as an undecidability or blind spot
that the system cannot account for by means of the discriminating
mechanism at its disposal. Since all of the concepts at hand necessarily cover over that blind spot, one can only point to it by means
of the operational concepts themselves if we put them into play in
a non-binary or aporetic way, erasing them as they are being
inscribed.[2]

If the deconstructive power of Derrida's text explains his aporetic writing style, then this observation only renders Nancy's
writing style more puzzling. If we agree that Nancy is not only
reaffirming traditional concepts such as freedom, sense, being, and
finitude but showing their traditional limits and putting them into
play in a new way, we must then ask how he can still (at least on
the surface of it) affirm the words instead of pushing them toward
their erasure. In *Rogues*, Derrida describes Nancy's use of tradi-

tional philosophical concepts, in this case the concept of *freedom*, in the following way:

> Never one to shrink from a challenge, he dares to call into question this entire political ontology of freedom, while still retaining the word ... and devoting an entire book to it. I, who have always lacked his temerity, have been led by the same deconstructive questioning of the political ontology of freedom to treat this word with some caution, to use it guardedly, indeed sparingly, in a reserved, parsimonious, and circumspect manner.[3]

Nancy's style is much more straightforward and affirmative, in an almost unsettling way. The most frequent logical structure of his sentences is an affirmation of the form "X is Y," or even more emphatically: "X is nothing but Y." These sentences seem to provide straightforward definitions. Yet, this affirmative tone only amplifies the enigmatic character of the concepts whose equivalence is asserted. Badiou, in a short essay titled *"L'offrande réservée"* ("The Reserved Offering"),[4] provides a careful analysis of Nancy's style. He shows, by juxtaposing a series of affirmations taken from Nancy's corpus, how concepts are brought into movement: finitude is sense, finitude is existence, sense is existence, thought is finite, freedom is the finitude of sense, etc. Trying to define finitude, we are going around in a circle. Yet, in these equivalences that form a circle, the master concepts are displaced so that none retain their traditional meaning. Again, the signification of any of these words captured in a definition of the type "X is Y" is not going to be very helpful in thinking through what finitude or freedom are. In doing this, we are merely going to be deferred from one concept to the next. Yet, in following this movement, the concepts start to *make* sense. It is worth emphasizing from the start that Nancy's concept of sense, as opposed to signification, is not only central to the content of his philosophy but also to the form of his writing. Essentially, signification concerns the relation of a signifier to its signified (of a word to its content, concept, or meaning); it concerns the relation of reference: a word signifies or means if it exemplifies this relation. Sense, on the other hand, concerns what happens *between* things, ideas, bodies, and people in their encounters, their movements of attraction/repulsion. We could say that the relation of signification is vertical while that of sense is horizontal. It is important to keep this in mind while reading Nancy's texts.

Nancy's intellectual development

Since Nancy's work will be presented in the body of the present study in a "systematic" or non-chronological order, the space of this introduction will be used to present Nancy's intellectual biography and situate his different works.[5] Jean-Luc Nancy was born in 1940 in Caudéan near Bordeaux in France. He obtained his *licence de philosophie* (the equivalent of the BA) from the Sorbonne in Paris in 1962, his *diplôme d'études supérieures de philosophie* (the equivalent of the Master's) in 1963 and his *agrégation* in 1964 (a competitive examination that allows one to teach in the public education system in France). During his time at the Sorbonne, Nancy worked closely with Canguilhem, a philosopher and historian of science, well known for his criticism both of vitalism (and the politics that arises out of it) and of the reductionist approach to life that tries to understand organisms on the basis of the mechanical model. Instead, Canguilhem argued that the organism is something whose sum is greater than its parts. (Nancy completed a certificate in General Biology alongside his philosophy degree.) Because of his interest in theology and religion, Nancy also worked with Ricoeur during the years when Derrida was his assistant. Ricoeur would supervise Nancy's Master's thesis on Hegel's philosophy of religion. Nancy also associated with a group of Christian students around Jesuit philosopher Georges Morel, who met regularly to discuss Hegel. After his *agrégation*, Nancy taught in Colmar before becoming an assistant at the Institut de philosophie in Strasbourg in 1968. He obtained his doctorate in 1973, again under the supervision of Ricoeur, with a thesis on Kant's analogical discourse. Soon after, he became *maître de conférences* at the Université des sciences humaines in Strasbourg, where he would spend his entire academic career until his retirement in 2004. Unlike most other French philosophers, Nancy was never much of a part of the centralized Parisian academy, but always remained on the margins, never integrating into one of the Parisian elite schools such as the École nationale supérieure (where Badiou finished his academic career) or the famous Sorbonne. He also did not participate directly in the event of May 1968,[6] which shook the academic milieu in Paris and led to the creation of the Centre universitaire de Vincennes, later known as the Université de Paris VIII, an experimental left-wing university, where philosophers such as Deleuze, Lyotard, Rancière, and Badiou taught. This marginal position gave him more freedom from academic disputes but also less direct impact.

Nancy published his first books during the 1970s. Two of them came out of his intense study of Hegel and Kant, *La remarque spéculative* (1973; translated as *The Speculative Remark*) and *Le discours de la syncope. I. Logodaedalus* (1975; translated as *Discourse of the Syncope: Logodaedalus*), while two others arose from his collaboration and are co-written with his long-term friend and colleague Philippe Lacoue-Labarthe: a book on Lacan, *Le titre de la lettre* (1973; translated as *The Title of the Letter*) and one on early German Romanticism, *L'absolu littéraire* (1978; translated as *The Literary Absolute*). In 1979, Nancy then published a book on Descartes, *Ego Sum*, which is only partially translated into English.[7] While these early works will not be directly discussed in the following chapters (except for the book on Descartes), it is important at least to underline their lines of questioning and their central problematic since these still inform some of the central motives of Nancy's mature work. In a word, the underlying question is that of the Subject. Nancy's postmetaphysical or deconstructive questioning of the Subject is well anchored in the intellectual context of the 1960s, which saw the rise of the thinkers, especially Foucault and Derrida, who would later become identified as post-structuralists.

The roots of this intellectual context, and hence of Nancy's first question, can be found in the event or rupture of western philosophical thinking marked by the proper names Nietzsche, Heidegger, and Freud. In Nietzsche's affirmation that God is dead and in his critique of Platonic and Christian metaphysics, in Heidegger's diagnosis of metaphysics as ontotheology and his attempt at overcoming metaphysics through poetic thinking and in Freud's psychoanalysis as the overthrow of the illusion of the subject as a pure, transparent self-consciousness, what is accomplished (or at least attempted) is a destruction or decentering of the foundation of thought. This rupture forms the background of Derrida's famous 1966 address, "Structure, Sign, and Play in the Human Sciences," in which he explicitly points to an "event" in the history of the concept of "structure."[8] This event occurs, according to Derrida, when the structurality of the structure comes into view or is reflected upon, in such a way that it becomes apparent that a structure necessarily implies a center around which it organizes itself (an empty center that can be filled with any transcendental signified: God, Reason, Man, etc.). This broad understanding of structure is not limited to what structuralist thinkers explicitly have in view but encompasses, for Derrida, all of western philosophy. The center of the structure, if it is to serve as its anchor, can only be an autonomous self-grounding presence, but this self-grounding presence will be unmasked as an illusion. That same year, Foucault closes his *Les mots et les choses* by announcing the crumbling of our arrangements of knowledge, for which the figure of "man" is central. This event would cause "man," a recent invention, to disappear "like a face drawn in the sand at the edge of the sea."[9] During the same years, Derrida, through a careful deconstruction of Husserlian phenomenology, shows how the pure self-consciousness that phenomenology relies on is always already pried open by an essential difference, or absence.

What Nancy and Lacoue-Labarthe propose in their first co-authored book, *The Title of the Letter*, is a deconstructive reading of Lacan's essay, "The Agency of the letter in the Unconscious or Reason since Freud." In other words, they show how the Lacanian subversion of metaphysical discourse fails, in that the text reinscribes the values it seeks to subvert, that is, the certainty of subjectivity, the ideal of scientificity and systematicity, and the positing of a ground. Lacanian psychoanalysis consists in a radicalization of Freud through a diversion of Saussure's theory of the sign. Lacan rejects Freud's theory of the unconscious and any depth psychology and insists rather on the fact that the subject is an effect of the signifier. According to the Saussurian theory of the sign, signifiers are what they are only through their differential relations with other signifiers, yet the relation that each signifier entertains with a signified, even though it is arbitrary, remains essential. This essential relation is the relation of signification. In the Lacanian appropriation of Saussure, the signifier is barred from its essential relation with the signified, so that the production of signification becomes problematic. The signifier slides in a field of signifiers without being able to cross the bar and reach the signified. Along with the signifying sign (that is, the relation of a signifier to its signified), the subject for whom the sign is supposed to traditionally function is destroyed. What we are left with is an "operativity" without referent and without subject, an indefinite deferral of meaning whose logic is that of lack and desire.[10]

Lacanian psychoanalysis as the science of the signifier is still, as Nancy and Lacoue-Labarthe show, a centered, organized system. Despite the diversion of transcendent meaning, meaning is maintained as the origin and the end of the movement of signifiers. As such, meaning cannot find its origin in a traditional subject since the subject instituted in and by the signifier can never identify itself as the subject of enunciation.[11] Despite this decentering, splitting or hollowing of the subject, a center rebuilds itself, which allows psychoanalytic discourse to "master" the logic of desire. This center is "the bar" that bars the signifier from the signified and launches the movement of desire; the bar is the halting point of the system. In this sense, Lacanian psychoanalysis is a traditional philosophical discourse whose center or organizing principle is a gap or a hole (whose name will be the Other as empty place). Nancy and Lacoue-Labarthe will call it a negative theology.[12]

Nancy's first book on Kant, *Logodaedalus*, also starts with a consideration of how a discourse that seeks to contest metaphysics is, by necessity, recuperated within metaphysics. And this also holds, as Nancy witnessed in the middle of the 1970s, for the deconstructive texts: the "signs" that arise out of deconstructive readings and point to the excess or overflow of the system are, as soon as they are fashionable, "converted into values and thereby erected into truths and hypostasized into substances."[13] Yet, if attempts at overcoming or exceeding metaphysics are always taken back into the orbit of metaphysical discourse, on the other hand, metaphysical discourses never succeed in establishing the foundation they desire.

Nancy's reading of Kant is interested in the failure of foundation. At the same time, the consequences of that failure allow us to think ground otherwise (rather than merely leading us to conclude that there is not ground). Kant's goal in the *Critique of Pure Reason* is to secure a ground or foundation for knowledge; in this sense, the critical project is foundationalist at the same time as it assigns limits to what can be grounded as knowledge. Nancy's anti-foudationalist reading of Kant focuses on the critical discourse as such, that is, on the manner in which it is presented or exposed. Nancy shows that the Kantian system articulates itself around a syncope. Indeed, the cornerstone of the foundation of knowledge, the condition of possibility of knowledge of object, is neither receptive sensibility nor spontaneous understanding, but the schematism that articulates one with the other. Yet, even though Kant recognizes the necessity of a presentation (a *Darstellung*) of schematism, this "secret art residing in the depth of the human soul,"[14] he shies away from it in the *Critique* itself. For Nancy, unlike for Heidegger, this is not just a failure on the part of Kant but the point at which the question of the relation and separation between philosophy and literature is posed within critical philosophy. The necessity of the schema points to the necessity of an articulation of the intelligible with the sensible and to the problem of presentation.

Unlike in mathematical presentation, where the presentation is adequate or equivalent to what is presented, philosophical presentation demands a literary device. Yet, as philosophical presentation, it strives for pure presentation and differentiates itself from literature. What interests Nancy is the way in which this failed presentation is inscribed in philosophical discourse in the form of a rupture, or better, a syncope of discourse. The figure of the syncope allows Nancy to think the "absence" of ground without turning this "lack" itself into a foundation. Foundation is thought as the interruption of identity and substance, as the syncope of the Same. The presentation of the foundation skips a beat so that, in the very enunciation of the philosophical discourse ("this is the ground"), the ground is withdrawn.

Nancy's early reading of Hegel in *The Speculative Remark* is also focused on the mode of "presentation" of Hegel's philosophical system. For Nancy, Hegel is not so much the thinker of totality and of the system but rather the thinker of movement, of identity as activity. In *The Speculative Remark*, Nancy does not look at the structure of the "Hegelian system" as such but starts from a remark of Hegel on the speculative proposition and the necessity of a "plastic" reading. In this remark, Hegel points to the threat that hangs over the speculative proposition: the difference between the subject and the predicate of a proposition threatens the unity of the concept. The reader's repetition of the speculative proposition should restore the "plasticity" of the author's exposition. Plastic reading is the ideal philosophical attitude since it frees the life of the concept from any congealed thought structure, especially from the artificial fixity of the grammatical proposition. In this sense, reading is neither passive nor active, but it is an act of both receptivity and formation. The question is: what is the status of the Hegelian text where we read the *Aufhebung*, if the very act of reading it (philosophically) requires that we already have understood its propositions? Again, Nancy pays more attention to the way in which the system is presented than to its argumentative legitimacy. This emphasis allows him to "read" *Aufhebung* not merely as the governing method of a totalizing and self-enclosed thought, but as a movement that dissolves and restores, fractures and reweaves.

Three years after the publication of *Logodaedalus*, Nancy returns, with Lacoue-Labarthe, to the problem of *Darstellung* or presentation in Kant. *The Literary Absolute* articulates the philosophical grounding of the romantic conception of literature in the Kantian philosophical problem of the sensible rendering of a concept. As we already saw, Kant addresses the problem of the sensibilization of the concepts of the understanding by appealing, in *The Critique of Pure Reason*, to a "third term," the transcendental schema. Schemata translate the categories of the understanding into forms that are intuitable by sensation. Yet, schematism is less adequate when it comes to presenting the Ideas of reason. This schematism, which Kant calls in the *Critique of Judgment* "symbolic," cannot provide an adequate presentation of the Idea but only an approximation of it.

In *The Literary Absolute*, Nancy and Lacoue-Labarthe analyze the specific manner in which the early romantics (especially the Schlegel brothers) responded to this crisis of *Darstellung* by looking to art, and more specifically to literature, for an adequate presentation and unmediated experience of the absolute. Literature becomes the realm in which the Idea attains to presentation and is hence superior to it. Literature is also the realm of the auto-production of the subject. If Kantian philosophy deprives the subject of its being-subject, of its presentation of itself to itself by emptying it out of all substance, literature will take the role of the subject's auto-production in and as work of art.

What we find in this early work of Nancy (and Lacoue-Labarthe) that is of particular interest in the context of Nancy's later development is the beginning of a thinking of fragmentary totality. For the romantics, literature not only presents the absolute but is itself absolute, the perfect closure of literature unto itself in the demand for the perfect and complete Work. The motif of the Work serves to arrest the proliferation of works and the necessarily fragmented presentation of the total Work:

> The fragmentary work is neither directly nor absolutely the Work. But its own individuality must be grasped, nonetheless, with respect to its relation to the work. . . . Each fragment stands for itself and for that from which it is detached. Totality is the fragment itself in its completed individuality. It is thus identically the plural totality of fragments, which does not make up a whole (in, say, a mathematical mode) but replicates the whole, the fragmentary itself, in each fragment.[15]

Romantic fragmentation is not the dissemination of the work into a play that exceeds totalization. The "absence of the Work" is equivocal, that is, it points in two directions at the same time. What interests Nancy and Lacoue-Labarthe in the romantics' conception

of the work is the point at which the self-identity of the subject
breaks down and the circle (of self-presentation, self-formation, the
closure of the absolute) does not close itself. Such a break points in
the direction of another thinking of the fragmentary totality, one in
which fragments are not thought of as fractured pieces of the Work
and the interstices between works do not sketch the contours of the
Whole. Here, the fragment is, as they say borrowing from Blanchot,
"unworked" (*désœuvré*) or interrupted. A decade later, Nancy will
reemploy this Blanchotian concept to think community as fragmentary totality without Work. Nancy and Lacoue-Labarthe conclude
that "what we have perhaps begun to learn from this is that the
future is fragmentary – and that a work-*project* has no place in it"[16]
so that what we are left with is "a sort of bottomless generosity of
the book and of books, a debauchery of works that would no longer
make a work, a proliferation that could no longer be numbered,"[17]
a dissemination as Derrida would say. This motif of the books
without Work will make itself heard again almost three decades
later in *Sur le commerce des pensées* (2008; translated as *On the Commerce of Thinking*).

Ego Sum is a continuation of both the problem of philosophical
discourse in *Logodaedalus* and of subjectivity in *The Title of the Letter*.
We saw that for Nancy and Lacoue-Labarthe the alterity (as hole
or gap) that alienates the subject and constitutes it as the subject of
desire is mastered by psychoanalytic discourse. In the 1970s, Nancy
diagnoses a return or a persistence of the metaphysical subject
conceived as substance in structuralism, psychoanalysis, and
anthropology. The decentering and overturning of the subject-of-
representation (in favor of a subject-unconscious, a subject-history,
a subject-text, a subject-language, a subject-machine, a subject-
desire), the declaration of the subject as an effect (of the text, of
desire, etc.) happens in relation to a ground, substance, or instance.
For Nancy, "it is clear that such an instance . . . forms the substance
of a new 'cogito': it is to it that all the representations of subjects
relate and it is it that identifies them" (ES 30). The question is: *who*
speaks of the subject as lack? Or *who* identifies the subject as lacking,
absent, split? This instance (e.g. psychoanalytic discourse) is itself
thought as subject or substance, as ground, and hence gives rise to
a theoretical discourse of mastery.

In *Ego Sum*, as in his reading of Kant and of Hegel, Nancy is
interested in the discourse of the cogito. If the cogito (in its substan-
tive form) represents the self-positing and self-grounding of the
subject of thought as thinking substance, then this subject must

enunciate and recount itself in a discourse. Descartes's *Discourse on Method* is the narrative of the self-grounding of thought. What Descartes's story brings to light is the noncoincidence of the instance that pictures the self-grounding cogito or recounts the enunciation "I think, I am," with the subject that is represented in this fable or story. What is presented or figured as substance is produced in the enunciation of the cogito as the residue of a convulsion or syncopation of the enunciating. Behind the ego as metaphysical subject, there subsists an enunciating "subject" that is not a metaphysical substance but a "dire-je-suis," a "saying-I-am," a gaping mouth. We will come back to this point when we discuss the relation between body and soul in chapter 5.

Nancy's early work circles around two related problems. First, there is the question of the presentation or exposition of philosophy or systematic thought that leads to the question of literature. The second is that of the subject of philosophy not only in the sense of the theme or content of philosophy but of what can ground the system of philosophy. In the late 1980s, Nancy will be guest editor of a special issue of *Topoi* on the question (chosen by Nancy), "Who comes after the subject?" In the introduction, Nancy explains what is at stake for him in a deconstruction of the subject as, to cite Hegel's definition, "that which is capable of maintaining within itself its own contradiction," that is, as that which "reappropriates to itself, in advance and absolutely, the exteriority and strangeness of its predicates." What is needed is not a return to the subject (in the face of its so-called liquidation) but a "move forward toward someone – *some one* – else in its place," "a punctuality, a singularity or a hereness (*haecceitas*) as place of emission, reception, or transition" that (or who) would not be a subject, but an "existent," a presence-to that is not to itself (or whose selfhood consists in this to or toward).[18] Understanding this "one" is the goal of chapter 1.

In the early 1980s, Nancy and Lacoue-Labarthe founded, at Derrida's suggestion, the Centre de recherches philosophiques sur le politique ("The Center for Philosophical Research on the Political"). Two collected volumes came out of the Center's work, *Le retrait de politique* and *Rejouer le politique* (the most important papers are gathered in English in *Retreating the Political*). The aim of the Center was to open a space to advance the question of the political dimension and implications of deconstruction that arose during the Cérisy-Colloquium on Derrida's work, *Les fins de l'homme* ("The Ends of Man"), organized by Nancy and Lacoue-Labarthe. Nancy and Lacoue-Labarthe sought to articulate a properly philosophical questioning of the political. Diagnosing what they see as the total domination of politics and economy in our contemporary world and insisting on the necessity of opening a space in retreat from this domination, from which vantage point the essence of the political could be questioned again, Nancy and Lacoue-Labarthe extend the definition of totalitarianism to include not only Marxism but also liberal democracies. The refusal of many participants to adopt a sweeping Heideggerian form of historical thinking, their uneasiness with Nancy and Lacoue-Labarthe's broad understanding of totalitarianism, as well as the problems arising from the separation between politics on one side and the political on the other, led to the closure of the Center only four years after its opening. We will discuss Nancy's work at the Center in more detail in chapter 4 of this book, when we take up the theme of politics. This early attack on liberal democracies as a form of totalitarianism will also provide a link to Nancy's most recent recasting of the concept of democracy in *La vérité de la démocratie* (2008; translated as *The Truth of Democracy*).

Some of the questions raised at the Center regarding the necessity of moving away from a metaphysical and transcendent grounding of politics, as well as the question of finitude and of relationality, lead directly into Nancy's work on community in *La communauté désœuvrée* (1986; translated as *The Inoperative Community*), which contains, aside from the essay of the same name, related essays on myth and its interruption, communism, literature, and being-in-common. Again, Nancy starts with the diagnosis of our contemporary situation (liberal capitalism, individualism) that leads to a recasting of "community" in ontological or existential terms. But if Nancy seems to affirm a sense of community against liberal capitalism (against mere juxtaposition and interchangeability), his major concern is to push the concept of community away from its traditional figure as pure immanence or fusion. What needs to be thought is a community that does not effect itself as work. To express this, Nancy borrows Blanchot's word *désœuvrement* (a word he had already used, as mentioned above, in *The Literary Absolute*). The question of community relates directly to the questioning of myth as the self-grounding of a community and of the interruption of myth as the opening of a being-in-common. The interruption of myth, the moment where myth is seen as fiction is also the beginning of literature, of literary communism. These problematics will occupy us in chapter 3.

Nancy's work of community might be the most well-known part of his work, not least because of the "critical" dialogue it prompted between Nancy and Blanchot. Nancy retraces the context of this dialogue in *La communauté affrontée* ("The Confronted Community"), a preface to the re-edition of the Italian translation of Blanchot's *La communauté inavouable* by S.E. Editions in 2001. In 1983, Blanchot published *La communauté inavouable* (translated as *The Unavowable Community*) in direct response to a short version of Nancy's "Inoperative Community" published in the journal *Aléa* the same year. The longer version that was published in the book in 1986, as well as the additional essays, can be read as Nancy's clarification of his position and a response to Blanchot's criticism. The disagreement essentially revolves around Bataille's Hegelianism (whether Bataille thinks community in terms of project, work, and synthesis or in terms of absence), Nancy's rejection of Hegelian terminology in favor of Heideggerian "being-with," Blanchot's insistence on the primacy of the relation to the Other (*à la* Levinas) and Nancy's clear rejection of Levinasian ethics and his affirmation of the primacy of ontology. This debate informs Nancy's reception in the English-speaking world, most notably by Simon Critchley (who definitely falls on the Levinasian side against Nancy). I will also take up these discussions in chapter 3.

From the late 1980s onward, Nancy will move more and more away from the word "community" and prefer words like "sharing" (*partage*), "being-with," "being-in-common," "ex-position," or "compearance." There are two reasons for this shift. The first one is related to the ambivalence or equivocation that plagues this renewed insistence on the word "community." This is nowhere as clear as in the history of the reception of *The Inoperative Community* in Germany. As Nancy mentions in "The Confronted Community," the book was smeared as national socialist when it was translated in 1988 but vaunted as communist in 1999 (CC 27). The second one is a move away from the social problematic toward a more thoroughly "worldly" one. It is not just our social being-together that must be rethought in terms of exposition and coexistence, but the world as such, with all the "beings" that inhabit it (C 37).

In 1987, Nancy obtained his *doctorat d'état* with a dissertation on freedom, *L'expérience de la liberté*, published a year later in English as *The Experience of Freedom*. His supervisor was Gérard Granel (a very influential but somewhat unclassifiable philosopher, who incorporated aspects of phenomenology, Heidegger, Marx, and Catholicism) and members of the jury included Jean-François

Lyotard and Jacques Derrida. In *The Experience of Freedom*, through readings of Kant and Heidegger but also Schelling and Sartre, Nancy tries to think freedom not as the property of an infinite self-positing subject but as the ontological or existential "ground" of finite, that is, shared existence, as the *surgissement* or coming-to-presence of finite beings. Coexistence in the world is the condition of free existence and not a limitation imposed on it. This book marks the beginning of a very prolific decade or so for Nancy, during which he will publish his major "ontological" works that will form the basis of our first chapter: *Une pensée finie* (1990; partially translated as *A Finite Thinking*), *Le sens du monde* (1993; translated as *The Sense of the World*), *Être singulier pluriel* (1996; translated as *Being Singular Plural*), *La pensée dérobée* (2001) and *La création du monde ou la mondialisation* (2002; translated as *The Creation of the World or Globalization*). These works, and especially *Being Singular Plural*, can be read as a critical engagement with Heidegger's fundamental ontology and an attempt at rewriting ontology starting from the essentiality of *Mitsein* or being-with. At the same time, Nancy completely transforms the Heideggerian concepts of world and sense and also opposes Heidegger's understanding of the end of philosophy and his attempt at overcoming metaphysics (defined as the thinking of Being in terms of the totality of what is and its ground in a being, e.g. God) through a poetic thinking. Nancy's thinking of the world aims at a non-foundational, hence non-metaphysical, thinking of Being that would still be philosophical through and through. It is therefore not a question of "overcoming" but of thinking at the limit of the closure of metaphysics. Nancy already expressed his distance from Heidegger on this point in *L'oubli de la philosophie* (1986; translated as "The Forgetting of Philosophy" in *The Gravity of Thought*).

During this time of high productivity, Nancy suffered major health problems, which forced him to interrupt his teaching career and step back from the academic scene. He received a heart transplant at the beginning of the 1990s and his recovery was slowed by a long-term fight with cancer. Nancy's small text *L'intrus* (2000; translated as "The Intruder" in *Corpus*) offers a touching personal account of his "illness" intertwined with a philosophical reflection on selfhood, on the integrity of the body, and on the originary exposition to what is foreign and heterogeneous. What Nancy works out in his major philosophical works of the 1990s, that is, the always renewed exposition of singularities to exteriority, is also for him a lived experience. As he writes in "The Intruder": "The empty identity of the 'I' can no longer rely on its simple adequation (in its 'I = I') as enunciated: 'I suffer' implicates two I's, strangers to one another (but touching each other)" (C 169). This book also served as the inspiration for Claire Denis's 2004 film by the same name.

At the end of the 1990s, Nancy begins to point to the necessity of pursuing a "deconstruction of Christianity."[19] The first programmatic text describing this enterprise appeared in 1998 and forms the starting point of the two volumes of *Déconstruction du christianisme: La Déclosion* (2005; translated as *Dis-Enclosure*) and *L'Adoration* (2010; translation forthcoming as *Adoration*). In the programmatic essays of these volumes, Nancy describes the deconstruction of monotheism as a loosening of the conceptual grid that conjoins monotheism, atheism, and nihilism in order to free up a thinking of the divine as the opening of the world. In this sense, the deconstruction of monotheism makes possible an ontology of the singular plural of the world in that it makes it possible to interpret the *nihil* of the creation *ex nihilo* as an opening instead of as the firm sediment of a ground. Thinking the world without appealing to a transcendent principle or falling into meaningless immanence, thinking the world as the infinite opening of (itself) unto (itself) requires a deconstructive engagement with the "text" of Christianity. I will discuss this deconstructive project in its relation to Heideggerian *Destruktion* and Derridean deconstruction in chapter 2.

Even though Nancy's explicit program for a deconstruction of Christianity has only been developed in the last couple of years, we do find an engagement with Christian motives earlier on. For example, *Corpus* (1992; translated as *Corpus*) starts with the phrase *Hoc est enim corpus meum* ("This is my body"), while two short texts, *Visitation: de la peinture chrétienne* (2001; translated as "Visitation: Of Christian Painting" in *The Ground of the Image*) and *Noli me tangere* (2002; translated under the same title) explore central scenes of the Christian tradition. The interest in Christian motives links up directly with Nancy's work on body. It might seem strange to look to the Christian tradition for a thinking of the body, since it can be thought to focus entirely on the sinfulness of the flesh. Yet, in the same way that, in his reading of Descartes, Nancy directs his interest to the way in which the "union" between body and soul puts the strict Cartesian dualism into question, in his reading of the Christian understanding of the body, he shows that Christianity is not so much a religion of the dualism between a fallen, sinful body and a pure soul but one of fusion or consubstantiality between body and soul. I will discuss this deconstruction of the Cartesian-Christian body in our chapter 2 and relate it to some of Nancy's reflections on materiality and thought in chapter 5.

Parallel to the work on the deconstruction of Christianity, more and more of Nancy's energy has been devoted to collaborative projects with various artists. Though even a rough periodization is somewhat problematic, we can separate Nancy's interest in "art" into four categories. The first two kinds of engagement were more prominent in the 1990s and early 2000s, while the last two are becoming more and more frequent. First, we find discussions of the essence of art in the light of Hegel's and Heidegger's aesthetics and of the so-called death of art in the "postmodern world." Thought according to the ontology of the singular plural, the question becomes not so much "What is Art?" but "Why are there several arts?" *Les muses* (1994; translated as *The Muses*) is the major text of this period. Alongside, we also find discussions of specific art forms: poetry (*Résistance de la poésie*, 1996; partially translated in *Multiple Arts*); painting (*Au fond des images*, 2003; translated as *The Ground of the Image*); the portrait (*Le regard du portrait*, 2000; translated in *Multiple Arts*), music (*À l'écoute*, 2002; translated as *Listening*), and drawing (*Le plaisir au dessin*, 2007). Every time, Nancy is concerned to overcome the thinking of art (of the truth or essence of art) in terms of representation or imitation. The goal of Art, of each art form and each artwork, is not so much to represent something (and hence it is not its role to signify anything) but to expose the event or passage of a singular material existence. Thirdly, we also find works on various artists, such as contemporary painters On Kawara (*Technique du présent*, 1997; translated in *Multiple Arts*) and Jean-Michel Atlan (*Atlan: Les détrempes*, 2010) and on Iranian filmmaker Abbas Kiarostami (*L'évidence du film/The Evidence of Film*, 2001). But the most interesting works are those written in direct collaboration with artists to accompany a dance performance, an installation, a series of lithographies, etc. Here Nancy can hardly be said to take the work of art as an object of study in order to produce an interpretation of it. Much more, we witness a thinking-in-common: the thinker thinks with the artist who creates with the thinker so that the thought is a response to the work as much as the work a response to thought. In this vein, Nancy has collaborated with choreographer Mathilde Monnier and their exchanges on dance have given rise to two co-authored books (*Dehors la danse*, 2001; *Allitérations*, 2005). Monnier and Nancy presented, in 2002, a "danced conference," also called *Allitérations*, where Nancy read a text to accompany the movement of bodies (or where the movements of the bodies accompanied Nancy's thoughts). Nancy has also written texts to accompany the photographs of Jacques Damez, Anne-Lise Broyer, and Anne Immelé, installations of Claudio Parmiggiani, and several works of visual artist François Martin. He wrote a poetic commentary of Virginie Lalucq's work *Fortino Sámano* and poems to accompany the lithographs of Bernard Moninot. He adapted Goethe's *Faust, Part One* for an installation by the artist Claudio Parmiggiani. We will discuss Nancy's understanding of art in relation to sense and the senses and of thought in relation to works of art in chapter 5.

Our presentation of Nancy's intellectual development would not be complete if it didn't address the close and complex relation it entertains with Derrida. Even though Nancy was never directly a student of Derrida, the influence of Derrida's questioning on Nancy's intellectual trajectory cannot be underestimated. In a sense, Derrida is the most important force in the milieu in which Nancy, the student and the young academic, comes to his own questioning. Nancy has often mentioned that he felt, when he encountered Derrida's thinking, that something new and very contemporary was born in philosophy. In an interview, he explains:

> It was through [Derrida] that I came to understand the irreversible turn in thinking taken by Heidegger, Wittgenstein, Bataille and Freud. This was because he opened up the space inscribed at the heart of *présence à soi*, being-present-at-oneself. He called it *différance* . . . : the irreducible separation from the present, from presence, the self – the "subject." . . . While Sartre – to take a hallmark of my student years – only offered the dialectic of the in-itself and the for-itself, and while just behind him was the ever functioning Hegelian machine that remained unaffected by the Nietzschean imprecations (for me, as far as I saw, like for many others at that time), there suddenly opened up, not a reductive or conciliatory force, but an instability that brought forward a new opportunity – and a risk! – for the adventure of thinking, that is, the opportunity of not closing off the circle of meaning, of not satisfying any end, be it a supreme or final end. . . . Philosophy suddenly found, for me, the actuality of its movement, of its act and gesture.[20]

Yet it is too simple to describe the relation between Derrida and Nancy as that between the rising star of contemporary French philosophy and a pupil, follower, or subordinate. In our discussion of Nancy's style, we already saw that Nancy, even though he might share the same deconstructive questioning of modern subjectivity and of foundational thought as Derrida, cannot be seen as a mere follower of "deconstruction." In a recent interview, Nancy describes Derrida's influence in the following terms:

> What I owe Derrida is a certain movement of thought, which is not a teaching or a doctrine any more than it is a corpus of terms, philosophemes, and citations. And that's where friendship plays a role in thought, the place of a friendship of thought; one stimulates, provokes, and nourishes the other, sometimes aggravates or irritates the other, but one also knows that each must do his own work, have his own style.[21]

Nancy indeed has his "own" style, but he also pursued his "own" work despite the sustained dialogue with Derrida up until the latter's death in 2004. There remain irresolvable points of contention between the two thinkers which will be outlined throughout the book. Schematically, we can say that these differences hinge on the way of thinking the interruption or spacing of self-presence, whether in terms of radical Otherness or in terms of touch. While Derrida is not uncritical of Levinas, he acknowledges the legitimacy of the Levinasian critique of metaphysics in general and of phenomenology in particular[22] and moves increasingly toward Levinas's preoccupations with the singularity, absolute secrecy and untouchability of the Other, the asymmetricality and verticality of the relation to the Other, and the absolute responsibility the Other imposes on me. Nancy, on the other hand, finds any thinking of the radical alterity of the Other, be it that of Levinas or Derrida, problematic with regard to community. In Derrida's thinking of the plurality of singularity, expressed in the aporetic formulation *tout autre est tout autre* (every other is absolutely other like every other), some absolute singularities must always be sacrificed in favor of some others. For this reason, Nancy moves away from the terminology of the "Other" (we already saw his criticism of that category in his reading of Lacan in 1973) in order to think being-with or being-together as contiguity, contact, and touch. For Derrida, the danger of this haptic ontology is that it fails to radically interrupt the circle of self-presence (and hence itself becomes a new avatar of the metaphysics of presence). The awareness of this danger orients Derrida's engagement with traditional metaphysical and phenomenological treatments of touching in general, and with Nancy's work in particular, in *Le Toucher – Jean-Luc Nancy* (2000;

translated as *On Touching – Jean-Luc Nancy*).[23] Derrida also expresses reservation toward the role that the concepts of "generosity" and "fraternity" play in Nancy's thought, both of which Derrida sees as pointing to some origin and some genealogy, despite the fact that, for Nancy, generosity is ontological and fraternity without father. Derrida's reservations, latent in *On Touching*, are taken up more explicitly in the first essay of *Rogues*. These points of contention will be discussed in more detail throughout the book.

This brief discussion of Nancy's intellectual trajectory is developed in the five chapters that follow. The first chapter presents all of the main concepts of Nancy's work, looking particularly at his ontology: what it means to be or to exist. In a sense, the four chapters that follow the first draw on the consequences of Nancy's thinking of being or existence to develop a thinking of monotheism, God, and the Christian mysteries (chapter 2), a thinking of community (chapter 3), a thinking of politics, sovereignty and democracy (chapter 4) and a thinking of matter, body and art (chapter 5). Chapters 2–5, therefore, rely on the key concepts laid out in the first chapter. Although each of these later chapters is more or less independent and can be read in any order, the reader may find it helpful to return, time and again, to the definitions and explanations, presented in the first chapter. Through this reading and returning, one will see how Nancy's work, although largely disconnected and divergent, circulates and builds upon the central questions of being, being-with, and community.

1

Ontology

The goal of this first chapter will be to present Nancy's ontology, his determination of what it means to be or to exist. In the course of this presentation, all of the central concepts of Nancy's thinking will be introduced: singularity and plurality, existence, world, creation, finitude, freedom, sharing, and sense. These concepts will then return in one form or another in the subsequent chapters. It is impossible to discuss Nancy's ontology without first addressing its Heideggerian filiation and situating it with regards to Heidegger's project. However, the proximity between the two thinkers should not be overestimated. Nancy often expresses himself in Heideggerian terminology but it would be a mistake to think that he simply repeats or prolongs Heidegger's project.

Nancy's "rewriting" of Heidegger's *Being and Time*

In *Being and Time*, Heidegger seeks to "reawaken" the question of the meaning of Being. In other words, he looks for the "horizon" in terms of which Being itself can be understood. This, of course, will be Time. But in order to pose such an audacious question, Heidegger sees it as a necessity to first put ontology (the study of beings qua beings or of beings insofar as they "are") on a secure footing. In order to grasp Being, or what "to be" means for any entity whatsoever, Heidegger first turns to the entity that in its relation to the various kinds of entities (including itself) understands these entities, understands *how* they are, *what* they are, and *that* they are. Heidegger calls this exceptional entity, which each one of us is, Dasein. This purely ontological name (in contrast to names such as "rational animal," "human being," etc., which in each case assign a predetermined essence to the human being) points to the fact that the "essence" of Dasein is to be found in its understanding of Being.[1] According to its inner constitution, it is simply impossible for Dasein not to relate "meaningfully" to entities. Heidegger will give this unavoidable pre-understanding of meaning the name *Existenz*. That Dasein exists means that while it is and each time that it is, its being is a task or an issue for it, something it has to take over in one way or another. It follows from this that the characteristics of Dasein are not *properties* (like blueness is a property or attribute of the table) but *ways* of Being. Doing science, being sad or opening doors are all existentiell (concrete, ontic, context-dependent) ways of Being for Dasein made possible by the structural constitution of existence (the *existentialia*). In seeking to clarify these existentialia, Heidegger hopes to be able to clarify not only the understanding of Being that lies in existence but its "meaning," the "horizon" upon which this understanding itself can be understood. If Being "is" the givenness or intelligibility of entities (to Dasein), then Heidegger's question concerns the givenness of this intelligibility itself, the givenness of givenness if one will.

Heidegger begins *Being and Time* by outlining the basic constitution of existence as Being-in-the-World. In order to avoid distorting this phenomenon, Heidegger insists that we take our starting point in the average, everyday Being-in-the-World; we should avoid superimposing any "theoretical" framework we might have acquired through our philosophical or scientific study. Heidegger's ontology is phenomenological in that it studies what appears (in this case, my everyday comportments in the world) as it appears, outside of any preconceived theoretical framework. It is important that the theoretical conceptuality we use to describe the phenomenon arises out of the phenomenon itself. Yet Heidegger's phenomenology is not one where I can will myself out of all my presuppositions and prejudices. Hence, Heidegger's ontology is also hermeneutical in at least two ways. First, the phenomenon we are trying to place into view is Being. I always already "understand" the entity I deal with in its Being (I relate to the hammer as a tool for hammering, as too heavy for me, as a weapon, or in scientific study as a bunch of atoms, or a piece of lead with a given density, or as something whose use and origin I don't understand, etc.). What remains at the forefront in all these ways of comporting is the hammer itself and this "presence" of the hammer obstructs not only presence itself (its Being) but also the peculiar way of Being of Dasein that makes the presence of the hammer possible. If Being is the phenomenon we want to grasp, then this requires an "interpretation," a wresting of Being from entities we deal with first and foremost. The second reason phenomenology must be hermeneutical is that Dasein cannot grasp itself outside of any relation to a given context. This seems at first counterintuitive. It seems easy to grasp ourselves: we just reflect on ourselves, turn the ray of consciousness toward this object that we are. Yet one of Heidegger's most profound insights in *Being and Time*, one that will pose a difficult methodological problem for the analytic of Dasein, is that what appears to be a "pure" self-reflection is in fact a mirroring back, a folding back of my understanding of innerworldly entities (hammers, other people, etc.) unto myself. The discussion of authenticity (*Eigeintlichkeit*, "propriety" or "ownness"), before being an "ethical" question of living in the truth (appropriating, owning up to the groundless entity that I am), will be a methodological question: how I can "overcome" the necessary distortion present in my average everyday understanding of myself.

A full account of the ontological constitution of Dasein uncovered by the existential analytic cannot be provided here. Only the moments of the analysis that help us situate Nancy's recasting of that analytic will be briefly sketched in what follows. Heidegger divides Being-in-the-World into three co-primordial moments: the Who, Being-in, and World. World is the space of intelligibility in which Dasein finds itself, the totality of significance, of relations between one thing and another thing, between a thing and an activity, etc. This totality of significance must always already be disclosed in order that Dasein be able to relate to something, for example, in picking up a hammer in order to hammer. The important point to keep in mind is that the world *is* only insofar as Dasein exists, because world is neither a container (a thing) nor the sum total of entities, but the coherent milieu wherein Dasein assigns itself to a way of being (a possibility of being, e.g. house-building) and through that assignment lights up some entities or lets them be encountered in one particular way rather than in some other way. Being-in-the-World therefore means "understanding." Being-in (existing) is characterized by "disclosedness" (*Erschlossenheit*). Disclosedness does not mean that this or that particular thing is simply somehow unveiled but rather that there is an understanding (and affectability) at the heart of Dasein itself, that Dasein is "opened up" to . . . , in a way that need be neither explicit nor conceptual.

Dasein is thrown into the world. This means both that Dasein exists but is not the ground of its own existence and that Dasein is not itself the source of the basic intuitive and discursive contexture of the world it always already finds itself in. Things have always already been interpreted in some way; possibilities of existence have always already been made available or been decided upon. By whom? Heidegger's answer is "the they" (*das Man*), anyone and no one, the average everyday understanding. Dasein understands itself and its possibilities for Being first and foremost from out of what one says, what one does, from out of the way in which the world has been laid out in advance. Dasein is itself as "anyone" else. This is the mode of Being-oneself Heidegger calls *uneigentlich* (inauthentic, improper, or ownless). The they, Heidegger insists, is an ontological structure of Dasein and not a moral or social phenomenon. It is "essential" to the way of Being of Dasein. Heidegger will describe the movement of thrown existence in average everyday understanding as a "falling" (*Verfallen*), the movement or tendency of everyday existence to be caught up with entities (things to take care of, things to look at, things to talk about, etc.).[2]

The more Heidegger emphasizes the existential structure of falling, the more difficult it becomes to find an access to my Being that is not always already caught up in average everyday understanding. This access, for Heidegger, is found only in a concrete, factical modification of falling: authenticity or "ownness." This modification is triggered by anxiety and the call of conscience. To exist in the mode of ownness, to exist properly, is to own up to what one is: thrown into a world with others and having to take over this existence. Ownness – and this is going to be essential for Nancy – is not an extraordinary or exceptional way of living that would set me apart from everyone else. Rather, it is making my own the fact that I am not the ground of my existence, my world, my possibilities. In other words, ownness consists of nothing more than merely existing as I already am, that is, exposed to limits that are not at my disposal: birth, death, world. Hence existence is essentially finite. It is this being-closed-off, this not being able to come back behind and appropriate one's own limits, that "opens up" Dasein for Being. To exist in the mode of ownness is to be properly disclosed, to be "decided" (or "resolute," *entschlossen*).[3]

Nancy's engagement with Heidegger starts from a problematization of the economy of the proper and the improper (the ownness and ownlessness of existence) in Heidegger's *Being and Time* in order to liberate the "with" from this double modality and place it at the center of ontology. On the surface, Nancy seems to only be pursuing Heidegger's analytic of Dasein but in a way that is more consistently Heideggerian than Heidegger himself. It is Heidegger who insists on the essentiality of the "with," and Nancy thinks that "no other thinking has penetrated more deeply into the enigma of Being-with" (BWBT 5). Yet, in the way the argument of *Being and Time* unfolds, the essential being-with is subordinated to an analysis of its improper face (inauthentic they) and its proper one (authentic people). Nancy's emphasis on the "with" of Being arises out of a critical engagement with ownness (authenticity) and its relation to everydayness and to the "each time my own" of existence. But it is important to keep in mind that the apparently simple recasting of the "with" in its essential position produces a complete overhaul of Heidegger's concepts (concepts Nancy will continue to use): existence, world, sense, finitude.

If to be-there, to exist, is essentially to be-with, how should we understand this "with," this being-there-together? That "with" cannot be mere juxtaposition, in which the juxtaposed terms remain closed off to one another (a pen with a book), nor can it be a sharing of the same essence (BSP 60–1). In both the pure exteriority of relations and the pure interiority of a common substance, in both the I-subject without any essential relation to otherness (the I that has its meaning in itself) and the We-subject that gathers all I's into itself (the We that is the meaning of all I's), there is no place for a "being-with." Yet, only these two possibilities seem to be developed in *Being and Time*. In everyday, common (in the sense of banal) existence, there is for Heidegger only improper being-with, similar to the juxtaposition of things. We do take care of things "together" but this "togetherness" remains external since it is determined by what one takes care of. Anxiety will tear me from this average everyday business by putting me in front of my own essential finitude, my own being-toward-death. Death is what individualizes me since it is the only possibility I have to take over myself. Authentic being-toward-death (what Heidegger calls anticipatory resoluteness) is not shared in common.[4] Here, the essential "with" seems to be lost. But Heidegger is clear that anxiety does release or free me for proper being-with-others-among-things. It allows me to properly take over my own existence in a way that is both "with" and "in." It brings me into "my Situation," that is, face to face with the communal, historical possibilities handed over to me, which I have to make my own. I exist in my ownness (I have a life that is "mine") by being communal-historical.[5] It is the community that bestows upon my existence its sense, integration, and wholeness, yet it does this by appropriating me to the common destiny (the destinal unity) of a people. My individual fate is brought into the common destiny of a "people," the shared having-to-be *our* own possibilities. In this case, individual existence is sacrificed to a higher instance. We will see later that for Nancy singular existence is not sacrificed but offered and it is in this (non-sacrificial) offering that meaningful existence lies and not in the sacrifice to a transcendent meaning.

What needs to be thought, according to Nancy, is a being-there that is essentially multiple and plural, that is not an individual "there," but a there, a coming to presence, a coming to the world that necessarily, essentially implies a multiplicity or plurality of "theres" that is neither juxtaposition nor fusion but com-position, ex-position, dis-position. To think the multiple there, Nancy will put into play the word "people" (the plural *les gens* and not the singular *le peuple*). Unlike the Heideggerian "one" or "they," *les gens* emphasizes both plurality and singularity, a plurality of "ones" that are not lost in the anonymity of indifferentiation, where one is like "anyone" else. Nancy writes:

> "People" clearly states that we are all precisely *people*, that is, indistinctly persons, humans, all of a common "kind," but of a kind that has its existence only as numerous, dispersed, and indeterminate in its generality. This existence can only be grasped in the paradoxical simultaneity of togetherness (anonymous, confused, and indeed massive) and disseminated singularity (these or those "people(s)," or "a guy," "a girl," "a kid"). (BSP 7)[6]

When we say "people are strange," we mean all of them but also each of them one by one in a different way so that "what is apprehended is nothing other than singularity as such" (BSP 8). This emphasis on "singularity" is also what will allow Nancy to give a positive description of curiosity. Unlike for Heidegger, curiosity is not the meaningless (indifferent) jumping from one thing to the next, the inability to tarry alongside anything, but the encounter with a singular "one" (BSP 19–20).

Existence, essence, being-to-itself

We have seen that to exist, for Heidegger, means to be "opened," to understand, to relate meaningfully. We also said that this openness or disclosedness is a function of Dasein's relation to certain limits. What does "to exist" mean for Nancy? In a sense, it also means to be unto-the-limit, to be exposed. At the same time, we will see that the limits Nancy has in mind are not horizons of understanding. As a result, existence is not a mode of Being limited to Dasein only. At first, Nancy defines existence in a traditional way, by opposing it to essence. An essence does not exist or it exists only when it is posited or positioned. This is the meaning of the Kantian thesis analyzed by Heidegger in *The Basic Problems of Phenomenology*: "Being is not a real predicate" or in its positive formulation: "Being is absolute position [*Setzung*] of a thing." Nancy explains, "Being is neither substance nor cause of the thing, rather, it is a being-the-thing in which the verb 'to be' has a transitive value of 'positioning,' but one in which the 'positioning' is based on and caused by nothing else but Dasein, being-there, being thrown down, given over, abandoned, offered up by existence" (OBC 2; BSP 12). But Nancy adds to the traditional Kantian thesis a further determination: "community is not a predicate of existence." It is not as if I could turn individual existence into common existence by adding the predicate "communal" to it. This operation presupposes that existence is essentially not communal and is transformed by the added predicate. According to Nancy, "*Community is simply the real position of existence*" (OBC 2). In other words, position (existence) is never the position of a single instance of existence that is independent and cut off from everything except the unity and unicity of its essence. Essence is nothing; it does not really exist, unless it is exposed or presented to itself and others. Tableness *is* only in the position of a table, its taking place, arrival or coming "here and now." What Nancy underlines is that this "being"-a-table (not tableness as such, but "that there is" a table) is of necessity a being exposed, being turned outside. That there is something means that some "ones" are posed, exposed, disposed.

The existence Nancy talks about in terms of "positing" is not something given once and for all, but it is the "giving" of something for existing. This giving, however, is itself without given, without gift and without giver. Nothing gives existence. Hence the giving gesture is not the origin of the existent, as if the existent was "given" or "posited" and then just lay there after that, stable and fixed. Existing takes on an active meaning: it is a *praxis* (that is, an activity that does not result in an external product but that aims only at itself). As long as something exists, its existence, its coming

to existence is constantly renewed. Existing puts into play existence, existence is at play in existing. Hence, Nancy will prefer
offering to giving. Offering keeps what is offered at the limit of
presence, "suspended," if one wills. It denotes the movement of
arriving of what is offered more than its having arrived, its being
given or present (EF 146–7).

A consequence of this definition of existence is that existence
cannot be thought on the model of the "Subject." The subject is for
itself; it folds into itself all exteriority and appropriates all otherness for itself, insofar as this exteriority or otherness is present for
it and makes sense for it. The subject, thought in terms of self-
consciousness or in terms of underlying substrate, is always that
which remains the same across all alterations, that which always
tends toward the stasis of self-identity. In Hegel, if it is necessary
that consciousness encounters and bumps against the not-I, this
otherness is nevertheless folded back into the self, through the
movement whereby the self recognizes this otherness as a result of
its own activity. If otherness is essential to the movement of the self
toward self-knowledge, this otherness is ultimately dissolved in
the realization of self-knowledge. In a similar way for Husserl,
consciousness is a totality: it is open to everything that can be given
to it, yet it is itself enclosed. In other words: it is absolute, it knows
no radical outside.

Nancy, here, following the Derridean logic of differance, seeks
to "radicalize or to aggravate Hegelian thinking about the Self until
it caves in" (OBC 3).[7] The word differance plays on the double-
meaning of the French verb *différer*, which means both to differ and
to defer. Derrida uses the neologism "differance" with an "a" to
emphasize the irreducible (or originary) difference at the heart of
the self, so that there is no self present prior to any differentiating.
Differance is not a relation between two things that would exist
prior to their being put into relation, a relation that would first let
them appear as different from each other (but only insofar as each
would remain identical to itself). Rather, difference is the openness
or spacing that first allows something like a self to identify itself.
Since this "identification" happens thanks to a "detour" through
an exteriority (a not-Self), pure self-identity or self-presence is
indefinitely deferred. Self-consciousness always lags behind: it
posits itself as having been there in a punctual, indifferent unity
prior to self-differentiating and self-relating, yet it does this only
"after the fact." The self has always already started by altering itself
so that it cannot catch up with what would have been a pure origin.

What both Derrida and Nancy emphasize is the irreducibility (absolute exteriority) of the "spacing" that allows for something to exist (BSP 30). This "spacing" *is* not. It is nothing that can be given in the form of presence. Yet it allows that there be things.

Following this logic, selfhood for Nancy denotes the "movement" of existence as being-unto-self or being-toward-self.[8] This means that there is no Self at the origin of this "movement" or this "exposition." Selfhood is an "effect" of an essential being-unto or being-toward, which can never fully reappropriate within itself what it is toward. It is what it is (self) only through an inappropriable exteriority. However, this inappropriable exteriority is not some other thing out there, but the limit or edge upon which it is exposed:

> To exist does not mean simply "to be." On the contrary: to exist means *not* to be in the immediate presence or in the immanency of a "being-thing." To exist is not to be immanent, or not to be present to oneself, and not to be sent forth *by* oneself. To exist, therefore, is to hold one's "selfness" as an "otherness," and in such a way that no essence, no subject, no place can present *this otherness in itself* – either as the proper selfness of an other, or an "Other," or a common being (life or substance). The otherness of existence happens only as "being-together." (BP 154–5, trans. mod.)

The "otherness" of the self that is not present as another self is the unappropriable limit or edge upon which I am exposed and that properly belongs neither to the inside nor to the outside.[9] This edge is the place "where" existence happens or is felt. If to be is to come to presence, then such a "presentation" or offering is essentially "*to-*" (itself, others, itself as another). There has to be a spacing or distance at the heart of the "thing" that allows it to be, to exist. If not, there is the black hole of immanence: pure essence that cannot even be said to be anything (itself or something else). Hence, Being for Nancy is neither in-itself (substance, pure immanence) nor for-itself (consciousness). To escape the constraints of this dichotomization of Being, Nancy will describe Being as to-itself or toward-itself (*à-soi*) and speak of the *aséité* of Being (BSP 40–1; BP 205–9).[10] Aseity is a term used in Scholastic philosophy to describe the self-existence of God (existence by or through itself alone). Nancy retrieves the concept not to point to the self-enclosure of the absolute Being, but to the necessary exposition of any enclosure unto a limit.

Finitude, absoluteness, freedom

We are now in a position to understand what Nancy means by finitude. To exist means to be enclosed within a limit, but it also means to be exposed at this limit. Hence, if Nancy insists on the finitude of what exists, this must not be taken to mean that each entity is encircled within a limit that separates or absolves it from all other entities. The finitude or limitation of the singular being must be distinguished from what Nancy calls "finiteness" (*finité*) (SV 87).[11] Finiteness (for example, Cartesian finiteness) is only thinkable against the backdrop of an infinite, against which the finite thing will then be essentially regarded as deficient and as engaged in an infinite process of finition or completion. The end or finition of finiteness can only lie in the finite being overcoming its limitation through the appropriation of what lies beyond it. The *telos* of the finite being will thus be only the bad infinite, an infinite that is never actually present but can only be achieved at the end of an infinite process. Unlike finiteness, finitude denotes that which exists at its limits or is affected by its end, not as something external imposed on it, but as something that is originary (SW 31–2). Since this finite being does not cease to be exposed at its limits, its exposition is endlessly repeated and therefore never finished once and for all. Finitude therefore will itself be the true infinite: "It is the good infinite or the actual infinite – the infinitude in act of the act itself as the act of exceeding oneself" (IRS 39; SW 35). Finitude is not a limitation imposed on a being by the fact that there happen to be other things outside of it and which press upon it. Rather, finitude consists in the fact that any being must be exposed to an outside in order to exist or be what it is:

> *Finitude* does not mean that we are non-infinite – like small, insignificant beings within a grand, universal, and continuous being – but it means that we are *infinitely* finite, infinitely exposed to our existence as a nonessence, infinitely exposed to the otherness of our own "being" (or that being is in us exposed to its own otherness). We begin and we end without beginning and ending: without having a beginning and an end that is *ours,* but having (or being) them only as others, and through others. (BP 155)

If a finite being has no proper end, no point of completion, then it cannot be either complete or incomplete. Rather, a being is always in every instant fully exposed, without holding anything back, without leaving anything to be actualized later. At the same time this being-offered is not a coming to stand in full presence; it is the movement of coming to presence. It is in this sense that a finite being is absolute. But "absoluteness" needs to be thought apart from any thought of the infinite. The finite character of the absolute is not its limitation but the necessary limit upon which (or to which) it exists or comes to be. A "pure" Absolute could not *be* or exist, since, having no exteriority, having no contact at the limit with any exterior, it would be unable to sense itself or relate to itself. Such an absolute totality would be, according to Nancy, an essential contradiction, since not only would it have to be separated from its outside by a limit, but this limit itself would have to be without relation to its outside (IC 4).[12] The logic of absoluteness leads the absolute to the black hole of immanence: "A total absence of exteriority, a non-extension concentrated in itself, not something impenetrable, but rather its excess, the impenetrable *mixed with* the impenetrable, infinite intussusception, the *proper* devouring itself . . . in an abyss where the hole absorbs even its own edges" (C 75).

Nancy's thinking of finitude requires a recasting of what history means: it will now have to be thought as essentially finite. History cannot be the progression of finite beings toward their *telos*; it cannot be the becoming-subject of a substance whose ultimate figure is that of the self-enclosed circle. In a sense, even when history is seen as necessary for the development of spirit as self-consciousness, it remains subordinated to a subject: history is what happens to something, that is, to the subject of history. History is "resorbed" (or accomplished, finished, and hence abolished as history) in the subject. History, thought of as the unfolding or accomplishment of an essence, necessarily "puts an end to history as the movement, the becoming, and the production" of this essence (BP 149). Here Nancy quotes Derrida: "The very concept of history has lived only upon the possibility of meaning, upon the past, present, or promised presence of meaning and truth."[13] Hence, history is something that originates or results in a presence and resorbs itself in this origin or end. What would it mean to think history outside of subjectivity and the accomplishment of self-presence? The model of historical time would then not be the continuity of a process of becoming (accomplishment or decay of some essence) but the discontinuity of a multiplicity of happenings (BP 162–3). To think history is to think finite and discontinuous happening, the opening of a space of time where we happen, we come to be. This space of time where "we" happen is without origin or end. To happen is neither to flow (to disappear), nor to grow, nor to be purely present, but to be continuously in the movement of arriving or "acceding." This can be easily explained with a concrete example: if I am arriving at your place, I am on the threshold: I am not absent but I am also not there. Once I enter your home, I am not arriving anymore, I am present; the movement of arriving is finished. This is why the happening of finite existence(s) for Nancy is linked to a thought of the limit or the threshold. To be finite is to never cease to "arrive" to the world; hence, it is to never cease to be exposed to "all there is."

It is impossible to speak of the finitude of being without thinking of Heidegger. For Heidegger finitude has to do with groundlessness and concealment.[14] The finitude of being ultimately points to the necessary non-appearing of Being itself, which conceals itself through and in the unconcealment of beings. When we ask "why is there something?" and put the emphasis on the "why," that is, when we ask this question metaphysically, we are led to look for a reason, a cause, or a ground for what is. This quest ultimately leads us back to an absolute foundation, a self-caused, self-founded entity (God), since only such an entity can truly "ground" what is without leading us back to a prior cause. The finitude of being means that being is not an absolute cause, foundation, or explanation for beings. When we wonder at the unconcealment of beings, when we wonder at the fact "that there is all there is" and sustain the groundlessness, the "without-reason" of the plurality of beings, we think the finitude of being. For Nancy, the finitude of being is (maybe more than for Heidegger) essentially linked to the "explosion of presence in the originary multiplicity of its partition" (BSP 21, trans. mod.) or the "free dissemination of existence(s)" without origin, ground, or reason (EF 13). The finitude of being is not the limitation of existence by other existences but the an-archy of what is, the rose without any why.

From Heidegger to Nancy, there is a subtle shift in the meaning of Being and in the significance of the abandonment or withdrawal. The crux of the problem could be formulated in the following way: in the withdrawal or abandonment of Being, is Being kept in reserve, hidden and withdrawn, or is it rather the case that Being is nothing more than the thing itself in its sheer existence? In a sense, Nancy sees Heidegger as holding on to the first option: Being withdraws, it is obliterated by the presencing of beings, it holds itself back and can only "appear" as nothing. For Heidegger, the "free gesture" of the disclosure of Being – the gesture that lets beings be encountered meaningfully in the world – is also at the same time a withholding, a holding back that is responsible for the history of Being as errancy. The history of Being is the history of the various ways in which Being is forgotten; it is the history of nihilism, the history in which Being can only be conceived of as nothing.[15]

Whereas Heidegger thinks Being as withdrawal, Nancy thinks the generosity of Being or the free dissemination of existence.[16] For Nancy, the withdrawal of Being holds nothing back, it is an expenditure without reserve. This also means that in existence, the ontological difference is annulled. "Ontological difference" means, for Heidegger, that Being is not a thing; it is nothing but its difference from beings. But at the same time, it is not something else, another being. It is nothing but the "that there is" of anything that is. The ontological difference is not (it is not a thing, nothing identifiable, especially not a relation between two things), but it happens.[17] But for Nancy, "nothing" (*rien*) does not mean "not a thing at all" but "the thing itself" (*res*) insofar as it is no thing, insofar as it empties out its essence. Here Nancy differentiates between nothingness (*néant*) and nothing (*rien*). "Nothingness" is what Being turns into as soon as it is posited. Being cannot be a being; it is nothing but "its own effacement that negates it and, while negating it, allows for the spacing of the concrete" (CW 102). "Nothing," on the other hand, is the thing taken in its sheer existence (and not in its essence, as this or that), "the thing tending toward its pure and simple being of a thing" (CW 103). At this point, the ontological difference is cancelled as a difference between two realities, Being and being, or as the abandonment of beings by Being (the withdrawal and reserve of Being); there is no difference between existence and the existent, the existent's "reality" is nothing other than the putting into play of its own existence.

"The experience of freedom" is the name Nancy gives to his "ontology of finitude." Once Being is freed from its metaphysical way of thinking, once the existence of beings is not deduced from any ground or principle, then we must think not only the abandonment of beings but also the "freedom" of such an abandonment. This is the proposition that opens *The Experience of Freedom*: "Once existence is no longer produced or deduced, but simply posited, . . . and once existence is abandoned to this positing at the same time that it is abandoned by it, we must think the freedom of this abandonment" (EF 9). For Nancy, freedom cannot be a principle that grounds beings. Traditionally, freedom is supposed to be the property of a subject or the structure of subjectivity itself. Freedom means the autonomy or the self-legislation of a subject. To be free means not to be subjected to any external determination. In this sense, I can be free only if I absolve myself from any contact with what is other and find the reason or determination of my existence within myself. The free being is the one that is *causa sui*, self-caused: it has its origin in itself or it gives itself the law of its own existence without any relation to what is outside of it; in other word, free existence is sovereign: a self-founding entity absolved from any relation with exteriority. Thought in this way, freedom becomes a ground: in Kant, it becomes uncaused causality, the ability to be the absolute origin of a causal chain; similarly in Sartre, it becomes the ability to be the origin of one's own life-project, one's own meaning. For Nancy, on the contrary, to be free is not to be absolutely self-determined but to be absolutely without "why." The thought of freedom leads to the deconstruction of any and all foundation and opens, as we will see, the thinking of the world or of the singular plural (EF 13). Freedom means that existence is "abandoned" without being abandoned by anything that would precede it (e.g. God or Being) nor being abandoned to anything other than its own existence. Freedom is the unfounded (*défondée*) factuality of an existence that surprises itself in existing. It is the deliverance from foundation and the releasing into existence.

If we think freedom as this deliverance and relate it to what we said about finite beings needing, in order to exist at all, a limit upon which they are exposed, it becomes clear why the freedom of a being is not limited by the "presence" of other such beings. If we think of freedom as a property of an individual subject, then the exercise of freedom in a common space shared by free subjects, the composition of freedoms, becomes problematic. We normally think plurality as limiting freedom: what I can do or be is limited by all the things that are outside of me. If I could be everything or if I could be with beings whose freedom is essentially in agreement with my freedom, I would be infinitely or absolutely free. According to this thought of freedom, either we have to show that absolutely free beings do not enter into contradiction with each other in the exercise of their freedom (for example in the Kantian Kingdom of Ends) or we have to appeal to a common constraint that guarantees the freedom of the individual (freedom can only be insofar as it lets itself be limited by the freedom of others). The antinomy between the free self and the common space of freedom is, for Nancy, not resolved in this sort of compromise but is only overcome by understanding that the self is essentially *with*. Freedom comes from the outside because freedom "is the name of this movement [of the breakaway of the self in the non-self], which does turn out to consist simultaneously in an emancipation (from the being-in-itself and to-itself) and in an availability, a possibility, or opening *to*."[18] Freedom is not a property of a subject but again, like finitude, the "property" of the self insofar as it exists in being exposed unto a limit. The "property" of the self is, consequently, a "property" of the "with."

Being singular plural

Up until now in our discussion of free and finite existence, the term "singularity" and the famous expression "being singular plural" have been avoided. This was done purposefully to forestall any curtailed understanding of the singular plural as some sort of banal expression of the multiplicity of particular things. Having examined the notion of existence, exposition, limit and finitude, we are now in a position to introduce this term and understand its range and impact. A singularity is anything that exists, anything that is exposed. We now understand what this means. It is important to emphasize that the logic of exposition knows no hierarchy and no individuality. It is not restricted to what we take to be individuals, but applies equally to supra-individual entities and infra-individual ones (BSP 8). Hence singularities are not just humans, and not just things; they are everything that exists: stones, cats, communities, books, thoughts, cities, etc. The "logic" of the limit (or of exposition) applies to any thing, to any "one," to any "I," to any "we."

Being singular plural means first of all that there is always by necessity more than one singularity. Since to exist means to be-unto-the-limit or to be-opened-to, this opening is necessarily "with": it is impossible to open oneself to oneself without exteriority. To be a singularity is not to be an atom, indivisible, and cut off from other atoms, but to be caught up in a movement of singularization and hence to be necessarily both entangled with and different from other singularities: "The concept of the singular implies its singularization and, therefore, its distinction from other singularities . . ." (BSP 32). To be oneself is to distinguish oneself from (oneself and others) and this movement of "distinguishing" is impossible without "two." One is always more than One (BSP 39). Derrida expresses something similar by saying that there is always "n+One," that is, no matter how many ones are gathered in n, there is always necessarily some other one to which n is exposed. That there needs to be two for singularities to "singularize" themselves does not only imply that there needs to be me and there needs to be you, but also that there needs to be an us and a something else, and that there needs to be a plurality within myself. I exist in relation/ exposition to you, an "event of me" exists in relation/exposition to other events, and our community exists in relation/exposition to some other community. A singularity is not a fixed point of identity but something that identifies itself through its exposition, something that is essentially caught up in a movement of identification (BSP 66, 149). Hence, Nancy's singular plural neither affirms a plurality of individual points, nor does it dissolve any fixed identity in the mere indistinction of pure differences. Being singular plural means: (1) that there is always a plurality of singularities; (2) that singularities have their "identity" in their movement of disentanglement; and (3) that a singularity is always itself a plurality of singular "events" or "strokes" of existence and hence not identifiable as such, not reducible to a fixed list of properties.

Nancy's "singular plural" requires that we rethink identities according to the double movement of entanglement/disentanglement, *mêlée/démêlé*. Nancy's rethinking of identities, especially communal identities, is most explicit in his "In Praise of the Melee," a powerful text written in 1993 during the war in Bosnia.[19] Asked to write in praise of mixture, Nancy instead pulls away from the idea of mixture, which mixes pure elements according to a set procedure, in favor of that of melee. A singularity (a human being, a city, a language, a culture) is always a melee of traits and not a definable unity. At the same time, it possesses its own recognizable tone and lets itself be identified in the process (or *as* the process) of disentanglement from other singularities. In "In Praise of the Melee," Nancy will name such singularities, ipseities.[20]

Sharing, rapport, sense

If there is of necessity more than one singularity, then what is there between these singularities? Nancy will give this "between" many names: articulation or exposition, sharing, relation (*rapport*), sense. Before we look at what these terms mean, the first answer that should be given is: the between is no-thing. The *with* or the *between* is not a third thing alongside and in the middle of the two relata (BSP 5). Nor is the *between* an empty space, a milieu, or container that would encompass or surround everything and within which singularities would come into contact. The "with" exists only as the articulation of singularities, as "the play of the juncture." We already quoted the passage in which Nancy explains this play in the Introduction, but it is worth quoting it again: articulation is "what takes place where different pieces touch each other without fusing together, where they slide, pivot, or tumble over one another, one at the limit of the other without the mutual *play* – which always remains, at the same time, a play *between* them – ever forming into the substance or the higher power of a Whole" (IC 76).

That there is nothing "between" singularities implies that Being (as pure immanence) withdraws and shares out existence(s): "there is no being between existents . . . and on the other hand, the being of each existence, that which it shares of being and by which it *is*, is nothing other . . . than this very sharing" (EF 69). Sharing means both that something is held in common and that it is partitioned or divided. If we share a pie, we all have a piece, yet this distribution requires first of all that the pie be cut. Nancy thinks the double semantics of sharing: having in common and being partitioned, but without relating this gathering/separating to a prior or underlying substance – there is no preexisting pie ("Being") waiting to be cut up.

Nancy first used the word *partage* in his reading of Plato's *Ion* in "Sharing Voices" with regards to the role of *hermēneia* ("interpretation") in the relation between the god, the Muse, the poet, the rhapsode, and the listener. Why this plurality of instances and why the necessity of a *hermēneia* (not understood as the retrieval or unearthing of a hidden sense, but as a retelling in another voice, another medium)? Nancy writes:

> [The voice of the divine] is first of all, principally (but that does not make it a *principle*; it is only *given* in this way), shared voices, the differentiation between singular voices. In other words, there is no *one* divine voice, nor perhaps a divine voice in general. . . . But *the voice*, for the divine, is the sharing and the difference. . . . This difference is the articulation of the divine with respect to and in the human. The man who is the poet is outside of himself, but the divine is there also outside himself – in the sharing of voices. (SV 236–7)

God, Muse, poet, rhapsode, and listener are outside of themselves, exposed, and what is shared or communicated between them is not some sort of universal message or signification that would emanate from God and be passed down from one to the other, but a movement of propagation, "the articulation and the announcement of this sharing" (SV 237). Meaning does not precede its sharing; it is not given prior to or outside of "our voices and our orations," but "abandoned in the sharing, to the hermeneutic law of the difference between voices" (SV 244).[21]

That existence is a sharing out or partitioning also means that between singularities there exists a *rapport*. The French word *rapport*, which is normally translated as relation, designates an action rather than a substance (IRS 16). Nancy thus prefers it to the French word *relation* (which could be translated as "relationship"), which designates the link between two subsistent things. Nancy develops the semantics of the *rapport* in a short book titled *L'"il y a" du rapport sexuel*. The title is a play on Lacan's famous assertion that there is no sexual relation. Nancy will say: there is *rapport* but not *relation*: the relationship destroys the relation. Since this text is not translated into English, it is worth quoting it at length. A *rapport*, Nancy explains, is

> nothing that is, it happens between what is. It is . . . of the order of that which the Stoics designated as the incorporeal. There were four instances of incorporeal: space, time, emptiness, and the *lekton* (the said, the enunciated). As we can see, these four instances of the incorporeal are the four instances or conditions of relation: indeed, relation presupposes the distinction between places, differences between times (including what one names simultaneity: where two tempi become synchronic or syncopated), the empty interval between bodies, and the possibility of emission and reception of a saying – of a saying-between or a saying-oneself-between [*d'un inter-dire et d'un s'inter-dire*]. . . . The relation makes sense: directional sense (relation of movement), then sensible sense (relation of one skin to another skin that touches it, one of an eye to the color that strikes it or that it strikes), and then the relation of signification. (IRS 21–2)

Nancy summarizes this explanation by saying that the *rapport* is "the happening of a distinction, a contact separation, in which the distinct is properly itself, and hence is itself only in relation to other distinct things" (IRS 22). We are by now familiar with this logic. The *rapport* is the between, but again it does not constitute a connective tissue or a bridge. On the contrary, "it opens the between as such: it opens the between-two by way of which there are two. But the between-two is none of the two: it is the emptiness – or the space, or the time . . . , or the sense – that reports or relates without gathering, or gathers without uniting, or unites without accomplishing, or accomplishes without bringing to an end" (IRS 23).

It is exactly this happening that Nancy calls "meaning" or "sense" (*sens*).[22] Meaning is normally thought of as a signifying event, as the relation of a signifier (a word) to a signified (a concept) or a referent (a thing). For example the word "table" signifies something by virtue of pointing to the concept "table." Its signification lies in its ability to lead away from itself to something of a different order: a concept or a thing. In the same way, if I say that the smoke signifies fire, I mean that it leads away from itself to its origin or cause. We can think of the meaning of Being, of existence, or of the world on the same model. On this model, the meaning of existence lies in some other thing outside of existence, which existence has to then appropriate to itself in order to make sense. Humanism is the school of thought that attempts to fix the sense of human existence, which human beings would then have to accomplish historically. But for Nancy (following Heidegger), to exist is precisely to have no such signification. This non-givenness of signification can be experienced as a loss of sense, but in fact it is only in the absence of any given signification that existence and sense are possible. Hence, Nancy will differentiate sense from truth: "Truth is being-such [*l'être-tel*], or more exactly it is the quality of the presentation of being such as such. Sense, for its part, is the movement of being-toward [*l'être-à*] . . ." (SW 12). Sense as the movement of being-toward is what makes it possible that a truth ("2 + 2 = 4" or "the table is blue") be exposed, communicated.[23]

Sense as this "happening between" requires more than plurality; it also requires that one "place of emission," as Nancy calls it, not be commensurable or interchangeable with the other. Suppose that we are both the same in the sense that we partake of the same universal rationality. Suppose further that I communicate to you a sentence whose meaning can be rationally and hence universally understood, e.g. 2 + 2 = 4. In such a communicative act, nothing happens. Rationality merely thinks itself, or humanity converses with itself. Speaking to you, in this example, is exactly like speaking to myself. Hearing you say something is exactly like hearing myself say it. But an event of sense is not the mere transmission of pre-defined content; it is a "communication" across the absolute incommensurability of speaking positions. This again relates to sharing: something happens, is transmitted or communicated between one voice and the other (the poet and the rhapsode, the rhapsode and the listener) because these positions are incommensurable. There is sense only in the sharing, the contact and separation, of voices, in their "contiguity" without continuity (BSP 5). This discontinuous contiguity is also what Nancy calls "syncope."

Sense at the limit of signification is what could be called *hermēneuein*: the transmission of a message, the announcement of news and its forwarding by the one who transmits it. The messenger is neither the signification of message nor its interpreter, but it is the address, presentation, and destination of a signification. The sense of sense is to present itself, to come to presence, to address itself *to*. Nancy gives a simple example: When you introduce yourself [*tu te présentes*], this has no signification: "there is neither distance nor intimacy; it is not a representation, nor is it sheer indetermination, since you stand out from both the world and significations. What happens there . . . is first of all the presentation of a place: that of your presence and your nomination" (GT 56), which precedes and exceeds signification. Sense is the condition of the presentation of significations, without which significations would be meaningless. Sense takes place between us and not between signifier and signified or sign and referent (GT 57). It does not come from anywhere, but is offered at the very level of our existence, in the movement of a presentation *to*. This movement is a rupture of presence, a departure or withdrawal, a "hollowing out of [pure] presence, which is the possibility and even the most proper nature of its coming," its presentation in its difference with itself (GT 64).

Another way of saying that sense requires the incommensurability of "places of emission" is to say that it requires an encounter with an exteriority or an alterity that resists its assimilation.[24] This alterity is not a big Other, or the other "as such," which would either remain inaccessible or which I would have to appropriate (either in making it my own or in making myself other). Rather, the other in question is an always singular and finite other that does not let itself be identified as other but infinitely alters itself and announces itself.[25] It is the alterity of another origin or another "stroke" of existence, another "one" to which I gain access (and this "access" is the event of sense) exactly on the mode of not gaining access (BSP 13). Gaining access is not "appropriating" (BSP 20), it is touching. Touching is a contact separation, a contact through a separation (BSP 81, 91, 97). It is what happens on the limit without belonging properly to either side (without either side being able to appropriate for itself what happens there as its own).

Yet it is important to see that if touching is the primary structure of sensing or existing, this structure is not one of proximity or simultaneity of the touching and the touched, but that of differance as the "origin" of space-time.[26] In Nancy's own words:

> In fact, simultaneity is not a matter of indistinction; on the contrary, it is the distinctness of places taken together. The passage from one place to another *needs time* [*D'un lieu à l'autre*, il faut le temps]. And the passage from a place to itself as such [*du lieu à lui-même*] also needs time: the time for the place to open itself as place, the time to space itself. Reciprocally, originary time, appearing as such, *needs space* [il lui faut l'espace], the space of its own dis-tension, the space of the passage that divides [*partage*] it. . . . The "together," therefore, is an absolutely originary structure. (BSP 61, trans. mod.)

This is the structure of differance we discussed above in relation to selfhood and also in the Introduction. "Together," that is, in the same place or at the same time, requires a certain distance, an originary spacing.

As Derrida argues in *On Touching*, the originality of Nancy's thinking of touch lies in the fact that he insists on a "*différance* in the very 'inside' of haptics" (OT 229) or an originary "technical supplementarity of the body" (OT 223; see also 96–7, 286–7). Here, using the term "originary" is misleading since the technical or prosthetic supplement undoes all thought of a simple, pure, "originary" origin. The supplement is one of these undecidable terms, analyzed by Derrida, which serves to undermine the dichotomies nature/technics (or culture), origin/effect, etc. The "strange structure of the supplement" is one where "a possibility produces by delay that to which it is said to be added."[27] A supplement is something that is added onto something else from the outside in order to complement or improve it, to make up for its faults. While the supplement would seem to be secondary and inessential, it is in fact what makes the thing be essentially what it is; it constitutes the primordial presence of the thing. If "touch" is the technical supplement of bodies or of singularities, it means that there is not first "a body" and then "organs of touch" added to it, which allow it to enter into contact with an outside. The supplement precedes that which is supplemented; there is a supplement at the origin. We will discuss the relation between sense, the senses, and the body in more detail in chapter 5. For now, it suffices to understand that "touch" necessitates the same spacing at the heart of presence as existence does.

With his recasting of sense in terms of sharing and touch, Nancy undercuts the problem of the "meaning" of existence in the face of an absurd universe. It is not the task of the human to give meaning *to* or impose meaning *on* the world. Rather, existing itself as being-toward-itself already "makes" sense. Sense is nothing but the singularities themselves, every time exposed to themselves and each other. Sense is "an outside that is open right at the world, right in the middle of us and between us as our common sharing out" (TD 18). It is also important to emphasize that the circulation of sense is not commensurable with the general equivalence of capitalism for reasons we touch upon briefly above. We will come back to this point in chapter 4, but for now it suffices to remember that sense presupposes the incommensurability (or the absolute value) of the singularities.

World as "totality of sense"

We have now seen that sense is "an outside that is open right at the world." But this leaves us to ask: what is "the world" for Nancy? "World" is a central concept in Nancy's thinking, but like the "singular plural," it is hard to grasp on its own and can give rise to misunderstanding. When we say "the world," we tend to think either of a big container (the universe) or of everything that exists taken together. In both ways, we think unity. For Nancy, on the contrary, the world is the dis-unified occurrence of all exposi-tions or of all events of sense. The world is formed of limits or edges between singularities, of their articulations, of the play of their junctures. This means that the "world" is neither pure immanence, since edges "open" right in the middle of the world, between singularities, nor is it transcendence, since the world does not refer to or open unto another world.[28] The dissolution of all transcendent positions with regard to the world is what Nancy calls the becoming-worldly of the world (SW 7), a dissolution which is linked to the death of God and the deconstruction of monotheism.[29] We will come back to this relation in the next chapter. For now, it is enough to explain how this disappearance of a tran-scendent position outside of the world allows us to think the world as such, its "worldliness," without referring it to another instance. It is in order to think this "worldliness" that Nancy reappropriates and displaces the Christian motive of creation *ex nihilo*. That the world is created out of nothing implies that it has no presupposition or precondition, no ground or reason, no origin or end. Creation *ex nihilo* is the expression of a "radical materialism" (CW 51) and not a religious doctrine. Creation implies that there is nothing but the world, nothing but the ever-renewed coming to presence, the *surgissement*, in each time and in each space, of singularities, each time other, each time with others (BSP 2–3, 16). We will see how the deconstruction of Christianity opens the way for such a thinking of the world in the next chapter.

There are two consequences to the dissolution of all transcendent positions with regard to the world. First, a world cannot be something I represent to myself (CW 43) since this would require that I can take a position outside of it and survey it with one glance. A world is "grasped" not in a vision or a representation but in sojourning, inhabiting, that is, sense-making. Second, the world cannot have a signification; it cannot refer to another instance in which it would find its meaning. As Nancy puts it: world *"no longer has* a sense, but it *is* sense" (SW 8).

Since the world is a com-position, since it is made up of edges that open right at the world, we can only speak of "the" world in the singular in a very specific way. The world is not the totalization of what is, an overarching horizon or a super container that would bring everything together: "That there is not everything (or not *the* whole) does not define a lack or an ablation, since there was not any whole before the not-the-whole. It means rather that all that is (since there is really all that there is) does not totalize itself, even though it is all there is" (IRS 25). Hence if we say that "the world stands by itself, configures itself, and exposes itself in itself, relates to itself" (CW 47), we must not understand by this that the world is a unitotality, but always hear the "itself" according to the logic of selfhood outlined above and according to the singular plural. Remember that the singular plural means more than the fact that there are many things. These things, these singularities, are caught up in the double movement of entanglement and disentanglement and it is in that movement that they find their "identity." According to this logic, the "one" world is a multiplicity of world-singularities; each world is a multiplicity of singularities exposed to each other and to others. There is no overarching, final, totalizing Singularity but only a plurality of being-toward (*être-à*):

> The unity of a world is not one: it is made of a diversity, including disparity and opposition is made of it, which is to say that it is not added to it and does not reduce it. The unity of a world is nothing

other than its diversity, and its diversity is, in turn, a diversity of worlds. A world is a multiplicity of worlds, the world is a multiplicity of worlds, and its unity is the sharing out [*partage*] and the mutual exposure in this world of all its worlds. (CW 109)

Despite this lack of final unification, the world has a stance: it holds together the multiplicity of expositions without itself standing on any foundation. In a similar way, we inhabit the world (a world, worlds) and this inhabiting is an *ethos*: "The art of standing, or what permits in general having or maintaining a standing in, including, and especially, where there is no longer any support or firm basis for whatever stance there is" (CW 90). The world is not something in which or on which this stance happens; it is the composition of all stances.

Mondialisation or world-forming points, for Nancy, to this composition of world(s): we (that is, singularities) form a world at our outer edges, we articulate ourselves. In this way, world-forming is not a human activity but an ontological one: *it* worlds, or *there is* sense, sense itself circulates. Here, a key difference between the understandings of existence, sense, and world held by Nancy and Heidegger can be highlighted. Existence for Nancy is not limited to Dasein, to the being that in its comportment toward entities cannot but "understand" that they are something in some way. For Nancy, this stone exists and so does this dog, this book, this thought, etc. This means that sense will have to be rethought. For Heidegger, the stone does not touch the earth because the stone is not opened to ground, it cannot make sense of the ground and of itself as being-on-the-ground, as not-being-the-ground, etc. Dasein can say that the stone is on the ground because it meaningfully relates to being-a-stone and being-ground and can let one be open to the other. But for Nancy, "access" to the concreteness of the stone "does not come about only when the stone is encountered, thrown, or manipulated by or for a subject" (SW 62). The stone is not *for* a Dasein that would let the stone be what it is in relating meaningfully to it. I can relate to the stone because it is there, exposed in its hardness, resisting my grasp (in both senses of the word).[30] The problem with phenomenology, according to Nancy, is that it thinks access (significance, light) only in terms of appropriation. This is true also of Heidegger's late thinking of the "gift" of the "there is," since the gift of the given is always thought in terms of its anthropocentric *telos*: the gift must be destined to a being capable of receiving it as such (*Dasein*). But this gift "for" Dasein hides another, more primordial gift, according to Nancy: the spaciousness of the world, the distribution or opening of places receiving a stone, a shadow, or a tree. For Heidegger, the world is a coherent milieu of significance already laid out in advance, the space of intelligibility, of the *a priori* meaningfulness of what is. In this sense, world is sense (or significance) and there is no significance outside of the world. Yet, for Heidegger, world is the wherein of Dasein's factical existence, so that there is no sense, no intelligibility or significance, unless a Dasein exists. For Nancy, world is also sense, but sense-making (and hence worlding) is not limited to Dasein, but is the sharing of singularities that are exposed to one another (stone, ground, dog, grass, star, and me, and you).

That the world makes sense means that bursts of sense happen in the spacings and articulations of singularities. The world does not make sense exclusively for us or through us. Yet Nancy does say that the human has a "special" relation to exposition and to world. Humans are not the world's composers, and, if they are its overseer, it is not in the sense that they have primacy over or stewardship of the singularities that compose the world but rather in the sense that they, humans, are the exponent of the world, the exposer of the exposing.[31] Humans are "those who expose *as such* sharing and circulation" (BSP 3, trans. mod.). "Humanity is the exposer [*l'exposant*, the exponent] of the world, it is neither its end nor its ground – the world [i.e. the exposing of singularities to themselves and each other] is what is exposed by and to humanity [*l'exposé de l'homme*], it is neither its environment, nor its representation" (BSP 18, trans. mod.; see also BSP 85). World is exposition; the human exposition is exposed to and exposes exposition. This exponential characteristic of the human means that the human is also potentially the unexposer of the exposing. If human existing takes on the active connotation of deciding to exist, it is because it is always possible for the existents that we are to close off exposition. The decision of existence is the decision to keep the spacing that allows for self-relation open, the decision not to close the gap that would close the entity upon itself. This decision should not be understood as a sovereign decision. I do not decide out of myself to exist. I do not give myself existence. I do not either decide to enter into relation with an exteriority as if I were first there in an interiority. But I exist, and as was said above, this existence is a *praxis*, not a brute given. To exist is to engage in, to be responsive to and responsible for existence as sense. Ultimately we have a tension between two movements: on the one hand, existence itself actively resists the closing off of sense; on the other hand, since existence is not a brute fact but an "act" or a "decision," sense must incessantly be reopened each time, at each place, at every turn. This (re)opening of the spacing, this (re)engagement of sense is, according to Nancy, a struggle for the world, so that the world can form a world (*faire monde*), so that it can truly be a world, that is, "that in which there is room for everyone: but a genuine place, one in which things can genuinely *take place* (in this world)" (CW 42).

What has been described in this chapter is Nancy's ontology. Yet an important remark needs to be made. Nancy often presents his ontological concept (being singular plural, world, finitude, etc.) as the structure of our current historical reality that imposes upon us a certain task to be fulfilled. If we are describing the ontological structure of existence, then it does not seem that we can be talking about either a historical event or a task to be taken on. With regard to the relation between the ontological description and "our times," it must be said that, if it is true that we have come to the end (end of sense as signification, end of the world as organized whole, end of community as communion, etc.), then coming to this end cannot first make us finite singular beings. It can only reveal to us that Being is finite and singular plural by rendering obsolete or impossible metaphysical thoughts of Being as absolute and infinite. That this is happening now is a function, as we will see in the next chapter, of the deconstruction of monotheism brought about by technology and capitalism. At the same time, if the singular plural is the ontological structure of everything that exists, it means that there never was a cosmos, or an infinite subject, or the pure immanence of community. Throughout our history, the drive toward the perfect accomplishment of an infinite subject, toward the perfect closure of a cosmos or a community, always reached a limit (this limit is the "with") upon which that desire undid or unworked itself. It is this self-disenclosing movement of any enclosure that Nancy seeks to uncover in the deconstruction of monotheism to which we turn in the next chapter. That same movement structures the tension between myth and its interruption, community and its unworking, which we discuss in chapter 3. According to Nancy, it is only in working through Christianity in a certain way, rather than simply rejecting it, that we will be able to think the complex movement of unworking or disenclosing beyond the opposition between immanence and transcendence, inside and outside. Nancy's engagement with Christianity is, hence, integral to the ontological categories that have been laid out here, and it is to this topic that we turn in the next chapter.

2

Christianity

The primary goal of this chapter is to explain what Nancy means by the "deconstruction" of monotheism or of Christianity and how it enables the ontology of finitude, and more specifically the "radically materialist" thinking of the world sketched in the first chapter. In order to do so, we will examine the first two essays of *Dis-Enclosure* and outline "the difficult and narrow path" ploughed by Nancy (D 13) in his deconstruction of the conceptual grid that conjoins atheism, monotheism, and nihilism. Nancy's methodological approach here needs to be situated vis-à-vis Heideggerian *Destruktion* and Derridean deconstruction. This will then allow us to see how Nancy's deconstruction of Christianity allows him to put into play a non-metaphysical thinking of God: a God that is not seen as the "first principle" of the world but as nothing but the world itself in its opening. The deconstruction of monotheism, according to Nancy, leads not to a simple rejection, but rather to a reinterpretation or retrieval of the divine, which is itself purely atheological and anarchical.

Nancy is attempting a rethinking of transcendence not as a movement toward that which is transcendent or absolute (God), but as the movement of opening-unto or of the self-disenclosing of existence. We will then see how, on the basis of this rethinking of transcendence, Nancy provides new readings of the theological virtues (faith, hope, charity) and of the three central mysteries of Christianity (Trinity, Incarnation, Resurrection). What these reconceptualizations of the central tenets of Christianity share is a new conception of the relation between body and the soul (or sense and matter). Though latent in Christianity itself, this alternative conception has been obstructed or covered over by traditional mind–body dualism, as we will see in chapter 5.

An explication of Nancy's project of a deconstruction of Christianity is rendered difficult by two related facts. First, the project is very much a work in progress, even though it has been anticipated since its announcement in the mid 1990s and the publication of a programmatic essay in 1998. The publication of the first volume of *The Deconstruction of Christianity*, titled "Dis-Enclosure," appeared in French in 2005 and the second, "L'Adoration," in 2010. Both volumes contain some programmatic essays that give an overview of the project as a whole and the second volume clarifies and develops particular questions that were left hanging in the first one (for example, that of the relation between Christianity and the other two forms of monotheism). Despite these developments, the expressed goals of the project are not accomplished in these volumes. What we find instead are gestures toward what such an engagement with Christianity would accomplish – that is, the overcoming of nihilism, not exactly a modest aim! – and some scattered texts that exemplify such engagement: texts on the epistle of James, the mystery of the Incarnation, God in Blanchot, etc. Nancy himself describes the first volume as "an open-air construction site," a series of texts that "turn around the same object without approaching it frontally" (D 12).

Second, what Nancy discusses here is nothing less than a fundamental mutation of civilization from polytheism to monotheism with all that it involves: philosophy, democracy, capitalism, and now nihilism. Nancy paints this history in broad brushstrokes and following all the details of his argument would require extensive knowledge not only of the history of Antiquity, but also of philosophy up to the present, as well as knowledge of what we could call "the text of Christianity," that is, the major teachings of Christianity and how they have been interpreted throughout history. Needless to say, such a thorough presentation cannot be provided here.

Monotheism, atheism and nihilism or the closure of the West

The implicit premise of Nancy's approach to monotheism is that the shift from polytheism to monotheism, the rejection and denial of the multiple gods present in the world, is brought about by a fundamentally atheistic impulse. As such, monotheism contains within itself the principle of a world without God, a principle which, pushed to its conclusion, can only morph into atheism proper and then into nihilism (D 36). If monotheism in itself and by its very nature conceals an atheistic and even nihilistic impulse, then it follows that atheistic or nihilistic gestures do not amount to the negation of monotheism but rather to the actualization of possibilities latent within monotheism itself. Yet, while monotheism is necessarily atheistic, the converse does not hold: one can conceive of an atheism that would not be monotheistic. However, the form of atheism we find today (the rejection of the existence of God) is precisely the monotheistic variety. It rejects a specific conception of God without rejecting the monotheistic way of thinking. What this means will become clear in what follows. Nancy's wager is that modern atheism will remain caught up within the monotheistic logic that it purports to negate so as long as we do not engage with the pattern of thinking that constitutes "the West," in order to explore the possibility of another way of thinking, another "atheism" hidden within modern atheism. Following Bataille, Nancy will call this other "atheism" "atheological."

In order to understand the intrinsic relation between monotheism and atheism, we must look at how Nancy understands the "birth of the Occident" as a shift from polytheism to monotheism. The birth of monotheism cannot simply be regarded as a shift in the quantity or number of gods, but rather monotheism implies a transformation of the very notion of "God," which entails in its turn a transformation of our very relation to God. The difference between monotheism and polytheisms, Nancy writes,

> is not due to the number of gods. In fact, the plurality of gods corresponds to their effective presence (in nature, in an image, in a mind possessed), and their effective presence corresponds to relations of power, of threat, or of assistance, which religion organizes through the entirety of its myths and its rites. The unicity of god, on the contrary, signifies the withdrawal of this god away from presence and also away from power thus understood. (D 35–6)

The polytheistic world is a pre-given, ordered, and animated world, populated by beings (by "presences") of heterogeneous qualities and statuses (D 15). The gods are present as active powers and stand in a differential relation of power to the mortals.

Against this background, monotheism occurs as a drastic and sweeping renunciation of the worldly immanence of the gods in the life of mortals. As Nancy notes, what perhaps most obviously unites Judaism, Christianity, and Islam is a rejection of the gods who are in the world, these gods now being called idols. (Christ seems to be an exception here, but, according to Nancy, his "presence" is of a special kind. We will come back to this below.) Nancy writes in the opening lines of a short text titled *Un jour, les dieux se retirent*...: "One day, the gods withdraw. On their own they withdraw from their divinity, that is, from their presence. They do not just go away or become absent: they do not leave for some other place, they withdraw from their own presence, they withdraw from within."[1] The statue that was once the full presence of the god (and not only its image or symbol) now ontologically shrinks into a false god, a mere representation that no longer has any self-presence. Nancy can therefore say that monotheism is "an aggravation of the relation to the incommensurable and a transformation of the relations with the inaccessible" (D 8). The word "God" no longer points to anything that is present but instead becomes a measure of the ontological distance between that which exists (the world, the creatures) and its principle, condition, or ground (God, the Creator) (D 15).

The gods are no longer immediately accessible so that the partnership between the gods and the mortals is replaced by a relationship of incommensurability. The world is ruptured into two realms so that the world is no longer a cosmos, an organized totality, but "this world here-below." Whereas it had been the place of the relation between mortals and divinities, this mundane world becomes the place of relations of exchange between humans themselves (A 75). The mutation from polytheism to monotheism is thus concomitant with the formations of cities (*polis*) or autonomous people and the invention of democracy. In "Of Divine Places," Nancy explains this relation between the withdrawal of the gods and the "birth" of community, or of the "question" of being-together:

> It is with the withdrawal of the gods that community came into being: a group of men facing its gods does not conceive of itself as a community, that is to say it does not seek within itself the presence of what binds it together, but experiences itself as this particular group (family, people, tribe) before the face of the god who holds and preserves in his innermost self the truth and the power of its bond. (IC 143)

This point will be elaborated in the next chapter. This mutation also gives rise to a new form of economic exchange, based on production and expansion instead of the reproduction of stable, hierarchical relations. What happens is a mutation in the under-standing of wealth from a "glorious and unproductive wealth" that is accumulated for its shine and splendor and that wraps what is sacred or valorous into its brilliance (such as the spoils of Roman conquest) into "invested and productive wealth" accumulated to be put to work in a process of infinite enrichment (A 30, see CW 47–8). In short, we witness a metamorphosis of the basic way in which we inhabit our world. We see the previously stable and given social bonds put into question and transformed according to a new experience of the divine.

In "The Forgetting of Philosophy," Nancy discussed this muta-tion in terms of the "entry into signification." This "entry" is an essential dis-orientation and hence contemporaneous with the demand for meaning. Such a demand assumes that meaning is out there, "present-at-a-distance" (GT 29), and must be pointed at, captured, signified. This is why signification lies essentially not in the sheer presence of things but in a representation that holds the world at a distance and directs us toward the fulfillment of its signification. The world is not present by itself, is not meaningful as such, but only as oriented toward the fulfillment of its given (but distant) meaning. While the desire for meaning necessarily repre-sents signification as something to be captured or recaptured (the movement of return or of progress exemplify the same distantce-presence), its fulfillment is by necessity impossible. The will to meaning is self-defeating because signification is itself the move-ment of desire and not the posited or desired end toward which the movement aims. Therefore signification exhausts itself in the movement of its desire (GT 52).

It is clear that the withdrawal of the worldly presence of the gods should not be understood as the liquidation of an occult world by the light of reason. In fact, it is this withdrawal that renders the world questionable in the first place: it makes it possible to ask why there is the world, where the world is going, etc. In other words, it makes it possible to question the principle(s) governing the world.[2] Before the withdrawal of divine presence, before the sepa-ration of the world into two orders (here-below and beyond), the closure of this system (the closure of metaphysics that we will discuss below) and the quest for meaning that results from it, there was not a night or a muddled signification but, as Nancy says, another kind of light, *another* day (GT 28). Before the monotheistic mutation, there was a way of being foreign to signification, to the division between the apparent world and the real world, between what is and the ground or meaning of what is. If this world appears to be a dark, occult world, it is because we do not understand how it made sense because sense for us takes on the specific form of signification (questionability, presence-at-a-distance) described above.

What Nancy wants to show is that monotheism, insofar as it consists in the renunciation of the worldly immanence of the gods, is already the undoing of theism and hence the origin of atheism. In opposition to the mythical function of the gods, monotheism establishes the one God as a radical alterity that serves as a first and final orienting principle upon which the world (or the totality of what is) is dependent (D 18).[3] This is the movement of the "will to signification" as described above. At this point, it is possible to replace God by other orienting principles that serve exactly the same orienting function, while remaining within this same mono-theistic framework.[4] Atheism is the rejection of a divine principle distinct from the world and it can take two forms. Either it claims that both origin and end (what is and its principle) are immanent to the world, a claim that, as Nancy just said, recreates the "tran-scendent position of the principle," or it claims that there ought to be no such origin, cause, or end. Humanism would correspond to the first type ("Ideal Humanity" as the principle that guides history). Scientific positivism (broadly: the doctrine that holds that the scientific explanation of reality must be liberated from first and final causes) would be an example of the second type, and so would capitalism, which knows no other final cause than the indef-inite accumulation of wealth. Scientific positivism and capitalism are thus forms of nihilism according to Nancy because they affirm that there is no orienting principle driving history toward a given end. Since meaning is found in principles (this is why we are here, this is where we are going), both forms of nihilism condemn us to live in a meaningless, chaotic universe. Despite their differences, all these "-isms" remain caught within a logic of the theological principle (D 23–4).[5] This logic condemns us to think the world as either dependent on a transcendent principle and hence as mean-ingless in itself, needing to receive its sense from elsewhere, or to think it as pure immanence, as lacking a principle and hence a meaning. Caught in this logic, we find two formally identical logical gestures, each of which is the inverted mirror image of the other. Either we think of the history of the West as that of a con-quest against obscurantism, religion, etc. and we see the progress

of atheism as the emancipation of reason, or we think that secularization and the progress of atheism are responsible for nihilism and
the lack of transcendent meaning in the contemporary world, and
we then appeal to religion to cure or save us. Nancy wants to throw
into relief the fact that neither of these patterns of thought genuinely allows to think beneath (and beyond) the closure of the West
since they both remain caught in a foundationalist logic. On the
one hand, supposedly enlightened humanism seeks to ground the
meaning and values of the world purely within the world itself. In
doing so, it is led either to reify humanity or reason itself (turning
it into a transcendent value, a God of sorts) or to confront the
absence of principle (and all we are left with is endless circulation
or exchange). On the other hand, reactionary nostalgia for the
comforts of religion appeals to a re-grounding of the meaning and
value of the world in a transcendent principle, since only
the solid foundation of the divine can put an end to general
equivalency and effectuate a true grounding. If both the emancipatory and the religious gestures can be seen as merely two sides
of the same coin, it is because they both assume that the questionability of the world in its principle, the search for a ground or a
sense of world outside of the world, can only be resolved by
a transcendent principle. Hence, philosophy and monotheism are
co-implicated and Christianity is nothing other than the name of
this co-implication. This is why, for Nancy, Christianity is the "most
Westernized form of monotheism" (D 35).

The Janus head of monotheism and atheism delineates the
closure of the West, which is what Nancy, following Derrida, identifies as the closure of metaphysics. The "closure" of metaphysics
means that metaphysics is total system with no outside, no beyond.
Or better put: it is precisely the system that sets up the opposition
between a "beyond" and a "here below." Yet this system, as we
will see, is not without play or without opening, and it is from
this opening that its self-deconstruction or self-disenclosing will
proceed. Nancy defines metaphysics as follows:

> "metaphysics," in the sense by which Nietzsche and Heidegger have
> marked this term, denotes the representation of being [être] as beings
> [étant] and as beings present [étant présent]. In so doing, metaphysics
> sets a founding, warranting presence beyond the world (viz., the
> Idea, *Summum Ens*, the Subject, the Will). This setup stabilizes beings,
> enclosing them in their own beingness [étantité].[6]…Everything –
> properly and precisely *everything* – is played out in the mutual refer-

ral of these two regimes of beings or presence: the "immanent" and the "transcendent"; the "here-below" and the "beyond"; the "sensuous" and the "intelligible"; "appearance" and "reality." Closure is the completion of this totality that conceives itself to be fulfilled in its self-referentiality. (D 6)

If metaphysics forms a total structure of reference between two realms or regimes of being, what does Nancy mean when he says that this structure discloses itself? Where does the spacing that allows for such an opening come from? In what way does it allow us to think beyond the Janus head of monotheism and atheism?

Destruktion, deconstruction, disenclosure

Let us pause here and try to bring to the fore Nancy's methodology, his strategy for posing the problem of the enclosure of the West within a monotheistic paradigm, all the while affirming the self-disenclosing or self-deconstruction of monotheism and of Christianity in particular. In order to do so, Nancy needs to show that Christianity, while it does reinforce the closure of metaphysics, also undoes it. According to Nancy a religion consists of rites and observances that establish a relation with the sacred in order to promise (or guarantee) another life after this life, which would replace and redeem it. If this is so, Christianity is the "religion" that complicates any properly religious understanding of itself according to which the world above or beyond (heaven, life after death) can be reached or achieved outside of this world and after this life through prayers, rites, and the observance of strict rules in this world. In other words, Christianity is the religion of the exit from religion because it erases the transcendent God, who disappears into his creation and becomes a pure relation (Trinity), and affirms the presence "here-below" of the divine alterity and of the other of life (Incarnation, Resurrection). This movement of becoming-atheistic, whereby Christianity undoes its own metaphysical premises (the separation of the beyond and the here-below), is where Nancy finds the necessary conceptual tools to think the world (and hence the divine in it) in a non-metaphysical way. It is not by thinking against Christianity that we move out of nihilism, but by thinking one Christianity against another.

Nancy's engagement with Christianity resonates with, while it at the same time challenges, Heidegger's *Destruktion* (destructuring, also translated as destruction) of the history of ontology and his notion of the overcoming of metaphysics. Heidegger mentions the necessity of engaging in a destructuring of the history of ontology in §6 of *Being and Time*. Fundamental ontology, the inquiry into the meaning of Being as such, and the destructuring of the history of ontology are essentially interrelated, even though only the first task is accomplished (and only partially) in *Being and Time* itself. While the first task provides us with the guiding thread (Being as Time) to engage the history of ontology, the destructuring of that history allows us to reach the soil (the primordial experience) from which to ask the question of Being as such by de-sedimenting or re-grounding the philosophical language we inherited from the tradition and which we employ in our ontology. For Heidegger, destructuring is a procedure that requires the retrieval or repetition (*Wiederholung*) of a possibility that remains potential since it has never been fully actualized. This "retrieval" demands that we work through the past, loosening up the sediment that covers over what has been transmitted to us, traversing "deficient conceptualizations to free up possibilities of questioning which the tradition has not yet explored."[7] Heidegger insists that the target of *Destruktion* is not the past but the present, the way the tradition is present for us. *Destruktion* is aimed at what has been handed down to us as ontology – i.e. the operative concepts we inherit and within which our understanding of Being operates. *Destruktion* seeks to free up the "elemental words of philosophy," by first rendering them puzzling for us again and by then bringing them back to their source in a primordial experience of Being,[8] which would be inaccessible to purely historicist or philological accounts. No ontology can forgo this engagement with its own history; indeed, as Heidegger shows with relation to Descartes, the philosopher who naively tries to break with the tradition remains all the more caught up within it. If Heidegger's *Destruktion* is closely linked, in *Being and Time*, to the possibility of reawakening the question of the meaning of Being, its implications will ultimately be spun out in Heidegger's thinking of the "destiny" of Being and of the necessity to "leap" (*Sprung*) into the "other beginning."[9] We cannot go into further detail here. Suffice it to say that ultimately, Heidegger will look for a possibility of thinking hidden underneath or on the hither side of metaphysics, rather than for the experiential source of metaphysics itself.

Heidegger never directly engaged in a *Destruktion* of Christianity or of monotheism. Christianity seems, for him, to fall fully on the side of metaphysics as ontotheology. Heidegger was the first to explicitly uncover the "onto-theo-logical" structure of metaphysics. As we said in the first chapter, metaphysics seeks to answer the fundamental question: "why are there beings rather than nothing?"[10] This question seeks "the ground for what is insofar as it is," yet this project of grounding splits into two. First, all that exists is interrogated with regard to its being (what does it mean for it to be?) and grounded in an ultimate sense of Being as that which is continuously present and explains the presence of what exists (e.g. Platonic Forms or Essences). At the same time, what is as a whole is brought back to a first cause or foundation, to a being who can ground not only what is, but also Being itself. This preeminent being will be called God (*theion*, the divine in the singular) because only a self-subsisting (uncaused and eternal) being can serve as highest principle for the totality of existing beings. As such, metaphysics is both ontology, the process of grounding beings in Being, and theology, the process of grounding Being in the highest being, that is to say, God. In both "branches," the ground or explanation for what is will be transcendent, yet it will be so in different ways. Given the double structure of foundation (God/Being) inherent to metaphysics, we can understand why Heidegger does not think that Christianity can be of any help in overcoming metaphysics. For Heidegger, there is no Christianity that does not understand itself through Greek philosophy. It would seem then that the thrust of Heidegger's engagement with the history of thought is to strip away the Christian veneer which has occluded our comprehension of the unique wonder before the coming into presence of beings that was experienced at the beginning of western thought. Indeed, the possibility of an "other beginning" depends on our capacity to "think the Greek from what is Greek alone," that is to say: apart from the Christian *and* apart from that which in the Greek "beginning" (Plato, Aristotle) already announces this conjoining of philosophy and Christianity in onto-theo-logy. The doubled structure of onto-theo-logy (Being/God) finds its possibility, as we just saw, in the necessity of grounding what is as a whole in both senses of ground: as common being and as highest being.[11] For Heidegger, a non-metaphysical thinking of Being would thus be beyond the scope of Christianity.

When Nancy describes his own deconstruction of monotheism as an "inquiry or search consisting in disassembling and analyzing the constitutive elements of monotheism, and more directly of Christianity, thus of the West, in order to go back to (or to advance toward) a resource that could form at once the buried origin and the imperceptible future of the world that calls itself 'modern' " (D 34), this sounds very much like a Heideggerian *Destruktion* of the ontotheological paradigm – i.e., a hermeneutic engagement with the Christian history of the West. Yet, there is one crucial difference between Nancy and Heidegger: the retrieval of the buried origin to be unearthed is not accomplished in an overcoming of Christianity or in a step back into the "ground" of metaphysics for Nancy. The originary possibility Nancy is trying to retrieve is internal to the framework of Christianity itself – the "heart" of Christianity "itself." This is made clear by Nancy's more structural or more Derridean description of his "deconstruction" as a taking apart, a disassembling, a loosening up of "the assembled structure in order to give some play to the possibility from which it emerged but which, qua assembled structure, it hides" (D 148). The deconstruction which belongs to any construction testifies to the excess of a structure over itself, to the opening of a closed system. (Hence, our characterization of Derridean deconstruction as structural by opposition to its historical or genetic counterpart is too quick. Deconstruction means that a structure is essentially open or that its "center" is empty, that is, that the structure is not tied down and hence cannot be brought back to a single origin or to a transcendental signified. This opening, as the inscription of the Outside or of absolute alterity within the structure itself is what ensures the structure its play and hence its history.)[12]

Nancy will say not only that the construct of Christianity deconstructs itself but that deconstruction is essentially Christian, that the movement of deconstruction is the movement of Christianity in its own action of exceeding itself (D 149). If Christianity is understood as a construction, then it is not possible to ask *which* Christianity is deconstructing itself.[13] Such an empirical objection simply amounts to a refusal to think the divergent strands and internal tensions of Christianity as interrelated terms within one single (and historically contingent) force field or structure. Nancy's point is that this structure itself is constantly moving, turning against itself, exceeding itself, doubling back on itself.

Where does the movement inherent in the structure of Christianity come from? If history does not befall Christianity by accident, then the law of this movement is what opens Christianity to history in such a way that there is no Christianity *per se*, no *essence* of Christianity prior to the opening of the supposedly closed system. The susceptibility of Christianity to history is so fundamental that Christianity consists in nothing but this opening itself.[14] This is what Nancy means when he says that Christianity is a subject (D 38). The impulse of the disenclosure can be found within the movement of Christianity itself, at the moment where Christianity exceeds "itself" and, in this excess, is itself. The "self" of Christianity is nothing but the movement of excess over what is "given" as Christianity (creeds, dogmas, etc.)[15] This same logic of self-disenclosure that Nancy essentially associates with Christianity as a con-struct was theorized by Derrida in his later writings using the trope of autoimmunity. Essentially, the movement of disenclosure runs parallel to the movement of autoimmunity: when the immunity of the self becomes so strong that it threatens the life of the self, the self, in order to stay alive, attacks its own immune system, its own system of self-protection. At this point, the self can only remain itself by destroying what protects it from invasion by foreign elements; it can only remain itself by being radically open to the non-self that threatens to destroy it. The pure life of the self (absolute immunity) is its death; the death of the immune self (autoimmunity) is its life. It is this aporetic logic that constitutes any "selfhood." The movement of autoimmunity is more complicated than a mere suicide of the self since the self finds itself (its life) in losing itself.[16]

Creation *ex nihilo* and the overcoming of nihilism

While for Heidegger the struggle against nihilism is likewise a struggle against Christianity, for Nancy this struggle requires a certain retrieval of notions internal to Christianity, which must be salvaged from their entrapment within the metaphysical closure. We could therefore say that Nancy's deconstruction of monotheism makes possible his ontology of the singular plural of the world in that it allows, as we briefly saw in the first chapter, for an interpretation of the *nihil* not as firm sediment or ground but as an opening. A deconstruction of Christianity, beyond the programmatic nature of the essays found in Nancy's book, would read the "text of Christianity" in order to show how, within it, the non-metaphysical or non-ontotheological interpretation of its major concepts or figures – for example the *ex nihilo* – runs in the background and unsettles its more "traditional" interpretation.

As we say in the first chapter, if we want to think the world as such, according to Nancy, we must rethink the couple "transcendence/immanence." Now we can understand why Nancy's thinking of the world as such (neither immanence, nor transcendence, but edges and junctures opening "right at" the world) require that we abandon the monotheistic logic of the "position of the principle." As Nancy says: "*Atheism is not enough. It is the place or position of the principle itself that must be emptied out*" (A 48). This also means that the "nothing" that occupies this position in nihilism has to be rethought. The death of God is the death of any reason that would explain the totality of everything that is. But the question is whether this lack of reason, which delivers the world over to contingency, necessarily condemns us to nihilism or whether it contains within itself the resources to overcome nihilism. For Nietzsche, the death of God means that our tablets of values, which were previously seen as objective, have now lost their power because they are seen as the result of humanity's subjective acts of valuing. Thus, values are not objective commands from without; values are not found but created. Nietzsche then concludes that what is essentially valuable are not values themselves, but the will – the valuing gesture – that gives rise to these values. The devaluation of all values (what could be called radical nihilism) leads to a completed nihilism, or what Heidegger calls "classical nihilism." Nietzsche understands this nihilism as the overcoming of nihilism. It consists in the disintegration of the transcendent realm and the affirmation of the phenomenal world as the only true world on the one hand, and the disintegration of all teleological narratives or purposive explanations in favor of an affirmation of the world as perpetual becoming on the other. For Nancy, going beyond nihilism necessitates, as it does for Nietzsche, a new principle of valuation. Nietzsche calls his principle of valuation the "will to power." Often mistakenly understood to mean that the will wills something outside itself, namely power, the will to power is the will that gathers itself and overpowers itself. The ability to gather and overpower oneself, to be one's own master and to obey one's own command, is what defines the will to power. If the will to power is the principle of all life, this means that life feels itself living not in achieving a goal and holding on to what is achieved, but in overpowering itself, in self-overcoming. Hence, life as will to power is constant becoming. It should be added that this self-overcoming need not appear as "positive growth." If the tree overcomes itself in growing, it also does so in decaying and turning into compost. It is our teleological understanding of life that makes us see things as growing, achieving their given goal, and then decaying. For Nietzsche, on the other hand, Being is understood as the constant becoming of life.

If for Nietzsche the will to power is what overcomes nihilism, for Nancy it remains essentially nihilistic because it reduces all evaluative gestures (all life) to a common denominator: the will. This is also why Heidegger will say that the completion of metaphysics is found in Nietzsche's will to power, whose truth is the sheer will to will. Everything becomes a value, that is, becomes something at the disposal of the will itself. Being is reduced to a value: to be means to be at the disposal of the willful activities of the subject. What truly is, then, is what becomes or wills, what uses what is given as the basis for its becoming or willing. If the will to power is, as Nancy and Heidegger thinks, nihilistic, then the overcoming of nihilism can only happen in a passage from the will to power to a different principle of valuation, one that presupposes the absolute distinction or incommensurability of evaluative gestures. According to Nancy, the dissolution of "the transcendent" does not abandon us to the world as the place of an eternal, immanent becoming, where everything is in the same way (becoming, willing, overcoming). It puts transcendence into play right *at* the world itself.

In Nancy's terms, the overcoming of nihilism necessitates a rethinking of the Christian notion of the "ex nihilo" creation of the world. Creation *ex nihilo* is, as was said in chapter 1, another way of saying that beings are only what they are, that there is nothing outside of the world (BP 196). That the world is created out of nothing implies that it has no presupposition or precondition – neither an undifferentiated prime matter nor an omnipotent creator capable of producing something out of nothing:

> The idea of *creatio ex nihilo*, inasmuch as it is clearly distinguished from any form of production or fabrication, essentially covers the dual motif of an absence of necessity and the existence of a given without reason, having neither foundation nor principle.... *Ex nihilo*, which is to say:...nothing but that which is [*rien que cela qui est*], nothing but that which grows [*rien que cela qui croît*] (*creo, cresco*), lacking any growth principle. (D 24; see BSP 16)

This world is without "God," that is without given reason, but not without opening, even if this opening opens unto nothing. The world opens from within to an unconditional alterity that is an "outside" of the world without being another world. This "outside" does not exist (it is nothing that "is") but it, as Nancy says, can "mobilize" existence (D 10). To think this outside or this alterity, we need a thinking that is strictly atheistic without being the simple denial of theism. We need a thinking that, in other words, is atheistic without being "absentheistic" (D 18). Such a thinking would not think the absence of principle as an *absence* pure and simple.[17] It would, therefore, not attempt to *save* the world from its meaninglessness or groundlessness since to ask for a meaning or a ground implies that the world needs to be saved by something outside or beyond the world. As was already said, this gesture remains caught within the metaphysical closure and its "desire for signification," which is the origin of our feeling the need for a transcendent meaning or ground in the first place (D 20).

In the same way that the becoming atheistic of Christianity (the dissolution of its theism) disencloses the world by opening it to an alterity that is not a transcendent principle but the breach or break of the here-below right at the here-below, this same becoming atheistic also disencloses reason and liberates it from its enclosure in the calculative forms of rationality that consists in giving reasons, in justifying. The movement that essentially constitutes reason is not that of a grounding but of an opening of reason to something that exceeds its power. It is a thrust toward something incommensurable. Reason seeks "reasons," "causes," or "explanations" because it is "in contact" with that which is greater than anything it can think. Here, Nancy provides an interesting reading of Anselm's famous "ontological argument" for the existence of God in the *Proslogion*. The argument goes as follows: Since "God is that, than which nothing greater can be conceived," and since a God that cannot be conceived not to exist is "greater" than one that can, God necessarily exists. Nancy's take on the so-called "proof" focuses on the movement of thought expressed by the "definition" of God: No matter what I think (no matter what object I represent or conceptualize, including God), "God" is in excess over that. God is that which, when I attempt to think it, brings my thinking beyond what it can think.[18] Nancy writes:

> The argument rests entirely on the movement of thought, insofar as it cannot not think the maximum of the being [*l'être*] it is able to think, but thinks also an excess to that maximum, since thought is capable of thinking even that there is something that exceeds its power to think. In other words, thinking (i.e., not the intellect alone, but the heart and the demand itself) can think – indeed, cannot not think – that it thinks something in excess over itself....In this sense, Anselm is much less a follower of Christianity than the bearer of a necessity that defines the modern world of thought, of the existential

ordeal of thought. "God" is for Anselm the name of this ordeal. This
name can assuredly be rejected for many reasons. But the ordeal or
trial cannot be avoided. (D 11; see also A 124)

Reason without this ordeal (that is, reason without the remainder
of deconstructed Christianity) is calculative rationality or understanding (*Verstand*). Hence, the disenclosure of Christianity, which
allows us to think a disenclosed world and a disenclosed reason,
is a transformation of the transcendent into a transcendence in
immanence. It is not a process of secularization, not the abandonment of any incommensurable alterity or opening for the sake of
pure immanence.

If the transcendent position is dissolved in favor of the movement of transcendence-in-immanence, and if "God" is the name
par excellence of the transcendent, does this mean that the
name "God" has to be abandoned? According to Nancy, this is not
necessary. Rather, Nancy thinks that it is possible to redeploy
the word "God" beyond its metaphysical (Christian/atheistic)
meaning as "God-principle" so that it comes to name not the transcendent, but transcendence in immanence.[19] In order to bring
about such a displacement, Nancy draws together Heidegger's
"last god," whose intimating gesture consists entirely in its step
(*pas*) or passing-by (*passage*), and the movement or play of Derridean differance, which we discussed in chapter 1 and whose
transgressive "a" points, for Nancy, toward the "*à*" with an accent,
the "toward" of an ad-dress (*à-Dieu*, toward-God or *adieu*, fare-
well). In order to justify naming this triple movement of passing-
by, spacing-out, and inclination "God" and "the Divine" (see CW
70), Nancy appeals to the etymological relation between the Latin
word for divine being or god, *divus/deus*, and *dies*, day or daylight
(a relation that can be traced back to the Sanskrit, *dēva*). "God,"
denotes neither a being nor Being but "the difference of day – *dies*
– and night, the division light/darkness by which everything
takes place, taking place *between* those two modalities, those two
accents or those two sides of the same peak or the same height of
being" (D 118). Divine is therefore the blink between presence and
absence, between night and day. Nancy is well aware that there
always remains the possibility that the triple movement of the
divine as passing-by, as spacing-out and as inclination be caught
and captured in a perception and become fixed in a look (*eidos*). In
that case, Nancy writes "the god no longer passes: he becomes
God. Then différance turns – not into transcendence..., but

into something transcendent installed as domination" (D 120, trans. mod.).

Reinterpreting Christianity:
Trinity, Incarnation, and Resurrection

To deconstruct Christianity, as was said above, means to point to the places where Christianity itself overflows its status as religion (rites and observances that bind humans to the beyond) and as metaphysics (the two-worlds paradigm). Nancy shows how the three Christian mysteries (Trinity, Incarnation, Resurrection) are not, or not merely, explainable metaphysically and how they thus open the thought of the world as a disenclosed totality. Two texts of Nancy are central to this reworking of the Christian mysteries: "Mystères et vertus" in *L'Adoration* and *Noli me tangere.*

The latter is Nancy's response to Derrida's reading of Nancy's work in *On Touching*. What Nancy is attempting to develop, according to Derrida in *On Touching*, is a "post-deconstructive realism" (OT 46). Nancy resists all idealism and subjectivism (we already saw this in our discussion of his transformation of the Heideggerian concept of sense) without falling back into naive realism. Schematically, we could say that philosophy moves from realism (the assumption that things are real and are really like we perceive them) to idealism (the recovery of the subject as the origin of all access to "reality") to phenomenology (the overcoming of the subject–object distinction in transcendental consciousness or *Ek-sistenz*) to deconstruction (the undoing of what in phenomenology still thinks of itself as an enclosed totality: transcendental ego, horizontal-ecstatic temporality). It is in the space or blind spot opened by deconstruction that Nancy's thought of the body as the "contact" between matter and sense situates itself. For Nancy, a singularity is a body and as such, it is always beyond the pure self-presence of a consciousness or the full presence of the thing itself. We will discuss Nancy's understanding of the body in more detail in chapter 5. For now, it suffices to recall our discussion of differance in the previous chapter to see that Nancy's thought is one where the logic of differance, the logic according to which something is "first" itself thanks to a spacing that allows it to relate to itself so that the self is an effect of spacing rather than the origin of the movement of self-relation, is explicitly applied to the body.

By calling Nancy's post-deconstructive realism "irredentist,"[20] Derrida wants to highlight two things. First, in touch, there is a certain desire to master or assimilate what is on the other side of the border upon which, or at the limit of which, touch happens. Second, such a desire to assimilate is predicated on an assumed homogeneity. In engaging with how the tradition of philosophy has thought about touch, Derrida wants to show how it partici-pates in what he calls "metaphysics of presence." Derrida defines the metaphysics of presence as follows: "The enterprise of return-ing 'strategically,' 'ideally,' to an origin or to a priority thought to be simple, intact, normal, pure, standard, self-identical, in order then to think in terms of derivation, complication, deterioration, accident, etc."[21] In *On Touching*, Derrida turns his attention to a certain strand of the tradition which he calls "haptological" (from the Greek *haptein*, to touch). This tradition is implicated in the metaphysical gesture insofar as it thinks touch in terms of identity, homogeneity, immediacy, and self-presence, even when it empha-sizes a certain interruption or distance. This is what Derrida's reading of Merleau-Ponty shows.[22] The question addressed to Nancy is: is his post-deconstructive realism implicated in this meta-physical gesture? Derrida's response is ambivalent. As was men-tioned in the previous chapter, Nancy's thinking of touch is, on Derrida's own admission, "neither intuitionistic nor continuistic, homogenistic, or indivisibilistic. What it first recalls is sharing, parting, partitioning, and discontinuity, interruption, caesura – in a word, syncope" (OT 156). Yet, if touching another is only possible insofar as I can touch myself, that is, insofar as I am present to or in "direct contact" with myself in this touch, we can wonder how touch can act as a figure of interruption. In the same way that Derrida shows that Husserl "hearing oneself speak" does not take place in the immediacy of the instant (an instant that would be without dimension and hence without exteriority), Nancy speaks of a "self-touch" as "self-touching-you" that does not happen in pure immediacy. Yet, Derrida worries that in *succeeding* to interrupt itself, this interrupted touch still presupposes the propriety and integrity of a self-contained body whose self-touch or self-sensing is itself immediate, that is, without detour through an irrecoverable exteriority. Even though for Nancy to touch is always to touch a limit (and hence not to penetrate into or merge with what is on the other side) and hence to touch the intangible, Derrida worries that this thinking of the intangible as that which is touched renders, despite all denegation, the intangible accessible (OT 38; see OT 295–6).

For Derrida, this thinking of the touch of the intangible or untouchable finds its roots in Christianity, and especially in the Christian doctrine of the Incarnation. What Derrida uncovers in *On Touching* is the unthought Christian underpinning of the tradition's thinking of the body and of touch (OT 99–100). Christ is the presence of the intangible; he is both the Toucher whose touch saves and heals us and the Touched, insofar as his wounds may be touched by the doubting Thomas. If his touch saves, it is because Christ is touched in another way, that is, touched by grace, so that he remains "saved, safe, unscathed, and free of damage" in the touch. Furthermore, the God that touches and may be touched is also the one who can still be touched in the Eucharist.

Nancy opens his *Corpus* with the phrase pronounced at the Eucharist: *Hoc est enim corpus meum*, "This is my body." In pronouncing this phrase, the Eucharist makes present here and now a something (God, the Absolute) that cannot be seen, sensed, or touched. This presentation, this "Here is," dissipates all our doubts regarding the world of appearances by giving us the Absolute, by presenting "the Thing itself," not as Idea but as Body, that is, as incarnate sense. Yet, Nancy points out that if we desire to touch, see, and participate in the body of Christ, this desire must be predicated on the felt absence of the Absolute. Our need to call the body of Christ to presence arises out of our anguish in the face of the intangibility, invisibility, and absence of this body, our anguish that this thing here (bread) might not be that (God) (C 3–5).

Nancy proposes a different reading of the Eucharist and of Incarnation. In the Eucharist, we do not participate in or touch the Spirit that would be made present in or by the wafer, no more than the Incarnation of God consists in the presence of the spirit in the flesh. God's presence in the world as a body (or as wafer) does not mean that the Absolute has fallen into the world, that the Idea has materialized itself so that it can now be sensed or touched. It only means that the Intangible is "here and now" and not hidden in a beyond. It is, here and now, this other body, that is, not a material body but the body of sense, the body that opens unto sense. Already in "Of Divine Places," Nancy discussed the mystery of Incarnation:

> The strict canon of Catholic faith lays down that in Christ "the two natures are not united solely by homonymy, nor by grace, nor by relation, nor by interpenetration, nor by naming alone nor by

worship, nor by the conversion of one nature into the other, but through subsistence (*hypostasis*)." There is only one hypostasis for the two natures of man and the god. There is neither fusion nor differentiation, but a single place of subsistence or presence, a place where the god appears entirely in man, and man appears entirely in god. This is neither a divinization of man nor a humanization of God. (IC 139)

Incarnation is not the materialization of an invisible Idea or Spirit; it is the irreducible ambiguity of all bodies as flesh – matter and spirit – in the same place. Hence the body is a visible image of the invisible, the manifestation of that which does not manifest itself. Yet, we should not understand this manifestation as a "sign" that points to a beyond, but as two dimensions of the same "thing," body. The incarnation is a becoming flesh that creates two natures (create again: separate and relate, relate by separating). Here, God empties himself out of himself, disappears as God to appear as the divine *in* humanity or *as* humanity. Hence, to say that the body is "not-of-god" does not mean that the body is sufficient upon itself, detached from God, but rather expresses the fact that the body has no founding presence, that it is not grounded in a presence. The body is neither the prison of the soul, nor the expression of a hidden interior, nor is it a full presence: it is an opened or gapping presence, an extension or a spacing, the "place" of an existence, an event of sense (D 82). Christianity then is neither the thought of the separation of body and spirit nor of their fusion but rather the understanding of flesh as the contact–separation between the two. Flesh is essentially ambiguous: both fallen, mortal flesh and the glorious flesh of the resurrected body. This ambiguous status of flesh explains, according to Nancy, Christian sexual morals. As Ian James explains in *The Fragmentary Demand*, "[i]f we were entirely fallen bodies there would be no spirit within us to sanctify, if we were entirely spiritual there would be no mortal fleshy desires to satisfy, and only in the touch *and* separation of the two does question of sexual ambivalence or indeed repression arise."[23]

As was said above, Nancy directly addresses Derrida's worries about the relation between touch and presence in its Christian underpinning in *Noli me tangere*. The phrase *noli me tangere* (Touch me not!) refers to a scene in the Gospel of John, where Jesus instructs Mary Magdalene, at the moment when she recognizes that the Gardener outside of Jesus' tomb is in fact the Risen Christ himself, not to touch him: "Jesus saith unto her, Touch me not; for I am not yet ascended to my Father: but go to my brethren, and say unto them, I ascend unto my Father, and your Father; and *to* my God, and your God" (King James Version, John 20:17). At that moment, between death and life, the touching–touched God has become untouchable. What is this scene teaching us? Does this taboo surrounding the holy Flesh mean that Christianity is the religion of the Untouchable? In light of what has been said about the Incarnation and the Eucharist above, this seems unlikely. To understand this interdiction of touch at the moment just before Ascension, Nancy questions the ontological status of the resurrected body. Death is not the separation of the body and the soul; if that were the case, there would be no resurrected *body*, no Glorious Body of the Ascension. What we have is not a division between a body and a spirit but rather two bodies (or rather, since as we saw above, these two bodies occupy the same place, two dimensions of the same "thing here"): the Glorious body of the Ascension and the body of mortal flesh. According to Nancy, the former is the raising up of the latter, its pivoting to the vertical. The Greek word for Resurrection is *anastasis* and it means, literally, to rise up. While the French borrows, like the English, *résurrection* from the Latin *resurgere*, to surge up or rise up again, there is no corresponding verbal form in French. Hence, instead of saying "He is resurrected," the French ambiguously says "*Il est réssuscité*," which translated literally as "He is resuscitated." Resuscitation comes from the Latin *resuscitare*, which means also to raise up but takes on the sense of "to reanimate" or "to reawaken," to bring back to life. Nancy wants to differentiate between these two senses of resurrection, one that implies a movement from the horizontal to the vertical of a body that remains dead and the other that implies a reanimation of the body that receives a new life. For Nancy, *anastasis* is "neither regeneration, reanimation, palingenesis, rebirth, revivification, nor reincarnation: but the uprising, the *raising* or *the lifting* as a verticality perpendicular to the horizontality of the tomb..." (NMT 18). It is only the tipping up (*basculement*) of sense (A 129). It "is not a second life, it is the erection (or rectification, *redressement*) by which the horizontal course of a life pivots into a vertical signal" (A 78). Hence, immortality is not to be sought on the other side of death, in another life, but in death itself: "In death, the definitive suspension of the sense (of existence) crystallizes eternally the brilliance [*éclat*] of this suspended sense" (A 45). She who is dead does not come back to life but the sense of her life tips up. Instead of going on living, of continuing the movement toward, "it stops and rises up, becoming at the same time final end and accomplished presentation of this 'sense of being I' " (A 129). But this "sense" is not an accomplishment; it does not confer on the life of the dead a greater "cosmic" signification. Rather, the resurrection is only the presentation of the contours of a singular life in its distinction and separation (see NMT 46). The mystery of salvation is not that one will be saved, in the sense of rescued, sheltered from the world and from death; it is rather the mystery of a singular opening of sense, a salutation that is "safe" or "intact," and saluted as such in death (A 79–80).

Why then this interdiction against touching the resurrected body? Because it is by "[n]ot coming into contact with its manifest presence," that one "accede[s] to its real presence, which consists in its departure": "To touch him or to hold him back would be to adhere to immediate presence,... it would be to miss the departing [la partance] according to which the touch and presence come to us" (NMT 15). To want to touch Christ would be to think of resurrection in terms of resuscitation, a beginning anew of presence. But the truth of the resurrection, for Nancy, lies not in the renewed presence of Christ but in the departure of presence: "Just as [a presence] comes, so it goes" and this is the law of its sense or its touch. Full presence blinds, paralyzes, fulfills. The interdiction of touch concerns the full presence of a body that would be fully in this world or of this world. It allows for another dimension to be touched: "this dimension from which alone comes *glory*, that is, the brilliance of more than presence, the radiance of what is in excess of the given, the available, the disposed [*déposé*]" (NMT 17).

This other dimension is not in another world. "What 'is not of this world' is not elsewhere: it is the opening in the world, the separation, the parting and the raising" (NMT 48). This is important since it allows us to understand what it means to live a Christian life, that is, to be *in* the world but not *of* the world (John 17:14–16). It does not mean to take leave of the world in favor of an elsewhere (a spiritual interior or a heaven) but to live in proximity to that which is not of this world and yet is not an alternative world. It means to feel the world according to its opening, that is, according to its irreducibility to any and all relations of force or to values defined by given common measures (A 60). The here-below and the beyond or elsewhere are not two detached realms but two axes or two dimensions of the same world. We have neither the cosmos, the ordered whole with its given hierarchies (the mortals, the divines, the dead in Hades, etc.), where religion regulates the relations between these different realms, nor the metaphysical separation between the transcendent and the immanent realms. Rather, we have, Nancy proposes, two ways of being in the world: *either* according to its all-encompassing and enclosing givenness, *or* according to its opening, breach, abyss, play or risk (A 37–8). There is nothing but the world, yet it is possible to relate to another order or arrangement of this world instead of adhering to the given. These two dimensions, the horizontal-mundane and the vertical-divine, intersect at a point, which is the opening of sense right at the world (A 60). This opening belongs to the world "like the mouth belongs to the body" (A 43); it is not outside of it and cannot be reified. Hence, Nancy will say that to speak of "*the* opening" is an abuse of language. We should instead say "it opens" (*ça s'ouvre*). In the second volume of *The Deconstruction of Christianity*, Nancy names this "experience" or "ordeal" of the opening that is not a thing but only a gap or spacing, "adoration," from *ad-oratio*, addressing, being turned toward that which exceeds the order of signification. He contrasts adoration with addiction: whereas addiction seeks to make present the elsewhere in order to leave the here-and-now, adoration restrains itself to the nothing of the opening, which is the condition for sense (A 18).

We have seen that for Nancy, Christianity undoes the metaphysical two-world paradigm by letting God disappear or empty Himself out in His creation. However, God does not simply disappear. Christianity also says that God is among us. God is the "among" of all of "us" and it is in this sense that He is the "creator" of the world, that without which there would be no "world," no "relation." The Trinitarian God is the God that is entirely relation (*rapport*), rather than an entity with definite properties (A 46–7). If religion establishes a bond with the sacred entity ("sacred" meaning "holy," "withdrawn," "unscathed," etc.), then the Christian Trinitarian God is nothing but relation itself. It is in this sense that the Trinity undoes theism and that the Christian God is atheistic: not posited as a being. God as Father, Son, and Spirit means that God is that which relates, not to itself in self-reflexivity (Aristotle's thought thinking itself) but absolutely. "The ternary structure or aspect goes from one to the other through another than the one or the other, which is the relation *between* them" (A 46). The "Son" opens the possibility of relation, of a reference of sense from one to the other. "Spirit" is the name of this dimension that presents the relata ("Father," "Son") one to the other and independently of which they do not subsist (A 76).

In light of this interpretation of the Christian belief system, what does it mean to have faith? For Nancy, the theological virtues (faith, hope, charity) are forces that pertain to relationality (A 82). Faith is not a weaker form of belief bred in the absence of certainty or knowledge. It is not of the order of belief but of trust (*confiance*). Faith is neither weak nor strong belief, but the absolute force of the trust in that which I cannot appropriate or know, that from which I cannot get a guarantee. Faith is a reason (I do not have faith in just anything), but it is the reason of the absence of a given reason (A 128).[24] Hence faith is a praxis, an act or a way of being in the world, more than the approval or assent given to certain dogmas. To speak of the content of "faith" is already to understand faith in terms of belief. This is why Nancy is interested in reading James' epistle rather than Paul's, since the former emphasizes the works of faith rather than its theological content. For James, faith without works is dead (James 2:17). Nancy elaborates on this relation between faith and works:

> These works do not stand in the order of external manifestation, or in that of a demonstration through the phenomenon. And faith does not subsist in itself. . . . Instead of works proceeding from faith, and instead of works expressing it, faith here exists only in the works: in works that are its own and whose existence makes up the whole essence of faith, if we may put it that way. (D 51)

Faith is not of the order of argumentation or logic (being convinced or persuaded by reasons or against all reasons) but of the order of the act as that which responds to a commandment or a demand. Faith is "the performative of the commandment" (D 53). It is not response to a presence, to something given, but rather "faithfulness to an absence and a certainty of this faithfulness in the absence of all assurance" (D 36). Faith has to do with the existence and the engagement (praxis) in the world insofar as both of these are without foundation. This lack of foundation requires that we abandon ourselves to the absence of signification (the givenness at a distance of meaning that we described above), so as to be able to engage or to create, in every instance, a sense.

3

Community

Nancy's writings on community are without a doubt the most well-known part of his work. Most of them were written in the early 1980s, after which Nancy moved away from the word "community" toward explicitly ontological terms such as being-together, being-in-common, and being-with (CC 31). Hence, the work around the concept of community predates the more developed ontological thinking that we discussed in chapter 1. In the following chapter, we will encounter some ideas that we already discussed: finitude, sharing, the absolute, singularity, etc. At the same time, we will see how Nancy's ontology arises out of a discussion of community that is informed by Bataille and Heidegger and remains in constant dialogue with Blanchot. We will focus first on Nancy's explicit discussion of community in the first eponymous essay of the book *The Inoperative Community*, in order to situate that discussion in relation to the three aforementioned thinkers. Then we will take up Nancy's discussions of the relation between myth and community on the one hand, and between the interruption of myth, the unworked community, and "literary communism" on the other. Since the next chapter will deal explicitly with the political, we will postpone the discussion of the direct political implications of Nancy's view of community.

The Inoperative Community

The essay "The Inoperative Community" was written in 1983 for a special issue of the journal *Aléa* titled "Community, Number" at the same time as Nancy was teaching a year-long seminar on politics in Bataille's thought (CC 28). The text was then revised and augmented, and published in a book by the same name in 1986, a book that also included two new essays: "Myth Interrupted" and "Literary Communism." Together, these essays attempt to think the relation between community, work, and death in dialogue with Bataille's thought. Between these two versions, Blanchot published a short book that took Nancy's essay as its point of departure, *The Unavowable Community*. Nancy's thinking of community and his reading of Bataille will be explained first, before being placed in relation with Blanchot's response.

In 2001, Nancy wrote a preface to the new Italian translation of Blanchot's *Unavowable Community*, in which he comes back to the context surrounding both his and Blanchot's texts on community in the early 1980s. We need to recall that these texts were written before the fall of the Berlin Wall and of the Soviet Union, at a time where real communism appeared clearly as the betrayal of the communist ideal. Putting the word community into play was both a way of questioning communism and of pointing to an undeniable communist exigency or demand within the contemporary situation. Communism was the name, for Nancy, of a desire to discover or rediscover a community beyond individualism and the socioeconomic divisions that plague the modern world. What happened to this ideal? What was the problem with it, which led it to slide toward totalitarianism?

Nancy's criticism of communism does more than put into question the embodiment of the communist ideal in reality; it questions the "basis" of that ideal itself, which Nancy identifies as a certain conception of the human being: "human beings defined as producers (one might even add: human beings *defined* at all), and fundamentally as the producers of their own essence in the form of their labor or their work" (IC 2). The community of communism had to be "one *of man*" and this, for Nancy, "presupposes that it effect, or that it must effect, as such and integrally, its own essence, which is itself the accomplishment of the essence of man" (IC 3). This is what Nancy (and Lacoue-Labarthe) called in the early 1980s totalitarianism, and what Nancy now proposes to call immanentism: the immanence of humanity to itself and of the community to itself, its production as self-enclosed totality. Hence the question of community is posed in the context of "the problem of 'totalitarianism.'" This problem is not, however, that of "good government," but rather an ontological one. But if communism shows itself as

totalitarian (or immanentist) not only its embodiment, e.g. in the
Soviet Union, but *as such*, what remains of community except the
proliferation, the sheer number or juxtaposition, of "individuals"?
What or where *is* community?

(i) Between individualism and communalism

Nancy's essay starts with a critique of our contemporary situation
– liberal capitalism as it dissolves social life into economic exchange
and social human beings into individuals, and communism as it
appeals to the self-production or self-formation of the human community – in order to move to an ontological description of community. Only the return to a philosophical discussion of community
can help us out of the impasse of the contemporary situation by
showing us how communism and liberalism are two sides of the
same logic and hence by offering a way of thinking community
that lives up to or addresses the communist exigency.

Nancy first directs his attention to the Romantic paradigm of
community, where community is thought in essentially nostalgic
terms as a paradise lost in the modern experience of the social.
Rousseau is, according to Nancy, the chief representative of this
paradigm,[1] but this nostalgic understanding of community informs
all the western philosophical thinking of community since its
beginning.[2] Even those who do not mourn the loss of community,
but welcome its disappearance in the birth of "society" (and hence
do not fit the nostalgic paradigm), take for granted the opposition
between a romantic view of a lost community and a modern view
of a rational society of interests. Such an opposition has been
explicitly laid out in Ferdinand Tönnies's *Community and Society*
(1887) and taken up by Max Weber in his *Economy and Society*
(1922).

Tönnies differentiates between communities (*Gemeinschaften*)
and societies (*Gesellschaften*, sometimes also translated as "civil
societies" or "associations") in the following way: whereas society
relates separated individuals on the basis of rational calculation
and self-interest, and thus allows these separated individuals to
live peacefully beside one another, community fosters a feeling of
belongingness, familiarity, and intimacy that joins its members
together. On the one side, there is unity on the basis of agreement
and contract, on the other of understanding and sympathy. For
Tönnies, the root and model of all communities is the family, and

the relations it entails (mother–child, husband–wife, siblings) contain the seeds of all the development of communities from neighborhoods and friendships, to clans and tribes and even the nation. It is not immediately obvious which of these two, society or community, should be privileged. Indeed, both can be invested with either positive or negative moral worth. For example, we can appeal to the critical function of communities against the material-istic and inhuman logic of advanced capitalism and its calculative rationality. On this view, communities are valuable and even neces-sary because they foster the intimacy, trust, and selflessness of which our social associations are so often deprived. On the other hand, we cannot deny that the irrational, emotional feelings of belonging to a particular group are responsible for much of the violence around the world and hence might want to appeal to the critical function of "rational" associations against the "dark" world of feelings. Even though Nancy focuses here on the first view, it is clear that both sides conceive of community as an ideal of self-presence, intimacy, immediacy, and identity that has been lost in modern society. Community is thought to be "not only intimate communication between its members, but also the organic com-munion of itself with its own essence" (IC 9, trans. mod.). The members are, in their plurality, impregnated with the same identity so that each member identifies himself or herself and each other by identifying with the living body of the community. The only disa-greement between the two views is whether or not this ideal is dangerous.

At the same time, what Nancy does in *The Inoperative Community* is not to appeal to "society" in order to criticize community (as in the second view outlined above), but rather to undercut the whole opposition between society and community altogether.[3] Commu-nity is not that which is destroyed by society; it is that which happens to us on the basis of, or starting from, society itself:

> *Society* was not built on the ruins of a *community*. It emerged from the disappearance or the conservation of something – tribes or empires – perhaps just as unrelated to what we call "community" as to what *we* call "society." So that community, far from being what society has crushed or lost, is *what happens to* us – question, waiting, event, imperative – *in the wake of* society. (IC 11)

Community is not something we have lost. Nancy's argument is simple: this experience of the so-called loss of community is an experience we make in common; hence we are there (in common) in the "absence" or "loss" of community (see OBC 6). Now, Nancy will argue that this is the only possible community, that is, the community that experiences its own absence, or the absence of fusion and communion. Community is the experience of the interruption of communion. Communion, on the other hand, would be the black hole of immanence. "What this community has lost – the immanence and the intimacy of a communion – is lost only in the sense that such a loss is constitutive of 'community' itself. It is not a loss: on the contrary, immanence, if it were to come about, would instantly suppress community, or communication, as such" (IC 12).

What informs our thinking of community as communion is the same logic that informs our thinking of the individual: the logic of "the absolute." We have already encountered this logic in the first chapter. The absolute is that which is detached, separated, without relation. Yet, if it is to be without relation,

> the closure must not only close around a territory (while still remaining exposed, at its outer edge, to another territory, with which it thereby communicates), but also, in order to complete the absoluteness of its separation, around the enclosure itself. The absolute must be the absolute of its own absoluteness, or not be at all. In other words: to be absolutely alone, it is not enough that I be so; I must also be alone being alone – and this of course is contradictory. (IC 4)

Why is it impossible for me to be alone in my being alone? Because I can only *be* alone, or feel myself alone, in relation to something else. If I am an absolute, I do not "feel" my limit and hence, I am not "alone." I am infinite, I am "all there is and can be."

What both individualism and communion cannot think is "relation," or what Nancy names in *The Inoperative Community*, following Bataille, "communication."[4] It is worth remembering that there can only be "relation" between finite beings since being finite means being concerned with or encountering one's limit, and hence being turned inside out. If community and finitude are essentially linked, it means that community does not raise the finite being to a higher, less limited form of existence. The community does not offer me the possibility of overcoming the limitation that my birth and my death represent for me; rather, it exposes these limits, or the excess that I am, to myself and to others (IC 15). Immanence or communion, on the contrary, is not exposition, but death. Only for the dead person or for the community of the dead is there no excess, exposition, or relation. This is why the community that seeks its own immanence ends up producing itself only as a work of death. Nancy gives some examples: the Hegelian State, the joint suicide of lovers, Nazism. In *The Inoperative Community*, Nancy develops this relation between immanence and death on the one hand, and community and finitude on the other, by reading Bataille and Heidegger against each other.

(ii) Community and death in Heidegger and Bataille

In Heidegger's *Being and Time*, being-toward-death represents an important moment of the deconstruction of the metaphysics of the subject. That is, Dasein is not a self-grounding subject but the entity whose ground is withdrawn: in thrownness and in death. Birth and death represent inappropriable limits: I am opened to these limits, in a sense I experience them, provided we do not think of this experience as one in which I appropriate these limits, but as one in which I am disappropriated, in which I slip out of myself (again, the formulation is imprecise; it seems to imply that I was myself before this slip, but on the contrary, I am only this slip). I cannot "come behind" myself in order to appropriate these limits: I am always too late for my birth and too early for my death. The problem with Heidegger's thinking of finitude is that he does not integrate being-toward-death into his conception of being-with. For Heidegger, death represents the limit of substitution. Even though I can substitute myself for the other in any matter of worldly concern, I cannot take over the other's death. I can sacrifice myself for the other, jump in front of the bus to save her life, but that does not take her dying away from her.[5] Death is the limit of community thought as substitutability; it makes us aware of our irreplaceability. Death individualizes:

> My death is that for which no other can substitute her care for mine. The other can only care by handing me over to my own care. . . . Be that as it may, the outcome is the same: it is an absolute solitude in death. On this level then, there is an essential limitation to the principle of the essentiality of the with. (BWBT 8)

Death is not shared; rather, Heidegger reproduces the most traditional understanding of "communal death" as sacrifice. When the individual is seen as having its truth in another (the lover, the State, the *Volk*), then this truth realizes itself in the individual giving her life for this other, that is, it realizes itself in sacrifice. But the question is: "Between the insurmountable death of a solitary dying and the sacrificial death in combat for the advent of the people – and for that matter without excluding those two extreme possibilities – how can a sharing of death be thought?" (BWBT 13).

What Nancy finds in Bataille is a thinking of death as that which reveals the community by revealing the impossibility of immanence or fusion, the impossibility of the community effecting itself as its own work through the sacrifice of individuality. The individual imagines that her death is reabsorbed in the community, which bestows upon her an infinite sense. Yet this community does not produce itself as infinite life, as the life of the infinite, but only as dead immanence. Death does not operate communion. The community cannot make a work out of death or make death work, except in becoming itself a work of death. For Bataille, the death of the Other is what reveals community, not in effecting it, but in disrupting, suspending or interrupting any communal project. In being exposed to an absolute loss or a meaningless expenditure such as the death of the Other, we experience our finitude as something that we cannot appropriate and that cannot be put to work into a higher totality (as if the limitation of a singular life were to be redeemed through the continuation of the life of the community). In this sense, what we experience in the death of the Other is community or sharing. What is shared (death) is not a property of a subject that would be common to all and make us recognize each other as the same, but an opening or an exposure.

Without going into the details of Bataille's thought and its development,[6] we can say that what interests Nancy in his reading of Bataille is: (1) how his interest in primitive communal relation and the experience of the sacred, even though tainted with nostalgia, moves past the modern understanding of the lost community; and (2) how he understands primitive communities as built on a form of excess or of aneconomical or unproductive "expenditure." A central form of such expenditure is the potlatch, to which Marcel Mauss devoted a study in his famous 1923 *The Gift*, a book that was influential on Bataille.[7] Yet, for Bataille, the most important form of such expenditure is sacrifice, and especially human sacrifice. What interests Nancy in Bataille's engagement with human sacrifice is his search for a sharing of death, for a way of experiencing *my* own finitude, *my* own death, by participating in the death of the other.[8] So what Bataille invites us to think, according to Nancy, is an idle or unworked community (CC 30),[9] one that is essentially tied to sacrifice, provided we understand sacrifice not as a form of economic exchange – I give this to the gods and I get that in return – but as a pure expenditure without recovery. According to Bataille, such a radical expenditure is the only thing that can resist or refute the Hegelian system: as pure negativity, it does not let itself be negated and integrated into the dialectical process. It is a negativity that does not let itself be put to work so as to give rise to a higher positivity (the community, the State). Bataille will say that it is an unemployed negativity or a negativity without use.

For Hegel, Spirit does not know itself in immediacy and hence it needs to externalize itself in another so that it can then recognize itself in this Other. This is the dialectical process: immediacy, externalization, reflection back into self. In the reflection back into itself, Spirit does not fall back into immediacy but achieves some determination by recognizing its own externalization (what it posited as not itself) as a part or moment of itself. History is therefore the process of Spirit rising up to complete self-consciousness, to absolute knowledge. This process is driven by negation, so we can rewrite the steps of this process as: immediacy, negation, negation of negation. The negation of the negation (or the negation of the separation between self and not-self) gives rise to a positivity; both moments are preserved in a higher unity. Bataille's question or puzzlement is the following: when, in the end, Spirit coincides with itself in full positivity, when the dialectical process has, thanks to the "work of the negative," worked itself out, what happens to this negativity? Since nothing is lost in the dialectical process of negation and of the negation of negation, this negation cannot merely disappear. What interests Bataille is the moment when negation is transformed into full positivity. At the moment of reversal, does negation itself erase itself or does it persist as unemployed, without work, inoperative (*sans emploi*)? Nothing escapes the power of the negative. Yet, if negation has the power to turn everything into positivity, it cannot, according to Bataille, turn upon itself and raise *itself* to positivity. This inoperative negativity is the remainder over and against the complete positivity of self-transparent Spirit it creates. In his 1936 "Letter to X" (addressed to Kojève, whose lectures on Hegel he is attending at the time), Bataille writes:

> If action is – as Hegel says – negativity, the question arises as to whether the negativity of one who has "nothing more to do" disappears or remains in a state of "workless negativity." Personally, I can

only decide in one way, being myself precisely this "unemployed negativity."... I imagine that my life – or, better yet, its aborting, the open wound that is my life – constitutes all by itself the refutation of Hegel's closed system.[10]

Bataille's life refutes Hegel's closed system at the moment where it reaches the awareness that it could as well not have been and that the Hegelian system would have lacked nothing. A singular life, the negativity or uselessness of an "unemployed" life, escapes the process of dialectics; it is an unsublatable remainder. Blanchot, in "The Limit-Experience," explains Bataille's question in this way:

> Man is the being that does not exhaust his negativity in action. Thus when all is finished, when the "doing" (by which man also makes himself [by which man, negating nature and negating himself as a natural being, produces himself in producing the world and hence reaches the absolute, that is, makes himself equal to the whole and by becoming conscious of the whole]) is done, when, therefore, man has nothing left to do, he must, as Georges Bataille expresses it with the most simple profundity, exist in a state of "negativity without employ."[11]

The recognition of "this surplus of nothingness, this unemployable vacancy" gives rise to "another exigency – no longer that of producing but of spending, no longer that of succeeding but of failing, no longer that of turning out works and speaking usefully but of speaking in vain and reducing himself to worklessness..."[12] The negative is recognized in the dialectics insofar as it is at the service of a positivity, insofar as it is put to work for the sake of positivity. What Hegel does not recognize is the negative *as* negative, what Bataille calls negativity without use (*négativité sans emploi*) and Blanchot, worklessness or inoperativity (*désœuvrement*).

The thought of sacrifice orients not only Bataille's thought of community but also the formation of the secret society *Acéphale*. Since this society was secret, it is difficult to know much about what took place in their meetings, but the principles orienting the society are enunciated in a journal by the same name. The goal was to put into practice the community without community that Bataille theorized, to find a new way of living the relations between inside and outside, between subject and community. The group apparently toyed with the idea of an ultimate sacrifice, a human sacrifice, but never put this idea into practice (for lack of a willing execu-tioner and not for lack of willing victim). It should be mentioned here that Bataille's thinking of sacrifice is set in opposition to the rise of Nazism. Whereas fascism demands the sacrifice of German blood for the purification of the race and in order to build a com-munity that would be the immanence of a shared essence or iden-tity united or held together by a singular principle, Hitler, the shared experience of death in *Acéphale* would not have been put to work or subordinated to any one power, but aimed instead at de-propriating the subject and liberating it from servitude, from the subjection to any function. Whether this is really the case is exactly Nancy's question.

What Nancy will oppose in Bataille is everything in his work that is still linked to a nostalgic figure of the loss of community or the loss of the sacred, and hence still risks putting death to work or creating a work out of death. First, the community is organized around a sacrificial *project*. Second, this sacrifice still serves the function of creating a community by operating a transfiguration of the subject, no matter how different this community imagined itself to be from the homogeneous and cephalic community of Nazism. As long as the executioner, the victim, and the spectator expect a transformation from this experience, there cannot be loss without gain. The only way in which a loss without gain could occur is if the participant would also commit suicide themselves. Here we find a similar logic to that exposed by Derrida in *Given Time*. For a gift without return to be possible, the giver must not retain the consciousness of the giving, since that consciousness (and the potential gratification that comes from it) already means that some-thing of the gift returns to the giver. If this is the case, the Bataillian community would result in collective suicide and hence in a work of death. While in the modern discourses about community it is always assumed that the desired position is that of the "presence to self of a realized unity," Nancy finds the same presupposition at work in Bataille's discourse, even though communion is asserted to be impossible so that the only community that actually remains is the one "of those who have no community" (CC 29).

Nancy acknowledges that the later Bataille moved away from any revolutionary project and from his nostalgia for archaic forms of community, and came to think of community, or of the commu-nal experience of excess or ecstasy, not in relation to the sacrificial experience and the sacred, but in relation to the erotic experience. The community of lovers "came by way of a contrast with the social

bond and as its counter-truth. What had been supposed to structure society – be it by opening a transgressive breach within it – was
deposited outside of it within it, in an intimacy for which politics
remained beyond reach" (CC 29, trans. mod.). The community of
lovers exposes the truth of community, the sharing of excess or
ecstasy, that society (social community) tries in vain to attain, but
as such it remains opposed to any other relation (social, political,
etc.) (IC 36–7). This also means that the social community remains
untouched by this truth and is left to "the exteriority of things, of
production, and of exploitation" (IC 36).

To the exteriority of "community" with regard to society, Nancy
opposes the logic of arealization. Nancy plays on the double
meaning of areality: a-real with a privative alpha and areal as in
"area." In the first sense, it means that the community is beyond
the dichotomy between the real and the irreal (in the forms of the
imaginary, the nonexistent, but also the ideal): it is not some ideal
to be realized. On the contrary, community has to be, or is always,
arealized. This arealization relates to the nature of community as
area, as formed space; it means that a community is spread out. A
community is "not a territory [not something delimited and closed],
but the areality of an ecstasy" (IC 20). Hence, Nancy speaks of a
double arealization of ecstasy and of community, the play between
them consisting in the resistance to immanence and to fusion.
Ecstasy opens up the subject and places it outside of itself: it is the
resistance to immanence. If community is the area or playground
where this ecstasy takes place or opens, then it means that community limits ecstasy, ensures that the ecstatic "subject" does not
pour itself out into the exterior, since what it encounters in its
ecstasy is another ecstasy. Hence community is the resistance to the
rebuilding of immanence at a higher level. This is what Nancy
names here and elsewhere "being-in-common" (IC 20): the double
resistance of the "limit" according to which there is neither a hidden
interior nor a fusion with the outside.

The logic of arealization also means that there cannot be any
"private" community (e.g. of lovers) that is not already "woven,
arealized, or inscribed" (IC 20) in a larger community, that is, in
the social and political community. Intimacy is necessarily spread
out so that the lovers are both within and without the community,
at its limit (IC 40). "If lovers harbor a truth of the social relation, it
is neither at a distance from nor above society, but rather in that,
as lovers, they are exposed in the community. They are not the
communion that is refused to or purloined from society; on the

contrary, they expose the fact that communication is not communion" (IC 37). Nancy thinks that Bataille remained unable to link
ecstasy to community and vice versa, and so remained with two
separate models of community: the communist model of the political community of equals, and the isolated, selective community of
the lovers (or of artists). The latter closes itself upon itself, and
hence withdraws from the former and holds no sway over it. The
point of contention is that of revolutionary practice: if the elective
community of lovers experiences ecstasy (true community) but
remains withdrawn from the political community, how is this latter
supposed to be transformed by the former (IC 20–1)?[13]

Blanchot's response to Nancy:
Levinas against Heidegger

Blanchot's *The Unavowable Community* is separated into two parts.
The first one, "The Negative Community," explicitly takes Nancy's
essay as its point of departure and seems, at least on the surface,
to advance Nancy's discussion of Bataille's "community without
community." The second one, "The Community of Lovers," proposes a Levinasian reading of Marguerite Duras's "The Malady of
Death." It is not easy to tease out the point of contention at stake
in the dialogue between Nancy and Blanchot from the texts themselves. Nancy and Blanchot agree that the importance of Bataille's
thought is that it identifies "insufficiency" or "incompletion" as the
"principle" of community. There are never any frontal criticisms in
their respective texts. Both Nancy and Blanchot quote each other
as if they were in perfect agreement, but this surface hides an
important dissension with regard to how community ought to be
thought.[14] While the first part of Blanchot's book restates the core
of Nancy's argument, it does so in terms of the Other (*autrui*), a
term that is more or less absent from Nancy's discussion.[15] His
alternative reading of Bataille, Blanchot thinks, does not fall prey
to the worries Nancy had raised in his reading. Ultimately, what
the debate clarifies is Nancy's rejection of radical alterity or absolute Otherness.[16] The question is: can the oppressive immanence of
human relations be broken only by the encounter with an absolute
Other or does Nancy somehow find in exposition an alternative
way to circumvent this pure equivalency of the Same? Blanchot
poses the dilemma in the following way:

However, if the relation of man with man ceases to be that of the
Same with the Same, but rather introduces the Other as irreducible
and – given the equality between them – always in a situation of
dissymmetry in relation to the one looking at the Other, then a completely different relationship imposes itself and imposes another
form of society which one would hardly dare call a "community."
Or else one accepts the idea of naming it thus, while asking oneself
what is at stake in the concept of a community and whether the
community, no matter if it has existed or not, does not always point
to the absence of community.[17]

We can rephrase the question in the following way: if the relation
"of man to man" is not an immanent relation but the encounter of,
or exposition to, an exteriority, should this lead us to rethink community as that which resists immanence, totality, foreclosure
(Nancy) or should it lead us to a completely different relation, the
asymmetrical relation to the absolute Other, one that could not be
the basis of any community worthy of the name? How are we to
think exteriority and the interruption of the economy of the Same?
How are we to think "the absence of community"? Does one insist
on the absence of community that would be community itself, or
does one move to a completely different relationship?
    Nancy, for his part, explains the point of contention between
Blanchot and himself in the following terms:

at the point where I claimed to reveal the "work" of community as
society's *death sentence* and, as a corollary, to establish the need for
a community refusing to constitute work, thus preserving the
essence of an endless communication (communicating to itself an
"absent sense", to speak once more with Blanchot, along with the
passion of this ab-sense, or rather the passion that this ab-sense
constitutes) – at that very point, then, Blanchot informs me of or
rather indicates to me the *unavowable*. Apposed but opposed to the
inoperative of my title, this adjective proposes to think that beneath
the inoperativeness or worklessness there is still work, an unavowable work. (CC 28–30, trans. mod.)

The danger is that the inoperativity of the community be seen as
presenting the unveiled secret of being-in-common: "Blanchot was
asking me," Nancy writes, "not to settle for the negation of com-
munial community, and to think further ahead than this negativity,
toward a secret of the common that is not a common secret" (CC

31). Simply put, Blanchot is uneasy with Nancy's ease at writing about community, and about absence as the "truth" of community. In Nancy's work, it looks as if the whole is negated (community is affirmed to be impossible), but this negation is taken back into the whole and affirmed as a moment of the whole and, more precisely, as its truth. The negation of community is turned into a positivity. For Blanchot, on the contrary, writing is not the profession of a truth, be it an absent or inoperative one, but the relation to the Other, to the unknown, to absence, a relation in which I experience my own solitude. Nancy, by remaining at the ontological level, seems to be able to define community, without having recourse to any experience of the impossibility or "exhaustion" of writing in the face of the absolute withdrawal or absenting of the Other. Nancy acknowledges the fact that what is needed are new practices of writing, discourses on the community which do not present the community but exhaust themselves in trying to indicate the sharing:

> Perhaps, in truth, there is nothing *to say*. Perhaps we should not seek a word or a concept for it [community], but rather recognize in the thought of community a theoretical excess (or more precisely, an excess in relation to the theoretical) that would oblige us to adopt another *praxis* of discourse and community. But we should at least try to say this…. (IC 25–6)

Even though a similar necessity of speaking in order to remain silent is also acknowledged by Blanchot at the end of *The Unavowable Community*, the problem is that Nancy's "perhaps" remains, for Blanchot, inadequate as an expression of the ordeal of the exhaustion of communication.[18]

The disagreement between Nancy and Blanchot can also be expressed with proper names: Nancy rejects the Hegelian language of subject/object in favor of the Heideggerian language of being-with. Whereas Blanchot also rejects the Hegelian language, he does so by adopting a Levinasian language instead. What is rejected by Blanchot is the primacy of ontology (of the language of being) in favor of the relation to the Other. Nancy, for his part, rejects an understanding of community based on the relation to the absolute Other. The danger of insisting on the primacy of the Other over being-in-common for Nancy lies in the fact that the community of the one with the Other becomes exclusive and sets itself apart from ordinary society. For Blanchot, the danger in Nancy's thinking of community lies in its lack of radical interruption of the production or work of the community and its potential for reproducing the economy of the same (or what Nancy calls immanentism). This disagreement about the primacy of the Other over being-in-common (and hence the primacy of ethics over ontology) and vice versa leads to different assessments of Bataille on (1) the death of the Other, (2) *Acéphale*, and (3) love.

(1) Both Nancy and Blanchot cite the following sentence from Bataille: "if it sees its fellow-being die, a living being can subsist only outside itself" (IC 15).[19] So for both, the death of the Other is what places me outside of myself. Yet Blanchot thinks this interruption of communion as substitution – to die the one for the other – while Nancy thinks it as sharing – to be exposed to the limit where the Other withdraws. Blanchot writes:

> What calls me most radically into question? Not my relation to myself as finite or as the consciousness of being before death or for death, but my presence in the proximity of another who by dying removes himself definitively. To take upon myself another's death as the only death that concerns me, this is what puts me beside myself, this is the only separation that can open me, in its very impossibility, to the Openness of a community.[20]

The death of the Other is the only death that I can die and in this dying I substitute myself for the Other, who cannot die, cannot experience her own death. Blanchot proposes the positive account of substitution to counteract what he sees as Nancy's purely negative conception of community (experience of a limit).

(2) For Nancy, *Acéphale* was a project grounded in nostalgia for the loss of the sacred and ran the risk of creating the community as a work of death. As such, it was doomed to fail and could only be experienced as a failure. For Blanchot, on the contrary, it is precisely the experience of this "failure" that is its success. Blanchot writes:

> The absence of community is not the failure of community: it belongs to community as its extreme moment or as the test which exposes its necessary disappearance. *Acéphale* was the common experience of that which cannot be placed in common, nor properly maintained, nor reserved for an ulterior abandon. . . . The community of *Acéphale* could not exist as such, but only as imminence and as withdrawal.[21]

For Blanchot, *Acéphale* was not a project or a work that would have sought to reach the point of unworking or inoperativity. On the contrary, Blanchot seems to be saying that the vocabulary of work and worklessness employed by Nancy implies that his thinking of community remains within the horizon of production, project, and ultimately, power and subjectivity. In the language of unavowability, Blanchot emphasizes the secrecy or the interruption of communication that surrounds the community. The community cannot name itself or present itself, it cannot exist as such. Community cannot be communication. The "subject" is stripped of its ability to communicate the relationship.[22]

(3) For Blanchot, the fulfillment of all genuine love is accomplished in the mode of loss. Yet loss here is not tainted with any nostalgia since one never possessed the loved one in the mode of presence. The lover and the loved one do not inhabit any common temporal framework. Their essential diachrony or interruption means that the community of lovers (like the community of artists, or the "spontaneous" gathering of the people in May '68, a gathering that was without leaders, without goals, absolutely "inoperative") is disruptive of society since society cannot do anything with it, cannot harness its energy, put it to work. The community of lovers disrupts both the "social" understanding of community as interest-based and the traditional understanding of community as face-to-face communion. The communal relation is not a face to face but a side by side, yet not the side by side of traditional societal relations since the lovers (or the artists) are not oriented, not turned toward, a common goal. What turns the lovers away from each other is their common solitude.[23]

The interruption of myth and literary communism

Up until this point, we have focused on the relation between death and community as it is developed in *The Inoperative Community*. We now turn to the relation between myth and community in order to further develop the logic of worklessness or inoperativity in terms of the interruption of myth. Myth, understood as foundational discourse, seems essential for community: it is thanks to the myth that we recognize each other as belonging together. Nancy's analysis of the functioning of myth, both as story and as foundation, points to an "interruption" of myth, which is both more and less than the "absence of myth" out of which the concept of "myth" originates in the first place.

Nancy begins "Myth Interrupted" with the "well-known scene" of the mythic foundation or origin of a community. Myths have the power to gather dispersed people into a community and make them recognize each other as belonging together. In listening to "their" story, the story of their origin, the listeners, who were up to now dispersed or indifferent, "understand themselves and the world, and they understand why it was necessary for them to come together, and why it was necessary that this be recounted to them" (IC 44). Myth represents, therefore, a community's attempt (or a people's attempt) at self-grounding or self-formation.

The understanding of myth is totalitarian in two ways. First in its form: myth is self-communication, that is, it communicates only itself and communicates that it communicates itself. In this sense, it does not tolerate anything outside of itself, especially not alternative (different, contradictory) myths. In other words, myth has the form of subjectivity (defined by Hegel as that which can include within itself its own contradictions, that is, as "remainder-less totality" [IC 56–7]). There can be only one myth pertaining to any given origin. Second, myth is totalitarian in its content: it always strives to provide a total explanation of everything that exists and assigns everybody (and everything, gods, mortals, animals, etc.) a role and a place: "myth represents multiple existences as immanent to its own unique fiction, which gathers them together and gives them their common figure in its speech and as this speech" (IC 57). The myth is therefore not a narrative to be interpreted, that is, a narrative whose sense would lie outside of itself or under its surface and would need to be retrieved through a process of interpretation. Rather, myth gives meaning to everything, completely, at once. Myth is full speech (*parole pleine*) or "tautegory" (as Schelling says), the "opening of a mouth immediately adequate to the closure of the universe" (IC 49–50). In this sense, myth is primordial *logos*: it fashions or molds the concepts or images that will form the basic vocabulary of the community by which that community will be able to name itself and the elements that comprise the world.

The first gesture of Nancy's analysis of the "mything" (that is, creative) power of myth is to move from myth itself to the myth of myth. What has been said of the communal or communitarian power of myth is itself a myth; it is the story that *we* (we, moderns or postmoderns) tell ourselves about myth. It is in this sense that myth might be understood as a purely western, or a purely philosophical, concept:

> Concentrated within the idea of myth is perhaps the entire preten-
> sion on the part of the West to appropriate its own origin, or to take
> away its secret, so that it can at last identify itself, absolutely, around
> its own pronouncement and its own birth. The idea of myth alone
> perhaps presents the very Idea of the West, with its perpetual rep-
> resentation of the compulsion to return to its own sources in order
> to re-engender itself from them as the very destiny of humanity.
> (IC 46)[24]

The concept of myth, as well as the desire for the creative power of myth, arises from the consciousness of a lack of foundation. This consciousness, coupled with the desire for an absolute foundation, is what gives rise to the myth of myth. Essentially, myth is the story we tell about the foundation we feel we have lost. Nancy explains: "To speak of the myth has only ever been to speak of its absence. And the word 'myth' itself designated the absence of what it names" (IC 52). In this sense, *muthos* and *logos* are not opposed to each other but imply each other. Myth is "the name for the *cosmos structuring itself in logos*" (IC 49), that is, myth names a "fiction" or a "story" that provides reason and structure (*logos*) to the world as a whole (*cosmos*). When, at the moment of the birth of philosophy, Plato famously opposes myths in the name of *logos* (in Book III of the *Republic*), what he rejects are stories insofar as they are false, and hence dangerous for the education of the people, that is, stories that give bad examples, the imitation of which would lead to the degeneration of the people. By appealing to reason, Plato seeks to found the *politeia* in truth. Hence the philosophic educator will be the teller of true stories, stories that are formed according to the true models (the *paradigmai* or Forms) and that therefore have the power to give true form to the people. Foundation in (false) stories and foundation in (true) reason, though seemingly opposed, are both foundations in *lexis*, that is, in a regime of "speech" or "enun-ciation." Plato's rejection of false story-makers acknowledges the forming or molding power of *muthoi*, stories, a power he tries to appropriate for philosophy.[25]

Hence, while myth seems to name the other of philosophy, it in fact names its most profound desire. This is why the appeal to a new mythology, to a new effective foundational story, can be heard throughout western history. Nancy names not only romanticism and communism, but also structuralism as the last traditions of myth. Romanticism attempts a re-inauguration or re-initialization of the origin in a primordial language (see IC 51).[26] Communism puts to work the myth of the worker (its figure or type) in an attempt to create or form a liberated, that is, a true humanity. In this sense, communism presupposes a total and complete definition of the meaning of the human.[27] It might seem counterintuitive to put structuralism alongside romanticism and communism here since structuralism studies myths scientifically and hence strips myth of "its mystery and its absurdity, of its magic and its savagery" (IC 48). At the same time, the structural analysis of myths actually produces the total structure of the mythic system of humanity, of which various myths are but exemplifications. In this sense, it produces the "meta-structure" of all myths which comes to take the place of myth as the absolute foundation of a "systematic, organizational, combinative, and articulative totality" (IC 48). If *muthos* is not opposed to *logos*, myth is also not opposed to science or structure. There is a romantic myth of the author-subject as the origin and end of the Work, but there is also a structuralist myth of "the structure" as a total explanation of what is.

We know that the myth is a myth, not only in the sense that "myth" is our invention, but more pointedly in the sense that the foundation, the creative myth, is a fiction. But this affirmation alone is not enough to interrupt the myth in the precise sense Nancy gives to this word, that is, to interrupt the *desire* for a fiction that would be operative as foundation. The myth of myth, the story we tell ourselves about myth, is that fiction itself is capable of serving as or bringing about a foundation. The realization that myth itself is a myth (that foundation is fiction) is not enough to bring us outside the "mythic" way of thinking about community. This "exit" can only come about through the interruption of myth, where myth does not disappear but stops working as the impetus for our desire for completion and fulfillment. At this point, the necessary incompletion (or unworking) of myth comes to the fore.

Historically, this point of interruption happened with Nazism. After "the fire of the Aryan myth," we cannot desire a mything, that is, a founding, humanity. Nazism brought mythic thinking to its limit, not because it tried to revitalize certain old Nordic stories, but because it attempted to produce the German people by putting to work the logic of the myth that was described above. In "The Nazi Myth," Nancy and Lacoue-Labarthe study this putting to work of myth in Nazism (NM 292). Fascism is the accomplishment of the logic of the Subject, that is, of "a subjectivity present

to itself, as the support, the source, and the finality of
representation, certitude, and will" (NM 294). Hence, fascism is not
irrational, but rather the most coherent setting to work of the logic
of the Subject. Myth is essential to this logic since it serves as the
apparatus by which a people identify itself with itself: myth produces the self-enclosed subject that is lacking to the Germans so
that the German people can become the "subject," the support,
source, and finality, of its own history. A myth is "a fiction, in the
strong, active sense of 'fashioning,' or, as Plato says, of 'plastic art':
it is, therefore, a *fictioning*, whose role is to propose, if not to impose,
models or types . . . , types in imitation of which an individual, or
a city, or an entire people, can grasp themselves and identify themselves" (NM 297).[28] This type is for Nazism the Aryan. But the
Aryan is not simply a type that would differentiate itself from other
types. The Aryan is the well-formed type, typed humanity as such,
the archi-type. The Jew is, following this logic, not just another
type, but the contradiction of the type, the absence of type. The Jew
is, for the Aryan, without form, because the Jew is without myth.[29]
The power of myth must be reawakened

> in opposition to the inconsistency of the abstract universals (of
> science, of democracy, of philosophy) and in the face of the collapse
> . . . of the two beliefs of the modern age: Christianity, and the belief
> in humanity (which, therefore, . . . are no doubt degenerate, perhaps
> "Jewified" myths, bloodless myths in any case, appropriate to an
> epoch that has lost the sense of race, of myth). (NM 307)

Myth is interrupted at the point where we realize that the total
accomplishment of myth as the logic of the self-foundation of a
people as Subject is self-defeating, that totalizing myth leads not to
community but to death, to the impossibility of living-with. Hence,
myth interrupts itself in being brought to its limit. Even as the community tries to produce itself as absolute, total immanence, it
remains exposed to its own outside. Mythic community represents
the attempt to appropriate the limits or edges between us, to turn
them into something proper, into a bigger Whole that would
subsume the edges. But a community, no matter how "united" or
"fused," remains, at its limit, exposed to other communities. If the
community's completion ends in the destruction of what we are,
of existence as in-common or shared, then this means that there has
never been and can never be a working myth. If myth works, it
destroys being-in-common; but at the same time, if we were not

in-common, we would not desire communion. "Being-in-common" explains both the desire of the effectuation or formation of "community" (as communion) through myth and the impossibility of any effective myth.

Yet, a question remains: is there a myth of the in-common? Bataille says that there is a kind of myth of the absence of myth. For Nancy, this formulation is problematic since it can always be heard in a nostalgic way. Nancy will therefore speak of the "interruption of myth" and of the "passion of community" it gives rise to. The interruption of myth undoes the community instead of producing it; it brings us to the edges, exposes us to each other and to ourselves. On these edges, where we exist, where we are turned toward the outside instead of toward a center (IC 60), there is a passion, a communication, or a propagation (all words Nancy borrows here from Bataille) of our being-in-common, which as we saw in the first chapter belongs neither to me nor to you, neither to us nor to them.

Nancy links the interruption of myth to what he calls "literary communism." The questions of literature and communism touch on questions of politics and art and we will have to come back to some of the ideas presented here in the next two chapters. Of course, what Nancy means here by "communism" cannot be the communism we linked above to myth. In "Literary Communism," reading a passage from Marx's *Contribution to the Critique of Political Economy*, Nancy shows how Marx thinks not a common nature of humanity but its being-in-common. Capitalism destroys community because it places the generality of production and of products at the origin of the organization of community. The community is divided and tasks are assigned on the basis of what is identified as the general task of humanity: the production of capital. The division of labor, the atomization of tasks, and the dispersion of individuals follow from the generality (and hence indistinction) of "abstract" labor in capitalism. Under capitalism, labor becomes a private activity or power, which belongs to the worker as her private property and can (and in fact must, since it is her only property) be sold in exchange for means of survival. Wage-labor, labor sold as a commodity and owned as private property, produces products that are the private, and hence exclusive, property of the capitalist. What this form of production and the "organization" of society it entails obstruct is the truly social character of human life. If the community of singularities, their articulation, is posited before production (this is what "communism" means), then labor is truly "social," or as Nancy says, "socially exposed" (IC 74), and "individual" property is "true common property," that is, the product belongs to the singularity only insofar as it articulates itself in-common (IC 75). Products do not separate individuals but rather articulate them, expose their being-in-common. Communism, therefore, "does not want to claim that one should put in common that which, by itself would not be so" (Com 378). It does not mean the common ownership of what is privately owned. "It wants to say that we are, insofar as we 'are,' in common. *That we are commonly*" (Com 378). In this sense, the "individual" for Marx (the singular being for Nancy) is not the opposite of "community." Community is, for Marx, according to Nancy, the pre-articulation of singularities among themselves so that, instead of the organization of production following from a preexisting general task, articulation (plurality) precedes and exposes socially all production and labor.[30]

What does this "communism" have to do with literature? Literature is not myth, or it is that which in any work interrupts myth. Each work has a share of myth and a share of literature (or of writing) (IC 63). Myth is the full speech of the community, enunciating itself to itself. There is no difference between what is recited and what is heard, between the reciting voice and the hearing ear since in myth the community speaks itself to itself. Literature or writing is what interrupts this self-presence. "Writing" is for Derrida the name of that which fractures consciousness understood as absolute transparent self-presence, rendering impossible its absolute self-enclosure. In this sense, writing is the mark of exteriority at the heart of interiority, which makes presence differ from itself and indefinitely defers self-identification. Nancy uses writing or literature in a similar way. Writing or literature exposes the mythic story, the "exemplary life," to the community, to each of us. It presents, that is to say, it offers or abandons, a fragment, a piece, without origin or end. Literature begins for no reason; it cannot be deduced from a subject-writer. Of course, we can produce a "total explanation" of the work of literature by appealing to the psychology of the writer, to her social condition, etc. But literature, the literariness of the work, is what interrupts these sorts of explanations by unveiling what they cannot explain: the "arbitrariness" of its *written*, that is, its *material*, character. Literature also ends arbitrarily. The voice of the "writer" interrupts itself for no reason, without being brought to completion. In other words, literature is "infinite": it is never finished but always has to begin again.

"Infinite" should not, again, be understood to mean "absolute" or "total." Thus, we should not speak of "Literature," but of "what is literary" in any work, literary or not, as that part which underlines its "inoperative" character, its non-accomplishment as work or myth. Of course, every book, every story, every work of art can turn into a myth, that is, into a founding speech. This is also true of philosophy: there is a mythic Hegelianism (a Hegelian system presented as complete and total explanation of everything that is) that is interrupted by the written, material presentation of this system.[31] Yet every work, literary or not, must also "be *offered*, that is to say presented, proposed, and abandoned on the common limit where singular beings share each other out [*se partagent*]. The work, as soon as it becomes a work, at the moment of its completion . . . must be abandoned at this limit" (IC 73, trans. mod.). At this limit, which is our being-in-common, the work is exposed, turned inside out. It is in this sense that literature, the experience "of writing, of the voice, of a speech given, played, sworn, offered, shared, abandoned," is necessarily "communist" (IC 70).

Literary communism does not have much to do with a communism or with a literature, and perhaps even less with a community of artists. The name is, as Nancy says, a "provocation" (IC 80). Communism names the necessary articulation of the singular beings, that is, a "being-together whose immanence is impossible except as its death-work." Literature names the articulation of a sense that is "shared," that is, a sense "whose transcendence or presence is indefinitely and constitutively deferred" (IC 80). Literary communism is a term that captures our ontological constitution. But it is also an imperative: "to defy at the same time the speechless immanence and the transcendence of a Word" (IC 80), both of which would put an end to "communication." Literary communism implies that we "not stop writing, or letting the singular outline of our being-in-common expose itself" (IC 41). "Writing" so as to expose the limit upon which we are exposed, to mark again and again the place where "I no longer (no longer essentially) hear in [the dialogue] what the other wants to say (to me), but I hear in it that the other, or something other [*de l'autre*] speaks and that there is an essential archi-articulation of the voice and of voices, which constitutes the being *in* common itself" (IC 76). Being-in-common is how "we" are, and this way of being makes fusion or communion impossible. But as we saw in chapter 1, to exist is not merely to be given as this or that, but to put existence into play; to exist must be heard in the active sense. This existence takes the form of "writing," what Nancy also calls "communication" or "the sharing of voices." As the interpellation from one finite being to another incommensurable being, "writing" is the "act" in which the in-common that we are is experienced as such.

4

Politics

Nancy's project is ontological in that it drives the originary existential structure of Heideggerian being-with toward its logical conclusion. To be is necessarily to be with, to be exposed to, to compose the plurality and sharing of the world. But, what are the political consequences of this ontology? Can such an ontology tell us how to orient our actions? Can it tell us how to organize our communities politically? We already saw, at the end of chapter 1 and then again in chapter 3, that Nancy's ontological description is also an imperative: we are in-common, we are world-forming, yet we must *be* or *become* what we are. What is or what we are, then, is given not as a bare fact but as an exigency that is at once *ethical* (we are responsive *to* existence, and hence responsible *before* and *for* existence) and *political* (existing is a praxis, a comportment). In this chapter, we will examine the relation between Nancy's ontology and politics.

We can distinguish three stages in Nancy's conceptualization of the political: (1) the withdrawal of the political as it is worked out in the early 1980s with Lacoue-Labarthe at the Centre d'études philosophiques sur le politique; (2) a view of politics as the praxis of (k)notting, as developed in *The Sense of the World* in the early 1990s; and (3) a discussion of democratic politics as developed in the recent book, *The Truth of Democracy*. Across these different stages, there is no radical break in the way Nancy conceives of the political and its relation to the ontology of being-with. What we do find though is a change in emphasis in that more care is taken to distinguish the ontological level of being singular plural from the political level and to describe the parameters of a political praxis. Consequently, Nancy's vocabulary is modified from the early to the later works, reflecting this changing emphasis.

In this chapter, Nancy's consideration of the political will be presented according to the three stages mentioned above: withdrawal, (k)notting, and democracy. Alongside these stages, we will also explore Nancy's views on labor and value (and hence his relation to Marx) and on sovereignty and justice. Finally, we will see how Nancy situates himself in relation to three other philosophers who have both engaged and contrasted with Nancy in their own redefinitions of politics, communism, and democracy: Badiou, Rancière, and Derrida.

The withdrawal of the political

Nancy and Lacoue-Labarthe called the Center they founded in 1980 "The Center for the philosophical interrogation of the essence of the political." It is crucial to understand what Nancy and Lacoue-Labarthe mean by this name. Their interrogation bears on "the essence of the political." It does *not* refer to "the classical appropriation of the political by philosophy" (RP 108). Nor is it a question of withdrawing from politics to a merely theoretical attitude in order to philosophically determine (or ground) the political. Interrogating the *essence* of the political philosophically means withdrawing to a position beyond both the philosophical and the political, and beyond their co-determination. Hence it is not a question of delimiting a new concept of the political on the basis of a "new" philosophy (or metaphysics), but of putting into question this founding gesture itself. It is possible to provide a philosophical foundation of the political and inversely to provide a political critique of philosophy (show that it is not neutral but politically interested), yet neither of these gestures unsettle the co-determination of the philosophical and the political.

This reciprocal involvement of the philosophical and the political is at the base of the institution of western thought (or of metaphysics). This is the case because philosophy in its metaphysical institution, as the science that provides a foundation for beings qua beings and beings as a whole, is itself already a political institution. Hence the *essence* of the political (the philosophical determination of what "politics" means) is not purely philosophical but is overdetermined by the political. The institution of the Greek *polis* is the institution of a space of relation and of a rational man, a man endowed with rational speech (*anthrōpos logikos*). Philosophy, defined as the pursuit of *epistēmē*, is both founded upon and founds the *polis*: philosophy can only take place within an open space of rational questioning, but it must at the same time furnish the essential principles of this opening. The philosopher is at once made possible by the institution of the *polis* and is himself the one who leads the *polis*, who is in charge of determining the good or the *telos* of the city.

In chapter 2, we discussed the closure of metaphysics: the fact that metaphysics is a total system of reference between two realms or regimes of beings. Concomitant with this closure, Nancy and Lacoue-Labarthe will speak of a closure of the political. That the political is completed or closed upon itself means that the progressive discourses of the reappropriation of man in his humanity and of the actualization of true humanity (the Marxian critique of alienation) have reached their limit. In this regard, Nancy and Lacoue-Labarthe speak of both a lacuna *and* an obvious presence of the political in Marx, such that he rejects the abstract form of the State in favor of a "material impregnation by the State of the content of all the non-political spheres."[1] This means that the rejection of the bourgeois State (and of its politics) happens in favor of the total immanentization of the political in the social or communal sphere. According to these discourses, politics disappears into the social or becomes coextensive with the social, but this completion takes the form of a self-fulfillment. Politics becomes total (which also means that it becomes indistinguishable) when humanity accomplishes itself as humanity, an act that corresponds to the achievement of authentic democracy, that is, the auto-regulation of humanity. At this point, every excess of the political is closed back upon itself, reinscribed in a figure of subjectivity.[2] Hence, the problem of the closure of the political is tied to the question of subjectivity. The subject, as we saw in chapter 1, is that which folds into itself all exteriority and appropriates all otherness for itself.

What disappears in the moment of the completion of the political is something like "the city," that is, a specific dimension of transcendence or alterity insofar as the city is a place that is not determined by "the factual given of needs and vital necessities," but by "this excess over 'living' – and over purely social 'living together' – of 'living well' which alone determines the *zōe* of the *zōon politikon*" (RP 134). In the past, this political dimension of transcendence assumed three forms according to Nancy and

Lacoue-Labarthe: (1) the articulation of power or material force with the heterogeneous dimension of the sacred, which produced authority, or "justified power"; (2) the relation of a community to immortality, which protected against the futility of individual, finite life; (3) the relation of community to itself, where it could present itself to itself as such (raise itself to self-consciousness). Under all these forms, what comes to disappear (Nancy and Lacoue-Labarthe will say withdraw) is sovereignty, understood as the supreme end to which "the political" as such destines each and every one of us. But this disappearance or withdrawal also lets something appear: it allows us to experience the essential absence of the unitary, total, and actualized community (discussed in the previous chapter) and allows us to determine the political anew (Nancy and Lacoue-Labarthe will say retrace) according to this essential withdrawal of sovereignty/community. This retracing cannot take the form of a renewed appeal to transcendence, since the withdrawal of sovereignty/community implies the collapse of any transcendent dimension whatsoever.

In light of the completion of the political, Nancy and Lacoue-Labarthe are led to re-define, in a controversial manner, the meaning of the word "totalitarianism" as the total domination of the political by means of the erasure of its own specificity. Under such a domination, the political has the non-appearance of obviousness. Such obviousness is a function of "the fact of the disappearance of all 'political specificity' in the very domination of the political, the fact of the political ceaselessly merging with all sorts of authoritative discourses . . . and everywhere converting itself into a form of banal management or organization" (RP 126–7). In this totalitarian phenomenon, no *specifically* political questions have the chance to emerge. In a more restricted sense, totalitarianism designates "the attempt at a frenzied re-substantialization – a re-incorporation or re-incarnation, a *re-organization* in the strongest and most differentiated sense – of the 'social body'" (RP 127) of which Nazism, Fascism, and Stalinism are the most notorious cases. In this sense, totalitarianism is a response to the crisis of democracy. Nancy and Lacoue-Labarthe underline many manifestations of this crisis, including:

> the disappearance of authority–tradition–religion triptych, the
> disembodiment of power, the collapse of ground or the loss of
> transcendence (mythico-religious or philosophical: reason, nature,
> etc.), the disruption of hierarchies and the customs of social

differentiation, the de-localization of the political (the 'empty space' of power, as Lefort has it) and the rule of political changeover, the desubstantialization of the body politic which no longer is one except in the pure dissipation of suffrage, politics eventually given over to the play of vested interests, etc. (RP 127)

If totalitarianism is a way of responding to this crisis, Nancy and Lacoue-Labarthe wonder whether democracy is not fostering, under the very domination of technical and productive criteria (what Nancy will later call ecotechnics), a new form of totalitarianism that the ready-made opposition between democracy and totalitarianism covers over (RP 128).[3] In this vein, western democratic societies aim at the same social homogenization (a homogenization of the body politics that is presupposed by democracy itself) as totalitarian States, but by other means: mass consumption and mass media.

We are now in a position to understand what Nancy and Lacoue-Labarthe mean by the equivocal expression *"retrait du politique."* Playing on the ambiguity between *"du"* as retreat *of* and retreat *from*, the expression means three things. First, it refers to withdrawing from the total domination of the political that is exemplified by the affirmation: "everything is political." More precisely, *retrait du politique* means withdrawing from the retreat of the "political as such" into obviousness. Through this withdrawal from the retreat, it becomes possible to re-trace or re-mark the political by raising the question of its essence (see TD 39). Nancy and Lacoue-Labarthe are quick to mention that this "withdrawal" is not a fall back into apoliticism; it remains a political gesture, through and through. Moreover, this withdrawal is the only possible gesture today since it is the only way of putting into question the total domination of the philosophical (metaphysical) determination of the political in terms of origin, foundation, authority, principle, etc. Determined metaphysically, the political is the putting-to-work, the accomplishment, of a self-founding, self-sufficient, and self-originating body. What needs to be put into question is not this or that form of politics but the way in which the political realm is subordinated to another instance that founds or determines it. This instance is the Subject of politics; it is the community thought as origin and principle (the kind of community that unworks itself, as we saw in the last chapter).

The question that appears in the withdrawal *from* and retreat *of* the political is that of relation. This is a question we have encountered before: how can we think of a relation (*rapport*) without either presupposing the relations or sublating those relations into a Subject of a higher-order. Emblematic of the first case are theories of the social contract, which always explain the institution of the State by appealing to a view of a "natural" state in which men are apolitical, that is, without relation, but also without *logos*. This is a problematic assumption: in our natural state we are not related, but we are at the same time not truly human (we have no *logos*) so that what makes us human is also what puts us in relation and makes us political in one and the same stroke. This amounts to saying that as human we are "naturally" related. Social contract theories, according to Nancy, always end up having to presuppose "relation" at one level or another. Emblematic of the second case is Hegel, for whom the State, as the realization of ethical life (of *Sittlichkeit*, or *politeuein*: willing to live together), is not merely the place of the external relations of citizens, based on individual needs, but the place of the absolute identity of particularity and universality,[4] where citizens live "the universal life." Here there are relations *between* citizens, but these relations are "internalized" or absorbed into the pure subjectivity of the (one) rational life. What this means is that "relations as such" can only be thought in the retreat *of*, or by subtraction *from*, the subject: "[t]he nature of relation (if it ever had a nature) is the reciprocal retreat of its terms, insofar as relation (but can one even speak of 'relation' in the singular?) is given by or proceeds from the division, from the incision, from the non-totality that it 'is'" (RP 119). What is at stake in the retracing of the political in subtraction from the subject is a "political" space, a *polis*. The organization of such a space cannot be based on the presupposed harmony or communion of its members, nor can it consist in the mere distribution of roles and functions according to needs and abilities (RP 119) since relations are in neither case essential. The political space is the space of originary relation(s) that makes it impossible to reduce the plurality to a single origin or principle.

As was said in the Introduction, four years after its inauguration, Nancy and Lacoue-Labarthe decided to suspend the activity of the Center. In the letter addressed to the participants, they mention that a certain consensus had been formed that had already foreclosed the possibility of an interrogation of the political by robbing it of its object. This consensus was not specific to the Center but was a general after-effect of what was seen as "the end of Marxism." This consensus concerned: (1) the designation of totalitarianism as the

sole political danger, embodied in the regimes of Marxist origins
(and hence the impossibility of questioning totalitarianism under
all of its forms); (2) the outdated character of the Marxian event
and the rebirth of economic neoliberalism and political neocon-
formism; and as a result (3) the end of the political as that which
has in view the identity, destination, and sovereign exercise of the
collectivity in favor of a more ethical, aesthetic, religious, or social
dimension over the political (RP 145–6).

Simon Critchley has criticized Nancy and Lacoue-Labarthe's
position during the years at the Center from a different perspective. For him, the problem is not so much that of a consensus
among the members, so much as the way in which the questioning was set up in the first place.[5] According to Critchley, Nancy
and Lacoue-Labarthe's reliance on the diagnosis of modernity as
the completion of metaphysics prohibits any passage back to politics, since all forms of politics are seen as complicit in this total
domination, and hence as forms of totalitarianism. Critchley
explains: "the diagnosis of the withdrawal of the political and the
reduction of *la politique* to *le politique* leads to an exclusion of politics, understood as a field of antagonism, struggle, dissension,
contestation, critique and questioning."[6] According to Critchley,
Nancy and Lacoue-Labarthe are left, like Heidegger, meditating
the non-metaphysical essence of the political and awaiting the god
that can still save us.[7] Of course, Nancy and Lacoue-Labarthe
would respond that it is only in thinking the disappearance (or
withdrawal) of the political into obviousness, and thereby in withdrawing from the political itself, that any truly political space –
a space of "relation" – can be opened anew. To which Critchley
might respond: "Perhaps political action is metaphysical, but how
exactly is this charge to be avoided without lapsing into political
quietism and despairing resignation?"[8] What Critchley sees in
Nancy and Lacoue-Labarthe's Heidegger-inspired meditation is a
decision in favor of essential thinking and a rejection of politics as
the realm of the battle over *doxa* (opinions). What Nancy and
Lacoue-Labarthe look for in their "essential" thinking is an
"essence" ("relation" by opposition to "subjectivity") that opens
the space for *politeuein*, live-with.

In what follows, we will see how Nancy develops his understanding of politics as relation or *rapport* so that it becomes first the
space in which our being-with is played out before being differentiated from being-with as that which ensures its possibility.

A politics of non-self-sufficiency

(i) Truth and sense, totalitarianism and ecotechnics

Nancy develops his understanding of the relation between ontology and politics in the sections of *The Sense of the World* titled "Politics I" and "Politics II." He begins with a distinction that is rather uncommon in his subsequent work: the distinction between being-with and being-together or being-in-common. Nancy describes being-with as the place of love and the expression of truth, while being-together is the place of the political and is on the side of sense. Nancy explicitly distinguishes between sense and truth in an earlier chapter of the book, where he writes:

> Truth punctuates, sense enchains. Punctuation is a presentation, full or empty, full of emptiness, a point or a hole, an awl, and perhaps always the hole that is pierced by the sharp point of an accomplished present. It is always without spatial or temporal dimensions. Enchaining, on the contrary, opens up the dimensional, spaces out punctuations. There is thus an originary spatiality of sense that is a spatiality or spaciousness before any distinction between space and time. . . . One is tempted to say further: truth is semantic, sense is syntactic. But one can do so only if one goes on to specify that syntax enchains, enchains itself, involves itself, and carries itself away *across* semantic punctuations – and that these punctuations in turn have value and validity only insofar as each is swept along toward, involved in, and even carried away beyond, the others. (SW 14–15)

From this long quote we must retain two things. First, if sense is understood as an opening *to*, an enchaining *with*, then both sense and politics will be linked to a spaciousness or spaciosity, while truth will be the presentation of what is *as such* in a given punctual present. Second, truth and sense, and hence love and politics, are described as two limits that are never achieved in their pure form. In other words, truth and sense always co-imply each other; sense needs to be punctuated by truth in order to be sense (or else it dissolves into pure, meaningless circulation) and truth needs to be exposed as sense for it to be true (or else it collapses into immanent punctuality). In the same way, love as the pure presentation of the two (the face to face of the one with the other) needs to come to make sense in order to last (SW 89). This is the becoming-sense of love/truth, its entering into the social and political realm in the family. At the same time, love's becoming-sense is a deformation and the potential disappearance of what love is. Reciprocally, politics starts in pure sense as the being-together of the indistinct, anonymous many and must punctuate itself into truth. This is the becoming-truth of politics/sense.

Politics in truth is, according to Nancy, what one calls totalitarianism: "the complete presentation of a sense in truth" (SW 89). This politics is necessarily sacrificial; it requires that one sacrifices one's individual life to the higher instance, such as the State, the People, or the Cause. Sacrifice, then, is linked to transcendence, as sacrifice is the only form of access to an absolute that transcends existence. Here again, Nancy does not oppose democracy to totalitarianism. Instead, he underlines the fact that democracy represents that last form of sacrificial politics, namely that form in which truth itself is sacrificed. Democracy is the figure of a politics without foundation, without Cause, yet this absence is still interpreted as truth: the truth of democracy is the absence of truth, mere circulation (IC xxxvii). Hence democracy is the form politics takes in the wake of what Nancy calls ecotechnics. Ecotechnics (or ecotechnology, depending on the translation) is the name Nancy gives to a world without reason, end, or figure, but whose loss of origin and end, whose loss of direction, is only effective under the names of "planetary technology" and "world economy" (BSP 133). This world without direction is made up of a single network of causes and effects, means and ends, so that it is impossible to distinguish between causes and effects, between ends and means. Everything is connected to everything so that there is no first or endpoint to circulation. Without an ultimate End, all ends are means, or alternately, all means are ends, without distinction.

In the world of ecotechnics, "politics" is coextensive with the management of production, exchange, and growth of the world (CW 94). That is, "politics" is not really a politics (remember that *politeuein* means living-with in excess over the mere social living together determined by our respective needs), but an economy. Nancy comes back to this point in a short text titled "Is Everything Political? (a simple note)," written in 2000. If it seems that even politics is now so dominated by economy that the affirmation "everything is economical" seems to ring truer than "everything is political," Nancy explains how what dominates is in fact what used to be called "political economy": the management of subsistence and prosperity on the scale of the city-state. The *polis* is taken to be an *oikos* (a natural order) and knowledge of the affairs of the city (*politeia* in Greek) becomes knowledge of the laws (*nomoi*) of the order and management of the city, now taken as a big household (*oiko-nomia* in Greek). If the Greek *polis* was the place of the production of a "more-than-life," or a "good life" beyond the mere satisfaction of needs and the natural order of the *oikos*, it has now become the global, all-encompassing *oikos*, whose management not only reproduces life, but also wealth. Importantly, this domination of the economical is only possible on the assumption that human beings naturally belong to one and the same *oikos*; this self-sufficiency of humanity is what sustains the total domination of the economical.

Nancy also points out, however, that ecotechnics undoes all presumption of the self-sufficiency of the human being, the self-creation of humanity as Subject, in that capitalism abolishes all final Ends. In doing so, it lets our naked, figureless, and meaningless being-together appear. Elsewhere, Nancy uses the term "*technē*" to name a "finish of being": the way something comes to be what it is fully and completely; *phusis* is the name of the other kind of finish. Both *technē* and *phusis* are ways in which what exists is brought forth as what it is (a tree, a chair). The *technē* of the ecotechnical world, on the other hand, acts as a "finish without end." The mutation of *technē* from pro-duction – the bringing-forth of something into its own end (*entelecheia*) – into the undoing of all ends means that modern technology need not necessarily be understood, as Heidegger does, as the bringing-forth that challenges and sets up all that exists in order to make it available as standing-reserve. It can also be understood as an unworking that has "as its ends not to make an end of sense" (SW 101). What is in question then is whether "ecotechnics takes on the sense of the autism of a 'great monad' in a process of indefinite self-expansion, and/or . . . takes on the sense of the disruption of all closures of signification, a disruption that opens them up to the coming of (necessarily unprecedented) sense" (SW 102).

The problem that lies at the heart of Nancy's discussion of ecotechnics is the ability to distinguish between two ways in which the link of politics to the values of self-sufficiency, subjectivity, and sovereignty, unties or undoes itself. One way remains caught in a sort of negative theology, while the other attempts to displace the entire schema. In other words, Nancy is concerned with whether there can be a "deconstruction" of the theologico-political that would be more than a mere secularization. What does this mean?

(ii)   The deconstruction of sovereignty and the politics of (k)notting

The discourse of the philosophical foundation of the political, where the *polis* is the site of the actualization of the essence of man, is at first overtly theologico-political. The monarch is the concrete and immaterial figure of the people or the nation; he is the embodiment or the presence of the political totality. This foundation in a transcendent principle is subjected to a process of secularization; sovereign is first God, then King, then the people, the workers, humanity. This process is not only the transcription of a foundational logic into a secular realm but, as we saw in chapter 2, also a process of immanentization: the loss of a grounding transcendence. In the move from monarchy to democracy, we have more than a transposition of the logic of foundation from the king to the people, as citizenship in fact displaces sovereignty. At this limit, the sovereign is seen not as that which provides a ground but as the place where the problem of auto-foundation (auto-poiesis or auto-formation) is played out.[9] Hence we must, according to Nancy, distinguish between the "becoming-secular" (putting a secular instance in the place previously reserved to God) and the "becoming-worldly" (dissolving the place reserved for God into the world) of the theologico-political (SW 93).

While the sovereign can be seen as the ground or foundation of the community, he is himself, by definition, without relation: free, detached, absolute.[10] Hence, we should actually differentiate between the sovereign and the suzerain, even though the two functions can be embodied in the same person. While the latter is the grounding authority, the ruler whose rule is authorized (e.g. by God), the former is the self-founding absolute (God himself). If the sovereign is "the existent that depends on nothing," the existent that nothing precedes or exceeds, then the institution of sovereignty is not the transcription of theological foundation into the secular realm, but "the creation of an atheological assumption" (CW 104). For example, the authority of the monarch is founded upon his election by God and the authority of the free people is founded upon Nature or upon God.[11] Sovereignty, however, cannot be founded upon anything but itself, "insofar as precisely, the 'itself' neither precedes nor founds it but is the *nothing*, the very thing from which it is suspended" (CW 103). This means that sovereignty is not the secularization of political theology, but its very end, the point at which the theological foundation of politics wavers. That is, even though we think of the sovereign in terms of the secularization of theological transcendence, the institution of sovereignty in fact opens, for Nancy, to the lack of any foundation; sovereignty is not founded; it is that which shatters itself in trying to found itself in nothing but itself. Nancy indicates that this is what Bataille has tried to say in stating that sovereignty is NOTHING. It cannot be an exterior thing to which a sovereign would relate or which a sovereign would appropriate for himself. Sovereignty cannot be what founds (justifies) the sovereignty of the sovereign. Hence, sovereignty at the end of the theologico-political opens onto the atheological, that is, for Nancy, onto being-in-common and the world. This is why Nancy can ask, evocatively: "What if sovereignty was the revolt of the people?" (CW 109).[12]

Consequently, we must distinguish a politics of sovereign self-sufficiency, whether it is totalitarian or democratic, from an "unworked" politics of knotting and tying. The latter becomes possible in the closure of the former. Our political thinking, according to Nancy, is organized and saturated by four key terms: subject, citizen, sovereignty, community. Put simply, the concepts of subject and citizen represent two ways of organizing community and claiming sovereignty. The subject is the figure of the theologico-political, the self-engendered substance circling back upon itself, while the citizen displaces this figure of the Subject, but without moving beyond the paradigm of self-sufficiency since citizens are indistinct and anonymous units without any essential relation or unity.[13] This gives rise to two ways of understanding community: one in which interiority reappropriates division and sharing, and one in which the sharing of space remains inappropriable. To these two senses of community will correspond two senses of sovereignty: the sovereign as self-engendered substance, and a notion of sovereignty in which the last instance of institution rests upon nothing. The question Nancy asks is: must we choose between these? Must we choose between the appropriative violence of the subject and the abstract spatiality of citizenship (SW 110)? If the politics of the Subject is the absence of politics "in the sense of a *being-together* into which one could *enter*, in the sense of a *knot to be tied* [lien à nouer]" (SW 91), the politics of the citizen appears as purely formal and hence is always at the mercy of becoming mere ecotechnical management.

The problem with both options is that they both rely on the same scheme of self-sufficiency: "In the different figures of self-sufficiency, sometimes it is the social tie itself that is self-sufficient, sometimes it is the terms or units between which the social tie passes. In both cases, ultimately the tie no longer makes up a tie, it comes undone, sometimes by fusion, sometimes by atomization" (SW 111). What needs to be thought is a "social bond" as an *act* and not as a thing to be instituted from an "un-tied" state (the so-called "state of nature") (SW 93). When the social "bond" is thought as a (k)not to be tied, community becomes sharing, sovereignty becomes no-thing, and politics becomes a question of the configuration of the space of sense:

> One would thus demand a politics without denouement . . . a politics of the incessant tying up of singularities with each other, over each other, and through each other, without any *end* other than the enchainment of (k)nots, without any structure other than their interconnection or interdependence, and without any possibility of calling any single (k)not or the totality of (k)nots self-sufficient . . . Politics would henceforth be neither a substance nor a form but, first of all, a gesture. . . . (SW 111–12)

The political sphere is the space in which a knot is to be tied but never tied once and for all. Such a space can only be open if room is made for all, for each and every one (not only humans, but all singularities) to tie themselves to themselves and to others. The political imperative is, as we saw already at the end of chapter 1, to "create a world," in which, Nancy writes, "there is room for everyone: but a genuine place, one in which things can genuinely take place, where there is place for being there (in this world)" (CW 42; see CW 112; RP 156–7).

(iii)   War and the desire for sovereignty

Before we discuss this imperative to "create a world" and the call to justice it implies, let us turn to Nancy's analysis of the 1990 Gulf War. Nancy's reading is interesting because it shows the difficulty we have in moving beyond the paradigm of sovereignty. Our world, Nancy writes, is one "encumbered by sovereignty," one that does not know how to displace or go beyond sovereignty (BSP 124).

The first striking feature of Nancy's analysis of the Gulf War is that it seems to provide an archaic "sovereign" reading instead of a biopolitical one. On the biopolitical reading, the Gulf War would be not so much a question of the sovereign declaration of war, the attack on a declared enemy and the control of a territory, but a question of the management of population, the mastery of life and life's processes. In "Note on the Term: Biopolitics," Nancy explains why he rejects the name "biopolitics" in favor of "ecotechnics": "The term *biopolitics* in fact designates neither life (as the form of life) nor politics (as a form of coexistence). . . . Both are, rather, henceforth subject to what carries them together into ecotechnology" (CW 94). Nancy does not deny biopolitical phenomena; instead, he wants to insist that they have nothing to do with either life as *bios* ("form of life" or "engagement with meaning") or with politics (form of coexistence). The life in question in biopolitics is not a *bios* but a *zoē* (bare life) that has become technical through and through. And the politics of biopolitics is the management of this technical life, its mere reproduction and maintenance (CW 94). Nancy identifies two misinterpretations that are latent in the word "biopolitics." First, it is always possible to interpret bare life as something that slides outside of the realm of the economic and social forces that dominate and manipulate it and to identify life itself in a figure (e.g. the worker, the pauper, etc.) whose bareness testifies to its truth.[14] At the other extreme, life can be interpreted as a self-produced whole that takes the place of the classical figure of the sovereign Subject (monarch or people). Neither of these interpretations addresses the problem of the ecotechnical world, namely the problem of an absence of figuration and totalization (the "finish without end" mentioned above).

The Gulf War might have been a manifestation of biopower more than sovereign power since it was not concerned with putting the enemy to death in order to protect or expand one's territory. But for Nancy this war was still that of a world desperately trying to enact sovereignty. War is "sovereignty's technology par excellence; it is its setting to work and its supreme execution (end)" (BSP 117). Technology, again, is not a means to an end but a mode of effectuation or execution. Hence a discourse that treats technology as a means and evaluates it according to its ability to reach an end exterior to it does not grasp the "essence" of technology, which, as Heidegger insisted, is "nothing technological." As such, technology does not have an extrinsic end but is an end in itself, a "finish of Being" that carries what is "to the limit of its own logic and its own good, that is to the extremity of its own Being" (BSP 118). If war is *technē*, it is not a means to an end but the ultimate way in which sovereignty manifests itself and becomes what it is. Beyond all questions of accomplishing a goal (e.g. securing a territory), war is the manifestation of sovereign brilliance (the flash of light of an explosion transmitted on a television screen, for example). In contrast, the laws do not possess this brilliance, but require the light of sovereignty and its founding event (BSP 107).

Even if appeals to sovereignty are intermixed with the expression of police intervention and appeals to international law and humanitarian principles, the rhetoric and symbolism present at the time of the First Gulf War (and others since then) attest to the difficulty of doing away with sovereignty (BSP 115). This difficulty itself manifests a desire for legitimation and finality in a global world, a desire to forget the world's lack of foundation and finality "in the sovereign brilliance that the power properly without power, which polices the world order and watches over the price of primary resources [Nancy is of course referring here to the US], borrows in the time of war" (BSP 137). In order to move beyond the death throes of sovereignty and to avoid a reinvestment of the sovereign place – as witnessed during the Gulf War – it is necessary not only to empty out the place of sovereignty but also to submit this place to deconstruction. For, as Nancy indicates, our world has not yet done away with sovereignty, with the desire for absolute self-foundation; it has only been able to replace the sovereign foundation with the absence of foundation of the ecotechnological totality. The problem is that once it imploded, the absolute height or inequivalence of the sovereign only left behind the general equivalence of all and the desire for an absolute value. But in a world become worldly, there can be no sovereignty since the world has no summit (CW 105), no highest, detached, absolute point. Thus, if there is to be any "absolute value" at all, it can only be found in the spacing of the world itself, which is the empty place of the common good and of justice (BSP 137).

(iv)   Justice and fraternity

The political imperative embedded in Nancy's ontology of finitude discussed in chapter 1 is that of "creating a world." Even though this task looks quite formal, it corresponds to an intransigent claim to justice. In *The Experience of Freedom*, Nancy defines justice as the measuring of the incommensurable: not measuring definite differences on a common scale, but measuring "differences" that are incomparable, incommensurable (EF 75).[15] In "*Cosmos basileus*," Nancy defines justice further as that which "must be restituted, returned, given in return to each singular existent" (CW 110), as that which is owed to each singularity as this singular "one." But since a singularity is never an isolated "one" but always plural – a plurality of traits that opens onto a plurality of worlds – justice is also what is owed to each singularity in their inherent and relational plurality. The "proper" measure of what one is owed cannot be separated from the "improper." Justice "rendered to the singular plural is not simply a demultiplied or diffracted justice. It is not a unique justice interpreted according to perspectives or subjectivities – and nonetheless it remains the same justice, equal for all although irreducible and insubstitutable from one to the other" (CW 61). There is one measure of justice equal for all, yet this measure is both immeasurable (how to measure the gift that each existent is?) and improper (how to decide where one singularity ends and another begins?). If no "proper" measure of justice is to be found, then the demand for justice cannot be met with a distribution of goods, places, or freedoms as if one could first properly identify and measure each singularity (individual or collective) and then give them their proper share (CW 111). Hence justice consists, first and foremost, not in laying out a just measure but in deconstructing all *given* measures: "*justice* can only reside in the renewed decision to challenge the validity of an established or prevailing 'just measure' *in the name of the incommensurable*" (EF 75). Existence has a common measure, but this measure is "freedom": the absence of ground or reason, the "releasing into existence" discussed in chapter 1. In other words, to exist means to measure oneself against nothing, or to measure oneself absolutely. Nancy will call this equality in the freedom or sharing of the incommensurable "fraternity" (EF 72). For him, fraternity denotes the absence of Paternal foundation; the delivery to freedom and equality.

It is here that we find Nancy both closest and farthest away from Derrida's own thinking of justice and community. Derrida is suspicious of a justice that relies on "what is appropriate" (*convenance*, Greek *oikeiotēs*), since "what is appropriate" is essentially linked with the hearth, the home, kinship, familiarity, property, and therefore "appropriability, proximity."[16] In *Specters of Marx* and especially in *Force of Law*, Derrida also questioned whether justice has anything to do with a measuring at all, and whether it is not instead linked to a certain *hybris* or excess over all laws and measures. Derrida insists on "a difficult and unstable distinction between justice and *droit*, between justice (infinite, incalculable, rebellious to rule and foreign to symmetry, heterogeneous and heterotropic) and the exercise of justice as law or right, legitimacy or legality, stabilizable and statutory, calculable, a system of regulated and coded prescriptions."[17] For Nancy, justice remains tied to the measuring and sharing of what is appropriated, yet this sharing is thought according to a measureless measure and an improper propriety, and hence aligns closely with what Derrida tries to think under the term "justice." Derrida's imperative to "calculate with the incalculable"[18] particularly resonates with Nancy's imperative to measure oneself against the incommensurable.

On the topic of fraternity, the difference between Nancy and Derrida is more marked, even though it may be possible to reduce it to a mere difference in vocabulary.[19] Nancy speaks of an ungeneric fraternity as the intersection between equality and freedom, or as the sharing of the incommensurable. Hence, Nancy does not have in mind "literal" fraternity. But this is not enough to quiet Derrida's misgivings about the political use of the figure of the brother. In *Rogues*, Derrida reminds us of his prior investigation, in *Politics of Friendship*, of such political use of the figure of the brother as Nancy's:

> In fraternalism or brotherhoods, in the confraternal or fraternizing community, what is privileged is at once the masculine authority of the brother (who is also a son, a husband, a father), genealogy, family, birth, autochthony, and the nation. And any time the literality of these implications has been denied, for example, by claiming that one was speaking not of the natural and biological family (as if the family was ever purely natural and biological) or that the figure of the brother was merely a symbolic and spiritual figure, it was never explained why one wished to hold on to and privilege this figure rather than that of the sister, the female cousin, the daughter, the wife or the stranger, or the figure of anyone or whoever.[20]

Despite the fact that Nancy's fraternity, and the community with which it is linked, is affected by something incommensurable (freedom), the risk remains that fraternity slides toward a genealogization and leads us back to autochthony, nation, birth. This is especially evident when Nancy writes that "fraternity . . . is . . . but the relation of those whose *Parent*, or common substance, *has disappeared*, delivering them to their freedom and to the equality of this freedom. Such are, in Freud, the sons of the in-human Father of the horde: becoming brothers in the *sharing* of his *dismembered* body" (EF 72, trans. mod.). Derrida worries that the common substance, which is dismembered and shared, is in the end reappropriated through a sort of "Eucharistic transubstantiation."[21] Nancy himself puts Freud's description into question (EF 168), indicating that Fraternity should not be thought of as the loss (or murder) of the father but as that which is without father, without ground or origin, without "given height" (CW 106; SW 115). Hence, in the absence of common origin, appeals to a generic identity are impossible. However, even with this defense, Derrida's question holds: Why then still name the sharing of unsharable freedom by the word "fraternity"? From *The Experience of Freedom* to Derrida's last texts, this is the point of contention that underlies the dialogue between Nancy and Derrida.

The delineation of the political against the in-common

In his contribution to the colloquium *Sens en tous sens* in January 2002 at the Collège international de philosophie, François Kervégan asserted: "There is no political philosophy in Nancy despite the constant concern." To which Nancy responded: "I have not thought the inclination or slope [*dénivellation*] from ontology to politics enough. To be with or in-common, that does not make up a politics, but it allows us to determine the sphere of the political. The political does not permeate the whole sphere of the in-common." In saying this, Nancy echoes his claims in an interview with Stanley Grelet and Mathieu Potte-Bonneville for the journal *Vacarme* in April 2000. Speaking of his essay "The Compearance," Nancy says: "I myself should have a turn at self-criticism: in writing on 'community,' on 'compearance,' then on 'being with,' I certainly think I was right to discern the importance of the motif of the 'common' and the necessity to work on it anew – but I was wrong when I thought this under the banner of 'politics.' "[22] He then hints at the space occupied by politics: "For me, then, politics is from now on submitted to a questioning that must first and foremost bear on the relation and distinction between 'politics' and 'being-in-common.' If you like: the ontology of the common is not immediately political."[23]

In "The Compearance," Nancy had equated "politics" with the multiple and expansive presentation of the "in" of the in-between and named as examples of such a presentation "art, thought, love, glory, the body" (Com 390). Politics, in this case, would be the *praxis* that keeps open and engages the space of our exposition. In

this sense, politics cannot assume or take over the meaning of existence as a whole, but only make room for the sense that existences
make in tying and untying themselves. In this context, Nancy discusses Marx's realization of politics, where the *polis* becomes coextensive with the whole of the real life of the community instead of
being a separate realm of activity, which has been appropriated by
the ruling class (Com 388). There are two ways to think this coex-
tensiveness of the *polis* with the real life of the community. Either
the *polis* is the same as the sum of all activities or it represents
something that is distinct from all other activities insofar as it is the
"in-common" or the "compearance" of these activities or practices
(Com 389). In the latter case, politics remains a distinct region,
while at the same time becoming equivalent to the in-common.
While it is not clear in "The Compearance" whether politics in
"propagating" the "in" comes to be identified with the flashes or
bursts of sense "produced" by praxeis of sense such as art, literature, love, and thought, Nancy is much more careful in *The Truth
of Democracy* to delineate the sphere of the in-common as the sphere
of sense-making against the sphere of the political.

(i)   *May '68, communism, democracy*

The Truth of Democracy was written in early 2008 to commemorate
the fortieth anniversary of May '68. May '68 likely represents the
most important event of the second half of the twentieth century
in France. For Nancy, May '68 was an event in the strong sense: a
"break" with "History," a breach or opening in the thought of time
as succession and progression where potentialities were encountered outside of or beyond the question of their feasibility and
realization.[24] At the concrete level, the name "May '68" refers to a
two-week long general strike, which started with student strikes
and protests in universities and high schools and involved at its
peak 11 million workers, that is, roughly two-thirds of the French
workforce at the time. There is little consensus as to the ultimate
meaning or impact of this event on French society, and it is hard to
find a single unifying thread indicating the general disenchantment
that animated the strikes. Protests were directed against traditional
hierarchical structures such as the university or the union movement, traditional moral values, modern consumerism, authoritari-
anism, and capitalism. In *The Communist Hypothesis*, Alain Badiou
emphasizes the diversity and complexity of May '68, identifying

four different but interrelated strands of events. The first involved the students' uprising, and especially the occupation of the Sorbonne university, while the second culminated in a massive general strike originating from outside of the "official working-class institutions." A third strand involved a "libertarian May" directed against the moral climate of the times and which brought about sexual liberation and cultural innovation, but it is the fourth aspect of May '68 that is most crucial for Badiou. This strand involved "the conviction that, from the 1960s onward, we were witnessing the end of an old conception of politics" and a "search for a new conception of politics."[25] For Badiou, this meant the need to reinvent revolutionary politics in the face of the ineffectivity of old models of emancipatory politics. The lasting heritage from May '68 is the formulation of what Badiou calls "the communist hypothesis," which asserts that "the existing world is not *necessary*," and that therefore "a different world is possible."[26] Even though Nancy will also link the events of May '68 to communism (as the necessary basis of democracy), he disagrees, as we will see, that communism is a *hypothesis*. For Nancy, communism is an *ontological fact*. Despite this divergence, the interpretation of the events of May '68 will lead both Badiou and Nancy to put into play a new concept of democracy that must be distinguished from the democratic pretension of what Badiou calls "capital-parliamentarianism."[27]

Nancy situates the singularity of the May '68 revolt in a certain disappointment with democracy itself, whose triumphal recovery after World War II failed to live up to its promises. As a result, student and worker protests targeted a "kind of managerial democracy" (TD 1); democratic politics, recognized as the lesser evil, sank "into a double denial: of justice and of dignity" (TD 7). The unquestioned consensus around democracy after World War II was caused less by an overall positive evaluation of its tenets than by its evaluation in relation to "totalitarian regimes" of all stripes. However, this unquestioned support for democracy obscured the fact that "most significant political catastrophes" of the twentieth century "were not the result of the sudden emergence of inexplicable demons" (TD 8) but rather the result of an intrinsic vulnerability at the heart of democracy itself. If democracy is part of the problem, then it is not enough to defend it; it must be *reinvented*. While a malaise with the democratic consensus was felt in 1968, this dissatisfaction did not give rise to an adequate thinking of what "had made democracy inadequate to itself"; what from the heart of democracy had made and continues to make democracy vulnerable to "totalitarianism." This, Nancy identifies as the "constitutive lack" in democracy, namely the inability to bring to light the *demos* that is supposed to be its principle (TD 6).

If democracy is to be more than just the management of necessities and expediencies, it must also, in some way, be "communist" (TD 15). Democracy names the "true possibility of being all together, all and each one among all" (TD 14). Communism, in turn, does not name the entity (the *demos*) which is to be organized or managed democratically, but the desire or spirit that animates democracy. Hence, the "democratic man" is not "the man of a humanism measured against the height of man as he is given" but the one who, as Pascal says, "infinitely transcends man" (TD 15).[28] What we need, according to Nancy, is Pascal joined up with Rousseau: the production of the human being in the production of a common body as developed in the *Social Contract*,[29] but where the human so produced is not simply given but is understood as being in a constant movement of transcending or of infinite exposition. For Nancy, Marx came close to thinking this synthesis since for Marx man produces himself in such a way that this production is "worth infinitely more that any measurable evaluation" (TD 16). The self-production of humanity through human labor is of a qualitatively different kind than the production of commodities. For Marx, free human labor is essentially social, whether that labor is individual or communal. That is, production and consumption are essentially human (social) activities that connect any individual producer or consumer to herself, to other human beings, and to humanity as a whole. In one of the *Economic and Philosophical Manuscripts* from 1844, Marx writes:

> We have seen how on the assumption of positively annulled private property man produces man – himself and the other man; how the object, being the direct manifestation of his individuality, is simultaneously his own existence for the other man, the existence of the other man, and that existence for him . . . . Thus the *social* character is the general character of the whole movement: *just as* society itself produces *man as man*, so is society *produced* by him.[30]

On the other hand, capitalism arises out of the private ownership of the means of production, giving rise to the abstract existence of the worker as mere labor power and obstructing the social (human) character of productive life since human beings relate to each other only through the commodities they own as private property.

(ii)   Value, equivalence, capitalism

For Nancy, capitalism is "the result of a decision on the part of civilization: value *is* in equivalence" (TD 21). What is the origin of equivalence? But more importantly, how does it relate to this other basic feature of capitalism, namely the accumulation of wealth (or capital)? Even though Nancy does not go into much detail in his discussion of capitalism, it is useful to go over some of Marx's basic analyses to clarify the origin of and link between equivalence and accumulation.

For Marx, the use-value of a commodity is its utility as it is expressed in the process of use or consumption, while its exchange-value is expressed in the process of exchange. The exchange-value of a commodity is the "mode of expression" of something contained in it, that is, labor time. Yet the labor that is embodied in a commodity and expressed in the process of exchange is not concrete; it is abstract labor.[31] It is not money that first renders all commodities commensurable and hence exchangeable; rather it is "because all commodities, as values, are realised human labour, and therefore commensurable, that their values can be measured by one and the same special commodity [e.g. gold], and the latter be converted into the common measure of their values, i.e., into money."[32] Aristotle could see that exchange required commensurability but he could not see how things as different as beds and houses could be commensurable because "Greek society was founded upon slavery, and had, therefore, for its natural basis, the inequality of men and of their labour powers."[33] The equivalence of commodities is a function of the equivalence of all labor and hence only possible on the basis of the equivalence of all labor power. But what renders all labor power equivalent?

The commensurability of human labor is a function of its commodification. It is because labor power is bought and sold, because it is "exchanged" for another commodity (food or shelter in the form of money), that it acquires an "exchange-value." This value is measured by the labor time necessary to produce or reproduce the worker's labor power and it takes the form of the wage that the capitalist gives to the laborer in exchange for his or her labor power. Out of this exchange of commodities, Marx is clear, there does not arise any surplus-value: "Circulation, or the exchange of commodities, begets no value."[34] Where then does the surplus labor that the capitalist appropriates in the form of surplus-value or capital come from? The exchange of labor power for a wage (commodity for commodity) does more than simply give rise to the commensurability of human labor. It also introduces an imbalance into the production process. While labor produces value, it is not the labor added to the raw material that produces surplus-value. When the capitalist who has paid for the labor power of the worker "consumes" this commodity (puts it to work in the factory), he releases its use-value. But using labor power is different than using a chair, for example. By putting labor power to work, more value is created. Hence the laborer is a commodity, whose use-value produces surplus-value: value producing value. If we have free human beings producing commodities, value is created, but no surplus: the value created corresponds to the labor time expanded. But when labor power is sold as a commodity, that is, when wage labor becomes necessary, then we witness not only the commensurability of abstract human labor but also the split between the value of the labor power exchanged and the surplus value produced by this power. This surplus is the profit made by the capitalist on his investment, and the accumulation or growth of this surplus under the form of capital is potentially infinite. While there is a limit to the use-value one can accumulate (one only needs so many tables), surplus-value knows no such limit.

For Nancy, this decision in favor of value as equivalence – which leads to the commensurability of all products of labor and the drive to accumulate more of that "equivalent value" – leads to nihilism. This is inevitable because, as we saw, for Nancy, sense is differential. The escape from nihilism is not found in the affirmation of new values but in a transformation of the evaluative gestures themselves. Remember that the Nietzschean criticism of values as transcendent markers that we discussed in chapter 2 condemns us to nihilism only if it reduces all values to perceived equivalencies between evaluative gestures (TD 22). If this is the case, the overcoming of nihilism can only happen via the passage to a different principle of valuation, one that presupposes the absolute distinction or incommensurability of evaluative gestures. As Nancy writes, "Only this provides the way out of nihilism: not the reactivation of values but the manifestation of all against a background where the 'nothing' signifies that all have value incommensurably, absolutely, and infinitely" (TD 24). Only on this assumption can we have a *rapport* or a *sharing out* instead of a mere substitution.

What has absolute worth or what is also called dignity because it is not of the order of measurable value? In a sense, we can say that it is "the infinite," provided we understand it in the right way. The infinite that has absolute worth is neither a given infinite (God, Reason), nor an indefinite growth (capital), but always the putting into play of existence: the infinite that is actual in the finite. As we saw in chapter 1, the finite is not the non-infinite but that which is infinitely open. This infinite opening does not progress toward a goal that would infinitely recede, but rather denotes the actual and effective presence of some *one*, of some gesture that engages existence, and hence creates sense, here and now, absolutely. The exit out of nihilism requires a new decision of civilization: "to make possible the finite inscription of the infinite" (TD 31).

(iii)   Democratic politics against general equivalence

In what way does this turn toward the infinite opening and the creation of sense prescribe a politics? What is the relation between politics and sense? Politics is neither everything, nor nothing, but arises in distinction from, and thus in relation to, the order of sense. This means that while politics opens up the realm of sense, it cannot take over this realm. The political necessitates in principle that we go beyond the political order and although such a going beyond starts out from the open space of the *polis*, its "object" is not as such political. Sense is decided in the sphere of the in-common, rather than in the political sphere, where the sphere of the in-common is not a unified sphere, but one of the multiple bursts of existence. Politics only gives the affirmations of non-equivalent sense their space and possibility (TD 26); it does not prefigure or determine the "Good" of the good life that makes up political life. Instead, politics allows each and all to "sketch out, to paint, to dream, to sing, to think, to feel a 'good life' that measures up incommensurably to the infinite that every 'good' envelops" (TD 27). At the same time, this figurelessness of the political sphere should not be thought of as a lack; it is the precondition for the proliferation of figures: works, gestures, bearings, thoughts, etc. This figureless and spacious politics takes the name of democracy, a democracy that is essentially an-archic insofar as the *demos* as such does not constitute a given *archē* or principle, but is to be understood instead as that which foils "any posited, deposited, or imposed *archē*" in favor of a plurality of absolute gestures (TD 31; see OBC 11). In this way, Nancy defines democracy paradoxically as an "egalitarian aristocracy" (TD 33).

At this point, Nancy's democratic politics seems not only abstract but barely political. Giving voice to this worry, Nancy writes: "Someone will say to me: So you are declaring openly that, for you, democracy is not political! And then you just leave us hanging, without any means of action, intervention, or struggle, as you gaze off dreamily toward your 'infinite' . . ." (TD 29). His response is that his position is quite the opposite: To think the inscription of the infinite in the finite is to nullify the thought of general equivalence and its indefinite appropriation. And for Nancy, to enter into this thought at all is "already to act. It is to be engaged in the praxis whereby what is produced is a transformed subject rather than a preformed product, an infinite subject rather than a finite object" (TD 31). Furthermore, this thought commits to certain "actions, operations, and struggles" (TD 31) that maintain the absence of given origin or measure – of a thingified common. Of course, this does not define a politics but rather constitutes the condition of possibility of a putting into play of existences whose precondition is social justice.

In *The Truth of Democracy*, we have a complex relation between, on the one hand, the in-common as sense and democracy as the condition of possibility of the in-common, and on the other hand, the sphere of the in-common and the concrete politics that arises out of our being-together in the world. This double relation should not be understood as one of foundation: democracy (which Nancy terms archaically as a "metaphysics" (TD 34) – though not one in which beings as a whole would be founded) opens a space for being-in-common without assuming its sense or destination. Democracy does not determine what form being-in-common will take; rather, it is the decision in favor of being-in-common, of the infinite opening of existence, against general equivalence. Being-in-common is the sphere of existence and sense and of their reticulated multiplicity. It is here that decisions about what it means to live a "good life" are made, that gestures of existence are affirmed. And it is from the place of being-in-common that policies – of health, culture, or otherwise – can be devised to respond to the senses or values that are affirmed in the sphere of the in-common. But again such policies are not determined by or derived from our common existence since this existence is not One. The two levels of politics (metaphysics and policies) are not only distinct, but each has, in its own way, being-in-common as its "focal point."

Nancy is not the only contemporary thinker to have recast the term "democracy" to rethink "emancipatory" politics in a radical way. Badiou's venture was briefly alluded to above. Two other

thinkers that come to mind are Jacques Rancière and Jacques
Derrida. For Rancière, in a vein similar to Nancy, democracy is
essentially an-archic: "Democracy is the disrupting of all logics that
purport to found domination on some entitlement to dominate."[35]
Yet Rancière does insist, maybe more than Nancy, on the fact that
the common is not given. While what Rancière calls "the police" is
the management of a given, common world, where each party has
its place and function, politics happens in the contestation of this
"sharing of the sensible." This contestation is enacted by those who
have no part in the governing of this common world; those who
cannot take part in the democratic process because they are not
recognized as "having logos," their speech being heard as mere
sonorous emission, and are therefore not recognized as a legitimate
part of our common world.[36] According to Rancière, politics is
fundamentally dissensus or disagreement. Yet, it is not disagreements on how to handle common affairs since such disagreements
already presuppose the appearance of actors on the political stage
and recognize the utterances of such actors as rational speech.
These disagreements are always based on a deeper consensus as to
the parts, roles, and functions that form the political stage. The
dissensus that constitutes politics is more fundamental: it points to
a division within the sensible itself. Returning to Nancy, being-in-
common is a given but, as we saw, this given is that of an exigency:
to become what we are. Hence, embedded in Nancy's account of
democracy is a contestation of the hierarchies and exclusions that
form our non-egalitarian "sharing of the sensible." This contestation is "founded," for Nancy, on our ontological constitution as
being-in-common and the freedom and equality it implies, while,
for Rancière, the democratic contestation is founded on a practical
inscription of equality by "the part of those who have no part."
Comparing the two positions, Nancy appears to be more optimistic
regarding the possibility of a "sharing of the sensible" that is adequate to our being-in-common. We could even say that it is this
possibility that drives Nancy's thinking as it was presented in
this chapter. For Rancière, even though politics can always irrupt
and shatter the claims of the "police order," an egalitarian,
non-exclusive sharing of the sensible does not seem possible.
Equality remains a supposition, a hypothesis, whose affirmation
destabilizes an existing order, but does not found a new one. Here,
Rancière is closer to Badiou than to Nancy.

Like Rancière's democratic dissensus, Derrida's democracy to
come is linked to a deconstruction of the sovereign *demos*, thought
as a self-enclosed, self-founding totality. Democracy names a certain

way of sharing power among a *demos*, but as long as we find the principle of the self-affection and self-definition of the people at the basis of democracy, the sovereignty of the people is not really divided since it always comes back to the same: each one rules, decides, votes, or obeys as a member of one and the same people. If there is another, "non-sovereign" democracy, it can only be thought by subtracting the *demos* from the Sovereign One.

According to Derrida, democracy has always been caught between an opening and a closing, between an immunization (against the exterior) and an autoimmunization (an immunization against its own defenses). He writes:

> democracy has always wanted by turns and at the same time two incompatible things: it has wanted, on the one hand, to welcome only men, and on the condition that they be citizens, brothers, and compeers [*semblables*], excluding all the others, in particular bad citizens, rogues, noncitizens, and all sorts of unlike and unrecognizable others, and, on the other hand, at the same time or by turns, it has wanted to open itself up, to offer hospitality, to all those excluded.[37]

The fraternal community reconciles these two imperatives through the process of fraternization, which renders the dissimilar similar. While this process permits the opening of the "closed circle of citizens" to all ("anyone can be my brother"), it does so by appealing to a certain exemplarity: "French" as the "exemplar" to be imitated to become a citizen of the world or "man" as the "exemplar" of the human that is to be imitated to become truly human. For Derrida, there is a difference between this opening of the *demos* thanks to universality and exemplarity and a radical opening to the "to-come": to "what or who comes" before (or beyond) any identifiable and calculable difference. "Democracy to come" is for Derrida neither the future arrival of democracy – the history of the amelioration of a certain political regime – nor the history of the progressive opening of citizenship to all human beings. It is instead the essential and unconditional opening of democracy to the Other, to what or who comes before or beyond being determined as friend or enemy, member of the family, human being, animal, or god. This democracy requires an unheard-of sharing/opening of sovereignty beyond its gathering into a People, a State, or Humanity.[38]

Both Derrida and Nancy attempt to subtract the *demos* of democracy from the Sovereign One. At the same time, two major differences can be highlighted. First, while Derrida thinks the radical opening of the *demos* in terms of the absolute (and hence singular)

Other, Nancy thinks this opening as the form without figure of the "in" of the "in-common." Nancy is critical of Derrida's understanding of singularities as "absolute secrets" and of his insistence on the absolute alterity of the Other because these limit Derrida's ability to think the plurality of others. Unlike Levinas, who resolves this plurality in fraternity as the basis for social justice, this plurality leads Derrida to the unbearable, yet inevitable, sacrifice of one absolute Other at the expense of another absolute Other, emblematized in Abraham's sacrifice of Isaac.[39] Though this sacrifice is not the sacrifice of the self to a transcendent Cause or Truth, as discussed above, it leads Nancy to believe that despite all disruptions and displacements of traditional politics, Derrida does not succeed in thinking being-in-common.[40] A second difference is that Derrida's "to-come," as the radical opening of any democratic system, remains dependent on the system itself and cannot be sustained as such. The other – "what or who comes" (*[ce] qui vient*) – is not anything that can be present; it irrupts in an instant without presence. Nancy's democracy, in contrast, points toward a way of sustaining the experience of the impossible, that is, toward the affirmation of singularities and of their multiplicity, as an alternative to both the total system of totalitarianism and the ecotechnical triad globalization/capitalism/democracy.

Stepping back from Nancy's analysis of politics, as discussed in this chapter, we can see that his discussion relies on some general conceptual gestures, familiar to us from the previous chapters. Nancy's understanding of politics presupposes his understanding of community as discussed in chapter 3: if community is not a thing, if it is not given, then we need to think politics differently. This is an approach we encountered early on in chapter 1 in the discussion of the "with" in Heidegger. We need to think neither the self-founding One nor the self-sufficient units, but the essentiality of the "with," of "relations." In political terms, this means that we have neither totalitarianism nor "ecotechnical" democracy, but something else. Nancy calls it "democracy." In terms of our discussion of the closure of metaphysics as onto-theo-logy in chapter 2, it means that we have neither ground nor lack of ground, neither monotheism (and its secular pendants, e.g. humanism) nor atheism (immanentization), but something else. Nancy calls it "world." Following from this, Nancy's ontology, his deconstruction of Christianity, and his understanding of community all tie into his recasting of political praxis as the imperative to "create a world."

5

From Body to Art

The discussions contained in this last chapter are gathered under the double heading "Body" and "Art." This chapter is concerned with drawing out the consequences of Nancy's ontology for a rethinking of the traditional dichotomy between Matter and Spirit/ Idea/Meaning. Our focus will be on the relation of materiality to sense, and hence on the triad "thing, sense, signification," whose complex relation Nancy thinks in terms of touch or exscription. Whatever body, sense, or soul mean, Nancy contends that they cannot be properly thought with the help of traditional dichotomies, in which either inert matter is spiritualized and infused with meaning or the intelligible Idea is incarnated or imprisoned in inert matter. In Nancy's vocabulary, the metaphysical understanding of Incarnation (whose deconstruction we undertook in chapter 2) is grounded in the two-world paradigm and must be replaced by a thought of "carnation," of bodies. The world that is created *ex nihilo* is necessarily a world of bodies. It is this "concept" of body that must now be clarified.

Such a clarification of the concept of body will lead us into Nancy's discussion of art. The link is obvious as soon as we recall that Hegel defines art as "the sensuous presentation of the Idea," a definition Nancy takes as his point of departure for the discussion of art. The fact that Nancy thinks body and soul not as two distinct substances but as mutual exposition, and that he thinks sense not as signification but as an embodied event determines his understanding of art in two ways. First, we will see that Nancy tries to develop a non-metaphysical concept of the "image" broadly construed. Metaphysics, we remember, distinguishes between the true world and the apparent world, the latter being founded on the former. Like the body, which is not the visible sign of an invisible interior, Nancy's image is not the representation or copy of another, higher, reality, be it sensible or intelligible. It is, rather, the presentation or exposition of sense. Second, we will see that Nancy emphasizes the irreducible materiality and plurality of art, in contrast to both Hegel's and Heidegger's understandings of art, both of whom have missed the material, sensuous aspect of art by subordinating it to a higher principle. Consequently, Hegel and Heidegger have reduced the essential dispersion of "Art in the singular" to an organized system or a singular origin. When art is liberated from its function as the presentation of the Idea or the manifestation of Truth, each work of art, each color, each sound, becomes a singular, material burst of sense.

In the Introduction, we said that Nancy's recent work is increasingly in "dialogue" with various artists or works of art. None of these recent writings will be directly addressed here. Rather, we will delineate a philosophical thinking of art (as non-representational and as singular plural) that will help us to better read Nancy's more "poetic" or more "artistic" texts. When Nancy writes on painting – for example on Caravaggio's *Death of the Virgin*, or on François Martin's *Semainier* – he does not (or not only) provide a theory of painting in general, or an interpretation of a painting in particular. He does not dissolve the painting's materiality in thought. Instead, by describing the painting, by exposing its materiality to language (and hence to the materiality of the word), Nancy assists or accompanies our encounter with the painting in its singularity.

Nancy's writings "on" art and "on" the body are not theoretical discourses *about* the body or *about* art, discourses that would turn them into concepts or ideas. Rather, these writings attempt to touch the body's materiality, and hence to touch the element that interrupts discourse itself. The driving question behind these writings is: how to make the incorporeal side of discourse touch the materiality of a given body, the color of this painting, etc. This explains why these texts are often obscure and difficult to read. At the same time, it also means that these texts cannot be summarized, but must be *read*. Only such a reading can give rise to the experience of the extremity of language, where "language loses itself" (BP 346) in shattering itself against materiality. No commentary can capture this experience.

Body and soul: reading Descartes
against Cartesian dualism

Before we delve into Nancy's thinking of the body, let us start by outlining his reading of Descartes's *Meditations on First Philosophy* in the text *Ego Sum*, and particularly in the last chapter, "*Unum quid*," which has not been translated into English. We will begin from this point not only because the *Meditations* are without a doubt one of the most well-known texts of philosophy, but also because, by working through Descartes, it will be easier to see how Nancy opposes "the body," or rather "bodies," to so-called Cartesian substance dualism, the doctrine according to which there are two substances, a thinking one and an extended one, mind and matter. Interestingly, it is in the *Meditations* that Nancy finds a way of thinking against the mind–matter dualism often attributed to Descartes.

The Cartesian Cogito, "I think therefore I am," is traditionally interpreted as the moment of the self-grounding and self-positing of the subject of thought and knowledge. For Heidegger, this is the inaugural moment of modern metaphysics, where the "I" becomes the *sub-jectum*, the underlying subject of representation, which is absolutely certain of itself. At this point, certainty becomes the measure of truth and the question of truth becomes that of the adequation between representations and objects that stand before the subject. Nancy's reading of Descartes disrupts this traditional reading by showing that the "ego" is not to be taken as the underlying subject in its self-certainty, the thinking substance, but rather must be understood as the gaping mouth that unfounds the subject in the very moment of its foundation.

First, Nancy emphasizes the fact that we should not speak of "*the* Cogito": the deduction of my own existence from methodical doubt, but always of *cogito*, "I think." The evidence that "I exist" is not based on a logical proof or a deduction, a proof that would be conducted by a (preexisting) ego. Rather, the evidence lies in, and is one with, the utterance. As such, we cannot speak of an enunciation *of* the ego in the subjective genitive (as if the ego is what enunciates). Rather, when we hear the expression in the objective genitive (what is enunciated is the ego), it implies that the ego is the *result* of an enunciation and hence not itself the enunciator. There is no underlying, preexisting enunciator that would precede the utterance. Before the subject of the *énoncé* (the I that is spoken of) and the subject of the *énonciation* (the I that speaks), there is the verb *énoncer*, enunciating, an action without subject, the opening of a gaping mouth that articulates "ego." If the evidence of ego is tied to an "I enunciate," then there is no "ego in general," no "egoity" that sustains the enunciation but only the "each time," the each time "such and such" a singular time. Ego is a "spasm or convulsion" without stasis or stance; it is always a punctual, local, discreet inflection and never a substance (C 25). For Nancy, the path of Descartes's *Meditations* is the path through which the "spastic" ego assures itself of itself by assuring itself of the distinction between substances. The purpose of the latter is to sustain the originary distinction that ego *is* by guaranteeing that it, ego, has the nature of a thing, and not merely that of a spastic stance at the extremity of its enunciation (ES 147). To assure itself of itself, ego must bind "the unbinding of its proffering" and install "continuous space, the indistinctness of the *times* of existence" (C 27).

According to Nancy's reading, it is not the thinking substance that pronounces "ego," but the human or the *unum quid* of the Sixth Meditation, the I which is itself not a substance but body–soul, the substantial union of body and soul (ES 157; C 25). If this is so, how is it then that this "ego" comes to identify itself with the thinking substance and cover over the evidence that it is I, body-soul, *unum quid*, who says "I exist"? The *unum quid* is not an immediate, substantial presence, but has the structure of "selfhood" that we discussed in chapter 1. Substantial presence, on the other hand, is the negation of presence-*to*-self; it is the point without extension. That I am extended means that I am exposed *to* (myself and others). It is thanks to this outside that I am, that I feel myself existing. But since there is no existence that is not "felt," there is no existence (no "ego cogito") that is not "ex-tended." Nancy explains using very common examples: "When I struggle or breathe, when I digest or suffer, fall or jump, sleep or sing," he writes, "I know myself only as being what struggles or sings . . ." (C 139). In this moment, there is an indistinction between the knower (the struggling I) and the known (that I am struggling), instead of a clear distinction between the I itself and the activity of struggling. When I reflect on the struggle, on the other hand, when I say: "I struggle," "I am this body that struggles," I posit a thing that struggles, put "the body" (a part of me) at a distance from myself (I distinguish myself, differentiate myself from my body) and hence weaken the evidence of the "union" (am I really that which struggles?), the evidence that body and soul are one, *unum quid*.

In Descartes, we seem to have pure extension on the one side and pure cogitation on the other. Yet, "thought is sensing, and as sensing, it touches upon the extended thing; it's touching extension" (C 131). Thought, in order to sense itself, to know itself as that which thinks (imagines, wills, senses, etc.), has to be opened to an exteriority, has to encounter an obscurity. If thought were only thought, if it were purely luminous, clear, transparent, it would not "feel" anything, and it would not "feel itself" think. Hence it would have no way of knowing itself as "something that thinks." It is by being exposed to the body, that is, to something impenetrable that does not think or know (without being ignorant or obscure [see BP 199; C 97]), that the soul knows itself: "The *psyche* is first psyche by its *extension, partes extra partes*, and by the opacity to itself in which it remains with respect to this exteriority-in-itself, or with respect to the to-itself that constitutes it" (GT 83; see also C 21, 159).[1]

At the same time, it is by being exposed or opened to thought, penetrated in some way by it, that the body senses itself. A body is not a mass; it is not something closed upon itself (C 123). It is an outside, something turned inside out: "A body accedes to itself as outside. . . . I am an outside for myself. . . . It's through my skin that I touch myself. And I touch myself from outside, I don't touch myself from inside" (C 128). Here Nancy picks up the phenomeno-logical analysis of self-touch in Husserl and Merleau-Ponty (my right hand touching my left hand) but points out (a point Derrida will develop in *On Touching*) how the phenomenologists "always return to a primary interiority" (C 128). For Nancy, on the contrary, I have to be completely exterior to myself in order to touch myself. Nancy gives the example of the organs: when I am healthy, I do not feel my stomach or my heart; they are silent. Here we can speak of an interiority or an intimacy, which is not of the order of the sensible/sensitive but rather of the mass. When I feel my stomach, it is outside. This is what is at stake in the word *soul*. The soul, in a certain strand of the tradition that includes Aristotle, Thomas Aquinas, Spinoza, and also Descartes, "doesn't represent *anything other* than the body, but rather the body outside itself, or this other that the body is, structurally, for itself and in itself" (C 126). What we have to think is not an opposition between body and soul but the soul as "the body's difference from itself" (C 126). The soul is that fact that there is a body, this body. The soul is the presence of the body, "its position, its 'stance,' its 'sistence' as being *out-side* (ex)" (C 128).

Hence, Nancy can conclude, against the traditional reading of Descartes, that Descartes's ontology is not one of the "cut between body and soul," but one of "the 'between,' of the swerve or exposition" (C 143). In order to think this relation between body and soul – which, it should be emphasized again, is not a relation between two things, since each is nothing but the ontological opening-*to* of the other – Nancy will redeploy the Cartesian *partes extra partes*: parts outside parts, but insist on the *ex-* of the extra. While Descartes thinks the "extra" as undifferentiated void, for Nancy the extra is the place of differentiation (C 97; see also C 29, 143). For Nancy, space is always and everywhere filled, a body always opening unto another, more or less subtle body. If this filled space does not collapse into a mass, a pure immanence, it is because of the "extra" that articulates bodies against bodies. Hence, "extension" is not the property of that which is spread out *in* mathematical space; it is an intension, a tension, a vibration, or frequency (C 17, 95, 134; SW 58).

Nancy will think this ex-tension of bodies in terms of weight rather than mass.[2] Bodies are not massive, but they weigh upon each other. "Their weight is the raising of their masses to the surface. Unceasingly, mass is raised to the surface; it bubbles up to the surface; mass is thickness, a dense, local consistency" (C 93). As spacing, bodies are "*places* of existence" (C 15; see BSP 18). Nancy gives the example of a newborn baby (but we should think that the phenomenon described is not limited to human beings but applies to each body in each and every place): "when a baby is born, there's a new 'there.' Space, extension in general, is extended and opened. The baby is nowhere else but *there*. It isn't in a sky, out of which it has descended to be incarnated. It's spacing; this body is the spacing of 'there'" (C 132–3). Incarnation, or what Nancy will prefer to call carnation, does not mean that what is merely ideal comes to occupy a place, but that a place opens itself or spaces itself out. Nancy's thought of "birth," or coming-to-presence, undoes any filiation (C 67, 83). Every body is absolute, not in the contradictory sense that it would be an immanence detached from every relation, but in the sense that a body exists without origin or end, that it arrives here without coming from anywhere and without holding anything in reserve: "like an image coming on a movie or a TV screen – coming *from* nowhere behind the screen, *being* the spacing of this screen, existing as its extension – exposing…" (C 63; see C 199, BP 187). The world of bodies is essentially atheological in the sense discussed in chapter 2.[3]

At the same time, we should not collapse Nancy's understanding of the body too quickly with the signifying body, the body proper (*Leib*) or the flesh (*chair*) of phenomenology, which is the zero-point of orientation in the world and the origin of all my intentional acts. In the case of phenomenology, the body is thought not as massive, obscure, or inert but as transparent, expressive, shot through and through with meaning. Against this picture of the signifying *Leib*, Nancy emphasizes the dis-location of the "body proper" into heterogeneous zones. The body that senses what Nancy also calls the enjoyed or delighted body (*le corps joui*) is a *zoned* areality. *Jouissance* (delight, enjoyment) is neither the pleasure that a subject can experience for itself, nor should it be understood as the moment where the I "loses itself" and dissolves into the Other. *Jouissance* happens at the moment of *rapport* or access, when the finite being is neither inside nor outside but on the limit. A delighted or enjoyed body is what Nancy will call a corpus, in opposition to the flesh or to the body proper (C 129; IRS 41). As he writes in the 36th of the "Indices on the Body: Corpus: a body is a collection of pieces, bits, members, zones, states, functions. Heads, hands and cartilage, burnings, smoothnesses, spurts, sleep, digestion, goose-bumps, excitation, breathing, digesting, reproducing, mending, saliva, synovia, twists, cramps, and beauty spots. It's a collection of collections, a *corpus corporum*, whose unity remains a question for itself" (C 155).

The relation between body, sense, and language: exscription

We have seen that the term "body" (or its equivalent, "soul") undercuts the dichotomy between matter and spirit and their relation in terms of "incarnation." In a similar way, it undercuts the dichotomy between mute matter and conceptual or linguistic meaning. As we saw in chapter 1, sense is not signification. Signification relates a word and a concept or idea, a thing and a thought, but sense happens between singularities, between bodies. As such, we can say not only that bodies are essentially local "events" or "bursts" of sense, but also that sense is always a bodily event. Yet, as was also mentioned in chapter 1, language is "the incorporeal of the world" (see BSP 84; IRS 21). What is then the relation between body and sense and between body and language?

The relation that sense and language entertain with material bodies is similar to the relation between bodies: a contact–

separation, a touch, an exposition. The polysemy of the word exposition is not overlooked by Nancy. Exposition denotes at once: (1)
bodily exposition, that is, bodies touching bodies and the "passibil-
ity" that ensues; (2) phenomenological exposition, that is, consciousness or thought exposing (and being exposed to) the
exposition of bodies; and (3) linguistic exposition, that is, sense
being inscribed in language, in ideal meanings. If language is
understood purely in terms of linguistic significations (words as
general concepts), it becomes an inessential part of the world. But
when it is understood more primordially as sense, it appears as an
essential "component" of the world. Language not only presents
something "as" something else, "for example, its essence, principle,
origin, or its end, its value, its signification" (BSP 88), it also presents
the "as" as such, or it presents the presence of the thing, its exteriority. Even when I point to this stone in front of me and say "this
stone" (instead of talking about "Stones in general"), what my
saying shows is the fact that this thing here is showable (and hence
neither ineffable nor unpresentable). Yet what is shown of the
thing, the "this" that it is, as Nancy says, appears only as the limit
of denomination: " 'This stone' is the stone that my statement designates and before which my statement disappears. Or, instead of
inscribing this stone in a lexicon, my statement comes to *exscribe
itself* in this stone" (BP 175). The failure of the name to capture the
thing does not mean that the thing remains ineffable. Rather, it
leads to the exscription of language. "Exscription is produced in
the loosening of unsignifying spacing: it detaches words from their
senses, always again and again, abandoning them to their extension. A word, so long as it's not absorbed without remainder into
a sense, *remains* essentially extended *between* other words, stretch-
ing to touch them, though not merging with them: and that's language as *body*" (C 71; see BP 175–6).

Exscription names both the relation between material body and
sense, and between sense and linguistic signification. Meanings,
inscribed significations (categories, concepts), are always already
beyond language, in contact with a material point:

> Sense needs a thickness, a density, a mass, and thus an opacity, a
> darkness by means of which it leaves itself open and lets itself be
> touched *as sense* right there where it becomes absent as discourse [or
> as signification]. Now, this "there" is a material point, a weighty
> point: the flesh of a lip, the point of a pen or of a stylus, any writing
> insofar as it traces out the interior and exterior edges of language. It

is the point where all writing *is ex-scribed,* where it comes to rest
outside of the meaning it inscribes, in the things of which this
meaning is supposed to form the inscription. (GT 79, trans. mod.)

What is inscribed – the meaning of the word "tree" for instance – is
at the same time exscribed, placed outside of language by its contact
with a material instance or a technical apparatus. Sense happens
as that which remains outside of or resists signification, that is, as
this singular material event. Sense as a singular material event is
at the outer limit of language and signification. In a similar way,
the body as impenetrable matter is at the outer limit of sense.[4] It is
through this double exscription of signification and sense, and of
sense and bodies, that thought can touch the thing. The concept
"tree" in its abstract meaning can come to touch "this tree here"
(impenetrable matter) through the exscription of its sense (as a
singular material event) (BP 338–9). At the same time, the *ex-* of
exscription reminds us that the thing is that which weighs *outside*
of thought (GT 79). Sense, as the middle term between material
bodies and ideal meanings, remaining beyond both of them but
touching them at their outer limits, is what allows for a "meaningful experience" of singular beings.

Nancy's rethinking of the material or embodied character of
sense undoes another Cartesian principle, namely the clarity and
transparency of ideas or thoughts. Thought, according to the Cartesian paradigm, should dissolve all obscurities and present its object
fully and completely. But Nancy asks: "Who would not want a
thought that blocks all passage through it, that does not let itself
be breached? Who would not want an impenetrable meaning, a
meaning that has consistency and resistance?" (GT 80) True thinking, according to Nancy, should not dissolve the materiality of the
thing into a purely intelligible concept, but should let that which is
outside of thought weigh on thought. This "experience" of thought,
Nancy writes, "remains a *limit-experience,* like any experience
worthy of the name. It does take place, but not as the appropriation
of what it represents; this is why I also have no access to the weight
of thought, nor to the thought of weight" (GT 76). This means that
thought cannot fold back upon itself and appropriate for itself the
weighty character of the thought that thinks the thing. It is exactly
this weighty character of thought/thing, of bodies against each
other and against thought, which phenomenology in general
(which thinks Being as sense and sense as intentional access), and
Heidegger's concept of world as significance in particular, obscure.[5]

As we already discussed in chapter 1, for Heidegger, Being-in-the-World is defined as having access to what is "as" what it is. I have access to the hammer in taking it "as" a hammer, and I display such an understanding in hammering. We also saw that according to Heidegger, the stone is worldless because it lacks such access to what it is "with" (the sun, the rain, the hand). What escapes Heidegger's thinking, according to Nancy, is the weight of the stone, its gravity (which need not be weighted *by* anybody), and so Heidegger's stone remains abstract: "Heidegger apparently fails to weigh precisely the weight of the stone that rolls or surges forth onto the earth, the weight of the *contact* of the stone with the other surface, and through it with the world as the network of all surfaces" (SW 61).[6] From Nancy's perspective, Heidegger's thinking of the thing, even in later essays such as "The Thing" (1951), remains appropriative and fails to let the thing weigh on thought. A true thinking of the thing is possible only because the thing itself is reduced to being the thing *of* thought. The question thus persists: can there be a thinking of things that is not appropriative, that does not usurp the independent existence of the thing, but rather comes into contact with the thing as it is in itself, that is, in its *weight* (BP 177–8)? Such a thought would "access" the thing only in touching "nonaccess, impenetrability" and would consequently remain on the threshold of access "at the entrance yet not entering" (SW 60; see also BP 169).

Presentation, representation, schema: the non-metaphysical concept of the image

Now that Nancy's "concept" of the body and the relation of exscription between matter, sense, and language have been explained, we are in a better position to explore Nancy's understanding of the work of art and of the image. The *ex nihilo* of the world, Nancy said, is the expression of a "radical" materialism, a materialism "without root" (CW 51). It means that what exists is not the embodiment of a higher, intelligible reality. It is all there is. If this is the case, what then is an "image"? Is it a secondary kind of presence that represents or imitates, and hence signifies what exists? Or does the image "make sense" in Nancy's use of the term?

Before we go over Nancy's own understanding of "the image," it is important to mention that his "definition" of the image should not be taken as a mere descriptive claim about the kinds of images

that we encounter in the world, or, even more specifically, about
the kinds of images that are considered artistic and are worthy of
being exposed in museums. Were Nancy's account a descriptive
one, it would suffice to point to images that do not fit Nancy's
definition in order to disprove his claims. But Nancy's discourse
on the "essence" of the image is normative. In other words, Nancy
can always claim that an "image" that does not display the essential features he attributes to images is not an image, or at least
not a good one. This procedure should be familiar to readers of
Heidegger. For Heidegger, the essence of something must be distinguished from a mere universal or generic category that would
be obtained by abstracting common features from a comprehensive
inventory of the species of that thing. To the contrary, a thing's
essence, for Heidegger, is its utmost possibility, what defines that
thing essentially, and this essence is always something that can be
forgotten or covered over in such a way that a thing presents only
the unessential face (*Unwesen*) of its essence. Hence, the description
of what a thing is essentially (a description best achieved by the
poet, who names more essentially than the philosopher who, as we
will see, deals only with universal abstract categories) has a his-
toric-normative purpose: to bring what exists into its essence.

Nancy defines the image as "sacred" or, in order to avoid any
confusion between the sacred and the religious, as "distinct" (GI
1). Religion consists in a set of rites or observances that establish a
bond with the transcendent. Religion relates two orders that are in
principle heterogeneous through a legitimated transgression, a sacrifice. Nancy does not want us to understand the "distinction" of
the image from worldly things on the model of the religious; images
are not transcendent, and our relations to them do not take the form
of transgression. What is, then, the kind of "distinction" specific to
images?

There are three ways in which Nancy speaks of the image as
something "distinct." First, the image "is distinguished from things
or from living beings, [second] it is distinguished from the image-
less ground from which it is detached, and [third] it distinguishes
itself insofar as it designates itself as an image" (GI 70). Let us focus
on the first two kinds of distinction for a moment. The image is
distinct first because it is withdrawn and set apart "by a line or
trait," a border, a frame, an edge. The line distinguishes the image
from what is present in the homogeneity of the world of tools
ready-to-hand, or of things present-at-hand (GI 2, 9). At the same
time, the image is not only cut out and framed, but also pulled

away, raised from a ground and brought forward (GI 7). The ground of the image is not the provenance or cause of the image, but a backside. This backside is the "indistinct" from which the image distinguishes itself so as to throw itself "out-in-front-of-itself," turning itself toward the outside (GI 21). In this sense, Nancy will also say that the image is evidence:

> Something is *seen distinctly* from far away because it detaches itself, it separates – like the two shapes or the double shape we see of Tahereh and her beloved [Nancy is referring to a scene from Abbas Kiarostami's film *Through the Olive Trees*]. Something strikes with distinction: always, a picture is also that which subtracts itself from a context and stands out, clear-cut, against a background. Always, there is a cut, a framing.[7]

Another way of expressing this evidence is to say that an image is not a thing but a force, the force of the thing that gathers itself unto itself, lifts itself up and cuts itself out from the homogeneous continuity of indistinct places and things, and offers itself as such to be seen (or sensed).[8] It is in this sense that every image is "a portrait":

> not in that it would reproduce the traits of a person, but in that it pulls and *draws* (this is the semantic and etymological sense of the word), in that it *extracts* something, an intimacy, a force. And, to extract it, it subtracts or removes it from homogeneity, it distracts it from it, distinguishes it, detaches it and casts it forth (GI 4).[9]

The image does not resemble the thing; rather, in the image, the thing is made to resemble or coincide with itself, is made to present itself in its resemblance to itself (GI 8; see also 24).

At the same time that the image shows something or makes something present, it also shows *itself* showing something. This is the third sense of "distinct." The image presents not only a thing, a flower for instance, but also presents the presentation itself: "that there is" (this or that). This is the primordial sense of the *re-* in representation, not the iterative *re-* of repetition, but the intensive one (as a performance is called a representation in opposition to the repetitions) (GI 35–6). The image "always says, simultaneously, 'I am this, a flower,' and 'I am an imaged flower, or a flower-image.' I am not, it says, the image *of* this or that, as if I were its substitute or copy, but I *image* this or that, I present its absence, that is, its sense" (GI 70; see also BP 347–50). It is because the image re-marks its own distinction as image that we cannot "enter" into it, but always remain on the threshold of it as before a "totality of sense" or a "world." This image is a totality because it does not hide any secret but is "all there is" (BP 357–8). At the same time, this totality of sense is not something that could be fully grasped in *a* vision. It is not a world placed in view and made available to a subject, but a groundless fragment that offers itself to be seen, provided we understand that "vision does not penetrate, but glides along swerves and follows along departures. It is a touching that does not absorb but moves along lines and recesses, inscribing and exscribing the body" (C 45).

If the image is what lets the thing present itself as *itself*, there is an "art of the image" or an "imagination" at the origin of the self-presence not only of artistic images but of all objects as they show themselves in their unity. This more fundamental art of the image is what Kant called "schematism," an art "hidden in the depths of the soul."[10] Kant introduces the schematism in the *Critique of Pure Reason* to solve the problem of the mediation or relation between concepts and intuitions. Since, as Kant famously states, intuitions without concepts are blind and concepts without intuitions are empty, human cognition requires both intuition and concept. Of the three types of concepts and their corresponding schemata discussed by Kant, it is the schema of the pure concepts of the understanding or the transcendental schema that interests Nancy. In order for the categories to refer to perceived, experienced objects, they must be schematized. But the categories are not abstract concepts of what is common to several objects of experience: red, flower, justice. As a priori concepts, they are not derived from experience but are essential characteristics of any possible object in general. Hence, the schema that will relate each category to a possible intuition cannot be the image of any specific, particular, individual object. Rather, it must be that by which the unity and unicity of a representation is possible in the first place (GI 81, 84), the condition of possibility of their being an image (a sensuous representation and not the chaotic flux of sensations).

The transcendental schema is, for Kant, a product of the productive imagination (*Einbildung*). Productive imagination does not produce images (reproduce or represent things in their absence) but is the a priori capacity to imagine, that is, to make-one or bring-into-one, *ein-bilden*. Or, in Nancy's words, it draws presence or "self-presence" (the thing in its resemblance to itself) from out of the "chaotic, general dissemination and the perpetual flux of a sensory multiplicity" (GI 23). It is the "force" that "forms" a world by producing the object in general. Hence, the imagination is the condition of possibility of both a subject that experiences a coherent world and of that sensuous manifold which is presented to the subject.

Every presence is an "image." Is it possible to understand this affirmation in a non-metaphysical way, that is, outside of the framework of the division between appearance and reality, between the world of appearance and the true world, a framework in which the image is understood as a secondary presence that hides or distorts what truly is? In *Being Singular Plural*, Nancy distances himself from the discourses on the "society of spectacle" (which assert that our "reality" consists now only of "media images") because these discourses, according to him, have remained incapable of thinking beyond the metaphysical framework, in that they have not drawn the proper conclusions from Nietzsche's deconstruction of "metaphysics." As Nietzsche famously wrote in "How the 'True World' Finally Became a Fable": *"in doing away with the true, we have also done away with the seeming world!"*[11] If the true world has slowly been shown to be an illusion, then the conclusion is not that everything is now a mere illusion, because the very notion of illusion itself is rendered meaningless by the disappearance of a fixed notion of reality. Nancy's understanding of the image is tightly linked with, and in fact made possible by, the deconstruction of metaphysics and its two-world paradigm discussed in chapter 2.

According to Nancy, our metaphysical understanding of the image is determined by the conjunction of the monotheistic ban on images and the depreciation of imitation in Greek philosophy. The ban on images is found in *Exodus* 20.4 and *Deuteronomy* 5.8. It reads as follows: "Thou shalt not make unto thee any graven image, or any likeness *of any thing* that *is* in heaven above, or that *is* in the earth beneath, or that *is* in the water under the earth" (KJV). As Nancy points out, the interdiction does not concern either figurative works of art or images of God but sculpted images, statues to be worshiped as idols. The commandment concerns "the production of forms that are solid, whole, and autonomous" (GI 30). If the idol is condemned, it is not because it is a copy or an imitation, but because it is a closed presence "where nothing opens (eye, ear, or mouth) and from which nothing departs or withdraws (thought or word at the back of a throat or in the depths of a gaze)" (GI 31).[12] The condemnation of images is based, for Nancy, on a certain interpretation of images as "inessential, as derivative and lifeless, as deceitful and weak" (GI 31). It is here that the biblical prohibition encounters the Greek problematic of imitation.[13] In the case of monotheism, we have a God who is Word or Logos and whose truth lies in the retreat of his presence, or, as Nancy puts it, a God who is "a presence whose sense is an *absense*" (GI 32). In the case of (Platonic) philosophy, we have a logos as intelligible Form or Idea (as non-sensible images). Nancy links the two: "In one respect, *absense* condemns the presence that offers itself as the completion of sense [the idol]; in another respect, the *idea* debases the sensory image, which is only its reflection, the degraded reflection of a higher image [the intelligible Form]" (GI 32).

Nancy's image, on the other hand, is neither a secondary presence replacing the absent thing, be it an intelligible Form or Idea, nor a presence asserting itself as completed sense (as thing or work). Nancy's image is an *ab-sense*, or a "sense inasmuch as it is precisely not a thing" (GI 36). A certain absence is constitutive of the image as what takes leave from sheer presence, in order to appear as a force withheld on its own edges, and rising from a groundless background. It is this image that Nancy calls a *"représentation interdite"* (as we say of a person who is stunned or dumbfounded and hence abstains from answering a question or entering a room, that she is *"interdite"*). Of course, one might try to exit from sheer, meaningless presence not through "ab-sensing," but by a sort of superpresence. Then, the image becomes an idol or a pure blow: a presence without opening or departure that merely dazzles (GI 47).[14]

Beyond Hegel and Heidegger: the plurality of the arts

While Nancy notes that his discourse on art remains in a "constant and problematic proximity" to the great modern philosophical statements on art (SW 194 n. 131), he also tries to conceive the work of art in itself and beyond the simple account of its production or reception. According to Nancy, what is left out of these traditional attempts at grasping art either from the point of view of its creation (poiesis, genius) or its reception (judgment, critique) is the birth or shock, the coming to presence of the image, its free offering without origin or destination. The consequence of the non-representational and non-metaphysical understanding of the work of art we have just outlined is that it liberates art from its subordination to any higher instance. Art, then, is neither the sensible presentation of the Idea (Hegel), nor the *Dichtung* or poetizing of truth (Heidegger). Rather, Art as such will dissolve into a plurality of singularities: art forms, artworks, materials, and techniques.

(i) Hegel: art as the presentation of the Idea

For Nancy, Hegel's definition of art as "the sensible presentation of the idea" captures the essence of art as it is thought from Plato to Heidegger (M 88). According to this definition, art is conceived as the presentation of universal Spirit in the form of an immediate perception in a sensuous shape. What makes a work a work *of art* for Hegel is not its sensuous materiality, but the fact that this materiality (which remains an essential moment of art) has been spiritualized into a form, organized into a composition produced by a human consciousness, and hence must be understood as an expression of the universal or the Idea. It is useful to remind ourselves here that the Idea, for Hegel, is neither something in my head, nor is it an abstract Platonic Form. Rather, the Idea (we could also say Reason) is the objective realization of the Concept. This means that the Idea is not opposed to reality or objectivity, but rather contains reality, truth, and actuality as essential moments of the dialectical progress of Spirit giving an account of itself. The Idea is the knowledge that Spirit has of itself; it is Spirit's self-consciousness (what Hegel also calls Absolute Spirit). It is this knowledge that art, religion, and philosophy express. Art is a way in which the Idea is realized in reality, a way in which Spirit knows itself, but it remains a limited way that will subsequently be sublated into higher forms of self-knowledge: revealed religion, and then philosophy.

According to Nancy, art occupies an unstable place in the Hegelian account of the dialectical progression of Spirit. Fine art is a way of expressing the divine or the absolute, yet this expression remains sensuous and immediate. For Hegel, it is this sensuousness and immediacy that constitutes the limitation and insufficiency of art. While art presents the Idea "as the immediate unity of the Concept with its reality," it does so "only insofar as this unity is present immediately in sensuous and real appearance."[15] Revealed religion will elevate itself above the determinations of sensuousness and finitude, and will express knowledge of the Idea in a form more adequate to its spiritual essence by giving the Idea the form of infinity and universality. At the same time, it will express this knowledge only in the subjective form of faith or fervor. It is philosophy, and specifically Hegel's speculative idealism, that will express the absolute in a form (the philosophical system) that corresponds to its true nature or content.

Hegel identifies three periods in the development of art: symbolic art, classical art, and romantic art. In each period, a specific understanding of the divine and of the relation between spirit and the natural world determines the conception of art. Symbolic art was the expression of a natural, abstract conception of the divine. Pyramids, stelae, statues (what monotheism will call "idols") represented or pointed to spiritual life without being able to find an adequate, living expression for it. In the Classical period, matter was infused with movement and life so as to express the Greek understanding of the perfect harmony between Spirit and Matter in the human form. Romantic art, finally, sought to embody a higher and more developed form of spirit, a conception of the divine as infinite. The adequate medium for the expression of such a conception of the divine is language since in language the material element (sound) is neutralized and becomes capable of receiving the most diverse spiritual significations. Linguistic sounds do not have any value as sounds; rather, they are external signs that communicate the spiritual content and signification of speech.[16] While the Romantic conception of the divine is for Hegel more adequate than the Classical one, it also leads to the "death of art." Sensuousness comes to be felt as a limitation to the expression of the divine. In Antiquity, it was artistic activity that defined and made explicit the Essence of Greek Spirit, as expressed in the norms of artistic beauty (the harmony between the whole and the parts, between form and content, between spirit and matter). For us – or perhaps, as Nancy will try to show, *we* have moved beyond Hegel's "we" – it is not art that is the normative center of our spiritual existence but rational thought, or philosophy:

> art, considered in its highest vocation, is and remains for us a thing of the past. Thereby it has lost for us genuine truth and life, and has rather been transferred into our *ideas* instead of maintaining its earlier necessity in reality and occupying its higher place. What is now aroused in us by works of art is not just immediate enjoyment but our judgement also. . . . The *philosophy* of art is therefore a greater need in our day than it was in days when art by itself as art yielded full satisfaction. Art invites us to intellectual consideration, and that not for the purpose of creating art again, but for knowing philosophically what art is.[17]

What interests Nancy in the Hegelian conception of art and of the history of art is the element of art that resists sublation into philosophy. Since for Hegel it belongs to the very essence of the Idea that it appear in actuality, art will be an essential moment of the development of Spirit. Yet art remains a moment that must ultimately be sublated into philosophy insofar as sensuous presentation comes to be understood as inadequate to the content of the Idea. The question is: what happens to sensuous exteriority, and hence to art, in this sublation? Nancy underlines a passage from the *Aesthetics* where Hegel seems to contradict the logic of the dialectical progress from art to philosophy. Hegel writes: "Thinking is only a reconciliation between reality and truth within thinking itself. But poetic creation and formation is a reconciliation in the form of a *real* phenomenon itself, even if this form be presented only spiritually."[18] Poetry is the dissolution of art, or of sensuousness, into signification. This is why the material nature of language (sound, mark) does not have the same value in poetry as it does in philosophy. Yet, since the Idea must appear, poetry seems to reappear in order to "give body" to philosophical thought. After art has been sublated into philosophy, it becomes poetry's task to take "speculative thinking into the imagination and give it a body as it were within the spirit itself."[19] Nancy explains: "There is a moment that necessarily and essentially joins the dissolution of art, as merely exterior element of the true presentation of the Idea, to the presentation of art, as sensuous destination of truth" (M 44). What this tension highlights, according to Nancy, is the irreducibility of the moment of sensuousness.

For Nancy, the logic of the externalization of the Idea does not lead to this exteriority being fully recaptured in its sublation (in a return-to-self of the Idea in a higher determination). On the contrary, in presenting itself, the Idea "withdraws as Idea" (M 92). Nancy admits that this insistence on a recalcitrant exteriority is not a properly Hegelian gesture, but he insists that it is the necessary consequence of Hegel's logic of externalization. If the presentation of the Idea "is not the putting of what was inside on view on the outside," and if, on the contrary, the Idea is what it is only when it is outside of itself, then it cannot remain itself but must, instead, efface its ideality so as to be what it is. But, then, "what it 'is' [i.e. ideal] by the same token, it is not and can no longer be" (M 92). This complicated logic can also be expressed in terms of sacrifice. The Idea sacrifices its own abstract interiority in order to appear and hence become what it is. The question is whether this sacrifice, this externalization, produces a return of the Idea to itself as concrete universality, or whether the sacrifice is without return, is dispersion into externality (M 93–4).

In the second case, art would be freed from its metaphysical interpretation. Instead of being the presentation of the Idea, art would then be seen not as the presentation of an absence of Idea, but rather as presentation itself, as the presentation of presentation as such. The Hegelian death of (religious) art is, paradoxically, for Nancy, the birth of (artistic) art, that is, of an art whose function as presentation is decoupled from the Divine or the Idea (M 47; see SW 130–1). Nancy locates this birth of art in the figure of "the girl who succeeds the Muses" in Hegel's *Phenomenology of Spirit*.[20] The works of art, which were sensuous presentations of the Divine, are now mere cadavers, but these cadavers are collected and presented in museums. What is offered, what remains, is their "un-conscious, in-animate" sensuous exteriority, their pure form, detached from any signification (M 50). At that point, "the image withdraws as phantom or phantasm of the Idea, destined to vanish in ideal presence itself" and becomes a "vestige," a withdrawn presence that refers to nothing (M 93). A vestige, from the Latin *vestigium*, is the remains of a step, a trace that shows the passage of a presence but does not reveal "who" or "what" has passed by in that passage. In other words, the withdrawal of the Idea, its dispersion into externality, is the withdrawal of the origin or cause of the work of art. At this point, art partakes in "the creation of the world" in the specific sense Nancy gives to that phrase. And if art still has a history, it is not in the Hegelian sense, but in the more radical sense of a finite history as we described in chapter 1: "not progress but passage, succession, appearance, disappearance, event" (M 86–7). Art does not progress from one form to the next but offers each time a perfection.

(ii) Heidegger: art as the poetizing of truth

Unlike Hegel, Heidegger is not interested in producing a history of the development of art and in systematically articulating the various art forms. Instead, he looks for the "essence" of art, which is the origin of the work of art, of all the arts, and of the artist.[21] While artworks find their origin in art, art itself stands in an essential relation to Truth understood as *aletheia*, as the unconcealing or unveiling of world, of the "there is" of Being. The work of art does not picture or represent something, for example, a pair of shoes. Rather, "[i]n the work of art, the truth of the being has set itself to work. 'Set' means here: to bring to stand. In the work, a being, a pair of peasant shoes, comes to stand in the light of its being."[22] In his discussion of Van Gogh's painting or of the poetic word of Hölderlin or Trackl, Heidegger shows how art gathers and discloses world. Art is, for Heidegger, essentially *Dichtung*. *Dichtung* is the German word for poetry, but, in Heidegger's work, it names the essential poetizing at the core of any art form, and not only poetry in the narrow sense (what Heidegger calls *Poesie*). At the same time, poetry in the narrow sense is the most originary form of poetizing. This is because poetic language first draws what is in unconcealment and hence opens the realm in which the other art forms operate.[23]

For Heidegger, art is essentially *technē*. By this, Heidegger does not mean that art is technical, that it is a specific know-how that allows one to mix colors to produce a painting or form clay to produce a sculpture. Rather, *technē* is (like *phusis*) a way of bringing-forth, of revealing (*poiēsis*). Heidegger's understanding of *technē* evolved over the course of his career. In the "Rectoral Address," for example, it is first understood as *epistēmē*, a thinking and questioning confrontation with beings, where the human being rises forth in the midst of beings to grasp beings as such and as a whole. The human makes the world his abode by gathering *phusis* (what exists) into the Open, by revealing or unconcealing it. Later, Heidegger moves away from an understanding of *technē* as "scientific" questioning toward an understanding of *technē* as art or artistic practice. What he is looking for is a way of being on the part of the human that retains the holding sway (or essencing) of *phusis* (that is, retains its unconcealedness), but without exploiting or overpowering it. This is why Heidegger will end up opposing *poietic* dwelling to modern technological enframing. The latter is also a way of revealing, but one that challenges forth, that sets to work only insofar as it exploits the force/energy hidden in nature. Technological enframing encounters only beings and forgets the "source" out of which beings become manifest, the origin of these beings in Being as such. *Dichtung*, on the other hand, holds the human in the Open in proximity to things. The poetic word, by naming things essentially, first lights up and secures what will then be available for scientific experimentation and everyday discussion.[24] For Heidegger, the importance of the poetic word is that it retains the "holding sway" (*Walten*) of what is, the movement of unconcealedness.

What is obliterated, according to Nancy, in Heidegger's thinking of Art as originary *technē* is the properly material dimension. It is true that Heidegger does pay attention to the materiality of the work of art (stone, pigment, sound, word). The materials are present in the work of art as *matter* or what Heidegger will call "earth": closed off and impenetrable matter. In contrast, the material used to make an axe, for example, is "present" only in its usefulness; it is subordinated to the *telos* of the axe, e.g. being hard enough to cut wood.[25] Unlike Hegel, who thinks that poetry can be sublated into philosophy (even though we saw the ambiguity with regard to the role "speculative poetry" plays in "giving body" to the system), Heidegger insists that the philosophical or thoughtful word cannot subsume or replace the work of art. But this impossibility is not due to the materiality of the work of art. The "philosophical" or thoughtful discussion (*Erörterung*, literally a situating, placing into its proper place[26]) of the poem seeks to open the possibility of a proper hearing of the poem by removing the sedimentation of everyday language and letting us hear the poetic word in its originariness and strangeness. At the same time, such a listening is entirely directed toward what is made manifest through the word (Being, Truth as Unconcealedness, Essence) and not toward materiality of the word, its contours, its sounds. Again, what is forgotten or brushed aside in the Heideggerian thoughtful listening is the materiality of the poem.

(iii)   Dislocation and fragmentation

We just saw that both Hegel and Heidegger, according to Nancy, do not pay attention to the materiality of the artwork, at least not in the right way. For both, materiality is an essential part of the work of art, but one that is at the service of another instance: the Idea for Hegel, the Truth of Being for Heidegger. According to Nancy, such a subordination of materiality to a singular instance, the Idea or the Truth, covers over the essential plurality of the arts. This happens differently in Hegel and in Heidegger. While Hegel affirms the plurality of arts only to produce a classification and hierarchization of the various types of arts, Heidegger affirms that there is at bottom only one art, *Dichtung*. In both cases, the plurality of art is reduced to, or controlled by, a single principle that allows us to order and explain this plurality. When art is liberated from its vocation as sensuous representation of the Idea or as the setting-into-work of Truth, when the sensuous, material, and technical aspects of the work of art are not subordinated to any "intelligible" or "sensible" principle, then art becomes essentially fragmented, splintered. We discussed fragmentation in the Introduction in relation to Nancy and Lacoue-Labarthe's 1978 book on the fragment in German Romanticism. We are now in a better position to understand what kind of fragmentation Nancy is after. In *The Sense of the World*, Nancy distinguishes again between an art of the fragment on the one side and the fragmentation of art on the other. Romantic fragmentation, which corresponds to the first kind, "consists in a certain recognized, accepted, desired state of detachment and isolation of the fragments. Its *end* is situated where the fragment collects itself into itself, folds or retracts its frayed and fragile borders back onto its own consciousness of being a fragment, and onto a new type of autonomy" (SW 124). This is Schlegel's hedgehog: "a fragment, like a small work of art, has to be entirely isolated from the surrounding world and be complete in itself like a hedgehog."[27] To this "logic of the hedgehog," which is similar to the paradoxical logic of the Absolute absorbing its own edges discussed in chapter 1 (C 75), Nancy opposes another logic, which should be familiar to us by now: the logic of exposition. Fragmentation, he writes, "is a matter of the fraying of the edges of its trace [*son frayage*]. It is a matter of the frayed access [*accès frayé*] to a presentation, to a coming into presence – and by way of this coming into presence" (SW 126). The second logic requires that we "think of an art not as an art *of* the fragment – remaining obedient to the work as finished totality – but as itself fragmentary and fractal, and of fragmentation as the presentation of being (of existence), tracing [*frayage*] of/in its totality" (SW 128).

Here again, it is Hegel's attempt at a systematization of the plurality of the art forms that serves as the starting point for Nancy's discussion. If the role of Art is to present the Idea in a sensuous form, then why are there many art forms, many ways of presenting this Idea: with sounds, with forms, with colors? The most obvious answer seems to be: because there are diverse material qualities and diverse senses, each apprehending a specific aspect of material nature. So it seems that we ought to be able to explain the plurality of the arts by appealing to the system of the five senses. Hegel discusses, but ultimately pushes aside, this possibility in the Introduction to the second volume of the *Aesthetics*.[28] There is no art of touch, taste, or smell for Hegel. This is because art "is not purely sensuous, but the spirit appearing in the sensuous." Hence, only the theoretical senses, sight and hearing, and the "sixth" sense, the sense that apprehends universal ideas, are adequate for the apprehension of the work of art.[29] This threefold mode of apprehension corresponds to the division of the arts into (1) the visual arts, (2) music and (3) poetry, which, "as the art of speech, uses sound purely as a sign in order by its means to address our inner being, namely the contemplation, feelings, and ideas belonging to our spiritual life."[30] Hegel does not pursue the division of the arts on the basis of the senses any further. Instead, as we saw above, he embeds the systematic articulation of the art forms fully in the dialectical progression of art from the symbolic to the romantic that corresponds to the progression of Spirit.

For Nancy, the plurality of the arts is a result of the plurality of the senses, but this plurality is in no way gathered into a systematic whole. There is no hierarchy or system of the senses, no transcendental sense that would make all others possible, no "sixth" sense or intelligible sense in which the sensuous senses would find their truth.[31] Sensing is always local and situated; it takes place within a world, between singularities. Hence, there is always "a" sensation, "this" sensation and never "the" sensation or sensation as such. This "there is not 'the' . . ." constitutes a major insight of Nancy's thinking of the body, of touch, and of art (see C 129) and forms one of the guiding threads of Derrida's analysis in his *On Touching* (see OT 287). If there is not "touch as such" but always the touch of this texture, this warmth, this hardness, etc., and not "sight as such" but the vision of this color, this hue, this brightness, etc., then the senses are properly infinite, always dis-locating the "as such." As Nancy says, the "principle" of the senses, like that of the arts, will be that of "discretion" or "discreetness," an "each time this," unique but repeatable:

> each time, this, this drawing, this stroke, this splash, this color. Each time unique, irrepeatable, irreplaceable: what the signs of discourse cannot be. And yet, like these signs, repeatable from one time to the next, substitutable.... Each time, this painting is unique, absolutely different, heterogeneous, and yet it forms a sequence, a suite, a series, a discourse. (BP 345)[32]

The plurality of the arts, like that of the senses, remains untranslatable, irreducible: warmth cannot be heard, red cannot be felt and a C-dur chord cannot be seen; an image cannot be reduced to a text or a piece of music to an image. Yet there is a relation or *rapport*

between sensations and between artworks, a relation of inter-pel-
lation or co-respondance (M 23). "The arts communicate only
through the impossibility of passing from one to the other. Each
one is at the threshold of the others" (SW 130). This "communication" or touching between one art and another does not produce a
synthesis, but only reasserts the diversity of the arts. Sight touches
on hearing and color touches on tone, but always as that which
remains exterior to it: colors cannot be translated into sounds any
more than into words, this stroke cannot be translated into that
stroke, and none of these will be reducible to a meaning or signification. Yet sight and hearing, the senses and sense, call or interpel-
late each other. A color resonates, a text brings forth images or
sounds, a painting tells a story, etc.[33] Art (capital A) is the tenuous
thread of translatability between the arts and between the artworks. Art is not before or above the arts, as their origin or organizing principle; it happens at the interstice between all of them (SW
130).[34] Hence, when Nancy's own discourse seems to be speaking
of "Touch as such," or "Art as such," be it to say that there is no
such thing, or that these things are dislocated, he is not contradict-
ing himself. He would be if he were committed to an inflexible
nominalist position, that is, to saying that Art is nothing more than
a word. But this is not the case. At the same time, Nancy's discourse
on art as fragmentation remains paradoxical, in a way similar to
his discourse on community, which named community only to say
that it remains always absent and consists of the interruption of
community. (Remember that this was Blanchot's criticism: Nancy
seems to be able to identify and point to the essence of community,
i.e. interruption.) Here again, by naming the fragmentation of art,
Nancy's discourse necessarily tends to totalize fragmentation and
turn it into a unifying, transcendental principle: "the principle of
Art is Fragmentation." Unless, of course, writing exscribes itself,
unless organized writing gives way to a corpus. This is important
to keep in mind when reading the texts where Nancy attempts not
to write *about* the Body or Art, but to "touch" upon it or let it touch
us. This is the premise of *Corpus* (C 9–13) and also, as we mentioned
in the Introduction, of so many of Nancy's recent "encounters"
with artists and works of art.

Conclusion

The present study has attempted not only to give an account of Nancy's corpus as a whole, but to do so in a coherent and systematic way. At the center of Nancy's thought, we found the thought of selfhood as differance, that is, as opened by a rift that inscribes an inappropriable exteriority at the "heart" of any self. We saw how this exteriority is thought not in terms of the transcendent Other, but as the limit upon which a self is exposed, and hence comes to feel itself existing. This thought of selfhood as being-unto-the-limit informs all of the central concepts of Nancy's ontology: finitude, sense, sharing, world, freedom.

Nancy's central philosophical intuition is more than a simple reappropriation of Derrida's notion of differance. As we have seen, in the context of Nancy's thought, differance is not (or not only) the fundamental movement of transcendental consciousness or of signification, but is always essentially a worldly, that is, an *embodied*, movement. It is the spacing of the body that is called "the soul." It is also the weight of singularities, a weight which is, as Nancy says, the "raising of their mass to the surface" (C 93). What this thought of differance ultimately undoes is the dichotomy between inside and outside. There is no hidden inside that would be either covered over or revealed by what shows itself. Every being is fully exposed, turned inside out. In its exposition, every being is "all there is" such that the world of bodies consists only of surfaces, folded in various ways. Despite this "lack" of depth, the world is not pure immanence. For if the world of bodies is "all there is" – without depth, but also without height – that world of bodies nevertheless implies an opening. As we saw, the edges between bodies, the *extra* of the *partes extra partes*, constitutes for Nancy the place of differentiation, and hence the locus of the event of sense, an event which is, as such, always plural.

Here, we can highlight a further difference with deconstructive thinking, and underline the unique place occupied by Nancy's thinking in the context of post-Hegelian philosophy in France. As Bruce Baugh has argued in his seminal study *French Hegel*, much of twentieth-century French philosophy from existentialism to "postmodernism," and in particular Derridean deconstruction, is the heir to a very specific reading of Hegel, first proposed by Jean Wahl, where the "unhappy consciousness" is taken as the driving force behind the entire Hegelian dialectic. The moment of "unhappy consciousness" is, for Hegel, that moment in the development of Spirit where Spirit is alienated from itself, internally divided, unable to reconcile the consciousness of its own essence (as unchanging and eternal) with its own finite, worldly existence. Self-consciousness is unable to reconcile individuality and universality, finitude and the infinite, but either sees the eternal as outside of itself (as a god it must blindly devote itself to), or sees the world as alien to itself and seeks to protects its "essence" from this alien world (through asceticism, for example). While the "unhappy consciousness" is for Hegel but a moment in the development of Spirit's self-knowledge, one that will give rise to "Reason" as the synthesis of the two sides of the antinomy, Baugh argues that it becomes for Derrida and other French philosophers an unsurpassable moment, "a condition from which there is no escape."[1]

For Derrida, any consciousness or any philosophical system that seeks to account for differences, to assimilate or reduce exteriority and otherness to something that can be accounted for by the system, always contains within itself, despite its pretension to totalization, an inassimilable exteriority, which is inscribed within the system itself as its blind spot, and thus provides the system with its opening and its movement. As we saw, it is because synthesis and reconciliation are always deferred that there can be a history that is more than the "play of the Same." At the same time, it is impossible to sustain what Derrida calls "the experience of the impossible," the moment of breaking through or breaking out of a totalizing system. Any such departure will always be reintegrated into the system. What we see then in Derrida's philosophy is a double movement of resistance similar to the one we found in Nancy, and described at the end of chapter 1 and again in chapter 3. For Nancy, immanence or fusion (synthesis if one wants) is impossible because we always encounter a limit: our "being-in-common." On the other hand, being-in-common is itself the very source of the desire for communion and fusion in the first place, a desire that cannot be eradicated since it is as essential to our existence as its fulfillment is impossible to achieve without the loss of this existence itself. We would seem again to be stuck in "unhappy consciousness": eternally divided between what we desire and what we are.

While such a characterization of Nancy's thought is certainly accurate, it is clear that Nancy is seeking a way of "living," or sustaining, this tension. It would be too simple to say that Derrida's thinking remains merely negative while Nancy's is somehow positive. Derrida is certainly affirming "the experience of the impossible" as a "positive" experience – despite (or by virtue of) the fact that this experience can never be made present. Derrida can affirm differance and the impossibility of enclosing oneself in a perfect circle of self-identity. Yet, Nancy, in a sense, shifts the question into a more concrete register by asking whether this impossibility can give rise to a different world, a world that would measure up to our "being-in-common." In a still more pointed way we could say that for Nancy, nihilism is not overcome merely by learning to affirm it, by ridding it of its negative character as *loss* of transcendent meaning or value. We do not overcome nihilism by learning to live in a world without transcendence, but by learning to "feel the world according to its opening" (A 60), that is, learning to live "within" the movement of transcendence or opening.

It is here that we can find the appeal or the transformative power of Nancy's thinking, beyond the impact it can have on various disciplines. Even though such an impact has not been developed in the course of the present study, it is easy to imagine how the conceptual resources provided by Nancy's thinking can be, and have in some cases already been, put to work in fields such as environmental ethics, social and political philosophy, art theory, and also, more concretely, in fields such as policy study or social work.[2] More importantly, Nancy's thinking has the power to transform not only the way we think about religion, art, community, or politics, but the way in which each one of us exists in the world as embodied, exposed, communal beings.

In a commentary on Bataille's work, Nancy writes: "In a writer's text, and in a commentator's text (which every text in turn is, more or less), what counts, what thinks (at the very limit of thought, if necessary), is what does not completely lend itself to univocality or, for that matter, to plurivocality, but strains against the burden of meaning and throws it off balance" (BP 336). If this is the case, if the part of a text that thinks is the one that throws signification off balance, then any encounter with Nancy's thinking cannot forgo an encounter with the text itself, with its materiality, its rhythm. This also means that a commentary such as the present one, which attempts to provide a coherent explanation of a work and present the arguments and theses it contains, will leave aside more than an inessential, merely aesthetic, dimension of a thinking. Hence, the voice that comments must, at some point, interrupt itself and give way to reading. In the same text, Nancy writes of reading that it must

remain weighty, hampered, and, without ceasing to decode, must stay just this side of decoding. Such a reading remains caught in the odd materiality of language. It attunes itself to the singular communication carried on not just by meaning but by language itself or, rather, to a communication that is only the communication of language to itself, without abstracting any meaning, in a fragile, repeated suspension of meaning. True reading advances unknowing, it is always as an unjustifiable cut in the supposed continuum of meaning that it opens a book. It must lose its way in this breach.

This reading . . . does not yet comment. This is a *beginning* reading, an *incipit* that is always begun again: it is neither equal to interpretation nor in a position to force any signification. Rather, it is an abandoning to the abandonment to language where the writer is exposed. . . . It doesn't know where it is going, and it doesn't have to know. No other reading is possible without it, and every "reading" (in the sense of commentary, exegesis, interpretation) must come back to it. (BP 336–7)

Notes

Introduction

1 Derrida lists a series of such definitions in *Positions*, 42.
2 For a concise explanation of deconstruction, see Derrida, "Letter to a Japanese Friend" in *Psyche: Inventions of the Other, Volume II*, 1–7. See also *Positions*, 39–47. For a more detailed discussion, see Gasché, *The Tain of the Mirror*, ch. 8.
3 *Rogues: Two Essays on Reason*, 43.
4 This was a talk presented at a colloquium on Nancy's work in January 2002. The contributions have since been published in French in *Sens en tous sens: Autour des travaux de Jean-Luc Nancy*, ed. F. Guibal and J.-C. Martin, but are not available in English translation.
5 For a short biography of Nancy, see *Twentieth-Century French Philosophy: Key Themes and Thinkers*, ed. A. D. Schrift, 171–2.
6 For an autobiographical account of his participation in the event of May '68, see "68, sans fin: Échanges avec Jean-Luc Nancy" with Carole Dely, *Sens Public. Dossier: Les héritages de Mai 68?* www.sens-public.org/article.php3?id_article=619. Nancy comes back to the events of May '68 in *The Truth of Democracy*.
7 Slightly different versions of the first three chapters, "*Larvatus pro Deo*," "*Mundus est fabula*," and "*Dum scribo*," have been published in English prior to the publication of the French book.
8 See *Writing and Difference*, ch. 10.

9   See M. Foucault, *The Order of Things*, 387.
10 See *The Title of the Letter*, 71.
11 See ibid., 70.
12 See ibid., 111 and 127.
13 *The Discourse of the Syncope*, 3.
14 *Critique of Pure Reason*, A141/B180. We will discuss schematism in more detail in chapter 5.
15 *The Literary Absolute*, 43–4.
16 Ibid., 124.
17 Ibid., 127.
18 See the "Introduction" to *Who Comes After the Subject?*, ed. E. Cavada, P. Connor, and J.-L. Nancy, 5–6.
19 We find such indications for example in BSP n. 52 and SW n. 50. Some earlier texts such as *Corpus* (1992) and "Des lieux divins" (1985, translated in *The Inoperative Community*), without explicitly mentioning a "deconstruction of Christianity," can be seen as initiating such a project.
20 "On Derrida: A Conversation with Sergio Benvenuto," *Journal of European Psychoanalysis* 19 (2004), trans. mod.
21 "Philosophy as Chance: An Interview with Jean-Luc Nancy," *Critical Inquiry* 33(2) (Winter 2007): 438–9.
22 See "Violence and Metaphysics" in *Writing and Difference*, especially 133.
23 A first, much shorter, version was published under the title "*Le toucher*: Touch/to touch him," *Paragraph* 13(2) (July 1993): 122–57.

Chapter 1   Ontology

1   See *Being and Time*, trans. Macquarrie and Robinson, H. 12/32. (The first number refers to the marginal number corresponding to the German pagination; the second refers to the page number of the English translation.)
2   See §27 for a description of the "they" as existential structure and §36 for a description of falling.
3   Anxiety is first discussed in §40. The discussion of the call of conscience and of authenticity as resoluteness is found in §§54–60.
4   Nancy takes issue with Heidegger's conception of death in BSP 88–91.

5   On the effect of authenticity on our relation to the world and to Others, see *Being and Time*, §§53 and 60, especially H. 264/308–309 and H. 298/344–5.

6   On Heidegger and everydayness, see *Philosophical Chronicles*, 38–43. Agamben develops a similar thinking of the "singular one" under the name of a *singularité quelconque* ("whatever singularity"). See *The Coming Community*, especially chs. I and V.

7   Derrida discusses differance at length in the interview titled "Implications" in *Positions* and of course also in the essay "Differance" in *Margins of Philosophy*.

8   On selfhood, see BSP *passim*, but especially 94–6. Here I oppose Selfhood to Subjectivity but Nancy will use "subject" for both the self that reappropriates all exteriority and the self pried open by spacing. The difference is normally evident from context.

9   On Nancy's concept of otherness, see Watkin, "A Different Alterity: Jean-Luc Nancy's 'Singular Plural,'" *Paragraph* 30(2) (2007): 50–64. See also Critchley, "With Being-with? Notes on Nancy's Rewriting of *Being and Time*," in *Ethics – Politics – Subjectivity*, ch. 11. Critchley accuses Nancy's ontological structure of being-with of dismissing the (Levinasian) alterity of the Other in favor of symmetry, solidarity, and reciprocity. Watkin's essay can be seen as a response to this accusation.

10 One should note that Nancy translates Heidegger's being-in-the-world with *être-au-monde* (with the preposition *à*) and speaks in the same way of an *être-à-plusieurs*. Nancy also translates Heidegger's *Sein-zum-Tode* (being-toward-death) with *être-à-la-mort*.

11 Nancy takes the distinction from Henri Birault's essay "Heidegger et la pensée de la finitude" in *De l'être, du divin et des dieux*. The theme of finitude runs throughout Nancy's work, but see especially the essay "A Finite Thinking" found in the book of the same name.

12 Again, Nancy sometimes uses the term "absolute" to denote the absolved being, the black hole of immanence, and sometimes to denote the finite being infinitely exposed to its limit.

13 *Dissemination*, 184.

14 For a thorough discussion of the finitude of Being in Heidegger, see Stambaugh, *The Finitude of Being*.

15 According to Nancy, Heidegger's history of Being is an ontodicy, a justification of evil, since the possibility of evil arises

out of the strife of Being (Being offered as refusal) but is "justified" or redeemed by the "new beginning." See EF 131–5 and
FT 191–2. On evil in Nancy and Heidegger, see Roney, "Evil
and the Experience of Freedom: Nancy on Schelling and
Heidegger," *Research in Phenomenology* 9(3) (2009): 374–400.

16   In *On Touching*, Derrida mentions that the word (if not the
concept) "generosity" makes him uncomfortable since it retains
connotations of power, virility, mastery, and filiality: generosity means to give what one has because one is naturally generous and has the power to give (OT 21–3). Derrida also worries
that this "generous offering" is linked to a "guarding" or
"keeping." Ironically, Nancy expresses the same worries
regarding Heidegger's use of guarding or shepherding. See FT
182–4.

17   The name Heidegger gives to the site of this happening is
Dasein: there, where an entity opens/is opened to Being.
Dasein is a being, an entity, but it is the entity that has its Being
as an issue; it is the entity that in relating to other entities
"makes the difference."

18   "La liberté vient du dehors" in *La Pensée dérobée*, 135.

19   This text appears in different translations in both *A Finite
Thinking* and *Being Singular Plural*.

20   Nancy is using *ipse*, "self," in the sense of to-itself or toward-
itself developed earlier. See BSP 94–6. Derrida is critical of the
thought of "ipseity" because for him *ipse* means power, potency,
and sovereignty, all values associated with the "I can" of the
free self-conscious (masculine) subject. See *Rogues*, especially
10–12 and 45.

21   On the difference of voices, see also "Vox clamans in Deserto"
in *Multiple Arts*, 38–49.

22   Across the translations of Nancy's works, *sens* is sometimes
translated as sense and sometimes as meaning. We will use
sense here since it captures more of the connotation of the
French word *sens* (meaning, direction, sensation, hunch, etc.)
The rationale for using meaning in some translations probably
comes from the fact that, even though the Heideggerian *Sinn
des Seins* is translated into French as *sens de l'être*, in English it
is rendered as the meaning of Being.

23   At the same time, truth punctuates sense so that it does not
become undifferentiated being-toward. On sense and truth, see
SW 14, 88–9. We will come back to this difference when we
discuss the difference between politics and love in chapter 4.

24 This will lead to a recasting of what thinking is and of its rela-
    tion to the thing in its impenetrable materiality in terms of
    exscription. See our chapter 5.
25 On the capitalized Other, see SV 246 and BSP 11–13.
26 Hence, Derrida remarks, in his long study of touching in
    Nancy's corpus, that "Nancy seems to break away from hap-
    tocentrist metaphysics, or at least to distance himself from it.
    His discourse about touch is neither intuitionistic nor con-
    tinuistic, homogenistic, or indivisibilistic. What it first recalls
    is sharing, parting, partitioning, and discontinuity, interrup-
    tion, caesura – in a word, syncope" (OT 156). We will come
    back to Derrida's discussion of embodiment and touching in
    Nancy in chapter 5.
27 *Voice and Phenomenon*, 45. See also Derrida, *Of Grammatology*,
    144–5.
28 In *The Sense of the World*, Nancy used the term "transimma-
    nence" to name this opening right at the world itself (SW
    55–6; see also SW 183 n. 48). He later abandoned this word
    (see A 31).
29 This is what Nancy will later call the world's *mondanisation*
    and differentiate from *mondialisation* or world-forming. See
    CW 44.
30 Nancy engages with Heidegger's affirmation that "the stone
    is without world" most thoroughly in SW 59–63. We will come
    back to this in chapter 5.
31 This is the role of language. We will come back to this in
    chapter 5 when we talk about exscription. For now, see BSP
    83–8.

Chapter 2 Christianity

1 Translation is mine but a different translation is available as
   "Beyond Story and Truth," *The Little Magazine* 2(4) (July/Aug
   2001). On the difference between monotheism and polytheism,
   see also "Of Divine Places" in IC, especially 111–12.
2 As we will explain below, there is here an undeniable complic-
   ity between monotheism and philosophy, both presupposing
   the "questionability" of what is as a whole.
3 The English clause on page 18, which reads "the reduction of
   the divine to the premise in a logic of dependence on the
   world," should actually read: "the reduction of the divine to

the premise [or principle] in a logic of the dependence *of* the world [*dans une logique de la dépendance du monde*]."

4   "Materialisms, positivisms, scientificisms, irrationalisms, fascisms or collectivisms, utilitarianisms, individualisms, historicisms, democraticisms even and juridicisms, without mentioning all the relativisms, scepticisms, logicisms – all duly atheistic – will have been the more or less pathetic and frightening attempts at occupying the place [of God] while making more or less believe not to do so" (A 49).

5   Here I use principle, in the sense of "first principle," to translate Nancy's use of *principe*. It should be noted that the translators of *La Déclosion* sometimes use the term "premise" instead of "principle."

6   Beingness, Heidegger's translation of Aristotle's *ousia*, is what allows beings to be meaningfully present. It is what explains the being-there of a being as this or as that. In this sense, beingness is the ground of the being, which "explains" *what* it is and *that* it is. Beingness represents the metaphysical understanding of Being, which Heidegger seeks to overcome.

7   See Greisch, "The Eschatology of Being and the God of Time in Heidegger," *International Journal of Philosophical Studies* 4(1) (1996): 24.

8   On elemental words, see *Being and Time*, H. 220/262. On *Destruktion*, see *Basic Problems of Phenomenology*, 23.

9   See especially the sections on inceptual thinking in the First Part, titled "Preview," of Heidegger's *Contributions to Philosophy: From Enowning*. In "Time and Being," Heidegger hints at the link between the early *Destruktion* and the later thought of the destiny of Being:

> Only the gradual removal [*Abbau*] of these obscuring covers [*Verdeckungen*] – that is what is meant by "dismantling" [*Destruktion*] – procures for thinking a preliminary insight into what then reveals itself as the destiny of Being [*Seins-Geschick*]. . . . [T]he only possible way to anticipate the latter thought on the destiny of Being from the perspective of *Being and Time* is to think through what was presented in *Being and Time* about the dismantling of the ontological doctrine of the Being of beings (*On Time and Being*, 9).

10 On this question, see *Introduction to Metaphysics*, 2–4.

11 "Not only does Being as ground ground beings, but beings in their turn ground, cause Being in their way. Beings can only

do so insofar as they 'are' the fullness of Being: they are what 'is' most of all [*das Seiendste*]" (*Identity and Difference*, 68–9).

12 See "Structure, Sign, and Play in the Discourse of the Human Sciences" in *Writing and Difference*, especially 278–9.

13 This is Christopher Watkin's question in his review of Nancy's *Dis-Enclosure*. See "Neither/Nor: Jean-Luc Nancy's Deconstruction of Christianity," *Research in Phenomenology* 37(1) (2007): 143.

14 As Derrida writes in "Violence and Metaphysics," "history . . . is the history of the departures from totality, history as the very movement of transcendence, of the excess over the totality without which no totality would happen" (*Writing and Difference*, 117).

15 In *L'Adoration*, Nancy explains in more detail why his focus is on Christianity more than on the two other strands of monotheism and why this focus does not amount to any privileging of one religion over the other. Christianity has less to do with religious observance than with this movement of excess in which religiosity undoes itself. See A 50–7.

16 *Rogues*, 45. Derrida relates the aporetic structure of autoimmunity to the possibility of religion in "Faith and Knowledge" in *Religion*, 44.

17 On absentheism, see CW 50–1 and *Philosophical Chronicles*, 20.

18 Levinas offers a similar reading of Descartes's ontological proof in *Totality and Infinity* and in "Philosophy and the Idea of Infinity" in *Collected Philosophical Papers*. Having the idea of infinity means having an idea whose content is nothing other than the "absolute distance" between an idea and what this idea is an idea of. The Infinite overflows the idea of infinity in me so that this idea is only the "idea of absolute excess." The idea of infinity is an idea without content, or whose content is nothing but the movement of transcendence.

19 See also A 70 and 114. Nancy also says that there is no necessity to keeping the name "god."

20 Irredentism, from the Latin *irredento*, refers to a position advocating annexation of territories administered by another state on the grounds of common ethnicity or prior historical possession, hence on the ground of a presumed homogeneity.

21 *Limited Inc.*, 93.

22 On Derrida's reading of Merleau-Ponty, see James, *The Fragmentary Demand*, 121–30.

23 *The Fragmentary Demand*, 140.

24 On faith, see Nancy's reading of James' epistle in "The Judeo-Christian (On Faith)":

> In the Epistle of James, everything unfolds as though faith, far from being a belief in another life, that is, some belief in an infinite adequation between life and itself, were the setting in act [*la mise en œuvre*] of the inadequation in which and as which existence exists. How did faith, one day, with the West, start composing a decomposition of religion? (D 59)

Chapter 3 Community

1 And this even though, as Nancy often notes, Rousseau is also the one who complicates the paradigm of this lost origin to be retrieved or re-enacted since "society" is what makes "man" truly human so that the state of nature is clearly not a state in which humans exist but a fantastical retro-projection.

2 Hence it all begins with the thought of a lost or buried origin prior to the beginning (as if the beginning came too late). This will be important for Nancy's discussion of myth below.

3 Later, in *Being Singular Plural*, he will explicitly reject these words (BSP 33).

4 Because of the misunderstandings it can give rise to, Nancy will abandon this word in favor of the word *partage* (see IC 157 n. 14). It should be noted that the communication of community is not the communication by which a plurality of subjects would assert their belongingness based on a common origin, a common property, etc. Communication does not create a link, but is the appearing of the between. Hence, it is opposed to communion (see IC 25–9).

5 See *Being and Time*, §47.

6 For more details, see *The Fragmentary Demand*, 178–9 and *The Unavowable Community*, 12–13.

7 This essay forms the basis of Derrida's engagement with time, economy, and the gift in *Given Time*. Derrida also proposes a reading of general economy – that is, an economy which includes practices of unproductive expenditure – and restricted economy in Bataille in "From Restricted to General Economy: A Hegelianism without Reserve" in *Writing and Difference*, ch. 9. For a detailed analysis of Bataille's reading of Mauss, see Richman, *Reading Georges Bataille: Beyond the Gift*.

8   The question as to whether it is the authentic relation to my finitude that allows me to relate to others in their finitude, or whether it is first on the basis of the mortality of others that I come to relate to myself as finite and mortal, is at the heart of not only Bataille's and Blanchot's disagreement with Heidegger, but also that of Levinas in his lecture course "Death and Time" (published in English in *God, Death and Time*).

9   Amanda Macdonald translates *désœuvrement* as unoccupancy and acknowledges the spatial connotation of the word: the fact that the community does not make a work out of itself means that the place of the community remains unoccupied and it is this emptiness that is the opening, thanks to which communication happens. See "Working Up, Working Out, Working Through: Translator's Notes on the Dimensions of Jean-Luc Nancy's Thought," *Postcolonial Studies* 6(1) (2003): 11–21, especially 11–13. *Désœuvré* normally means of a person that she or he is idle or out of work, unemployed. Peter Connor translates the word both as unworked and as inoperative, emphasizing its relation to work as an activity rather than as an object with dimensions, e.g. as we say "work of art." The community, thought here as a machine or organism, is inoperative in the sense that it does not work or function well.

10 *The Bataille Reader*, 296.

11 *The Infinite Conversation*, 205.

12 Ibid., 206.

13 Nancy also wonders if Bataille really succeeds in overcoming Hegel since he expresses the excess of subjectivity that undoes the subject in the Hegelian language of the *fusion* of the subject and the object. Without going into the details, it means that the Other, or exteriority, takes the form of an object of representation for a subject so that the subject is not outside of itself in the fusion with (its) object and the place of community (as the place of fusion) remains that of a Subject determined as self-presence (IC 25). Yet, for Nancy, this not a criticism of some inadequacy in Bataille's thinking: this limit is also our limit, and hence what we need to think.

14 Bernasconi writes that "[t]he debate can also be offered as an illustration of the somewhat discreet forms of criticism that often operate between French thinkers, in marked contrast to the rather more direct approach that is customary in Britain and the United States." See his "On Deconstructing *Nostalgia*

for Community within the West: The Debate between Nancy and Blanchot," *Research in Phenomenology* 23(1) (1993): 3–21, here 7.

15   The term appears but most of the time in the plural: *la communauté des autrui* (the community of Others), which implies that I am also an *autrui*, other than myself (see IC 15). The plural of *autrui* is unusual in French since *autrui* is an indefinite pronoun. It would certainly make no sense in the Blanchotian–Levinasian context.

16   This is also Bernasconi's argument in the article cited above.

17   *The Unavowable Community*, 3.

18   Blanchot's style in *The Unavowable Community* is filled with indecision and open questions: is it this, or maybe that? Even though it is easy to recognize that Blanchot leans more toward one side of the alternative than the other, there are never any decisive answers.

19   *The Unavowable Community*, 9.

20   Ibid.

21   Ibid., 15.

22   It is interesting to note that in "The Limit-Experience," Blanchot provided a different, more negative, assessment of *Acéphale*. For the Blanchot of 1962, the experience of sacrifice was still based on the "I can" of the subject and did not succeed depropriating it of itself. See *The Infinite Conversation*, 208.

23   For an account of Blanchot's response to Nancy written from the Blanchotian perspective, see Hill, *Blanchot, Extreme Contemporary*. For a discussion of the disagreement between Nancy and Blanchot with regard to Bataille's (and Hegel's) understanding of negativity, see James, "Naming the Nothing: Nancy and Blanchot on Community," *Culture, Theory and Critique* 51(2) (2010): 171–87.

24   This is an idea we already mentioned in chapter 2 in relation to the birth of the West and the will to signification. See "The Forgetting of Philosophy," especially in chapter 9, where Nancy writes:

> There is nothing "before" the West, if the very idea of the "before" is already caught in a network of metaphysical significations (the prior, the causal, the archaic, the primitive, the originary, the naive, the repressed, the forgotten, the recalled, etc.). And yet, the West has taken place; it has happened and

there was not nothing when and where it happened; but its occurrence consisted in signifying that the "before" was lost, that it was this lost meaning (Egypt, the gods, Homer, Solon . . .) and that the process of signification was initiated on the basis of this loss (or else, which amounts to the same thing, that meaning remained mute, unarticulated, not yet signified and presented). (GT 47)

25 See Lacoue-Labarthe, "Typography" in *Typography: Mimesis, Philosophy, Politics*, 43–138, especially 131–2.
26 On the basis of this, Lacoue-Labarthe will argue that Heidegger is heir to the Romantic project and that "myth" forms the blind spot of his thinking of art, and especially of poetic saying, which leads him to fascism. In this sense, Heidegger's politics is an "archi-fascism," not an adherence to the content of Nazi ideology, but of a certain way of thinking about myth and community. See his *Heidegger, Art and Politics: The Fiction of the Political* and also his *Heidegger and the Politics of Poetry*, especially the Prologue and ch. 1.
27 Even though in the Marxian text itself, things are more complicated, as Nancy acknowledges in "Literary Communism."
28 Lacoue-Labarthe analyzes the relation between mimesis and the metaphysics of subjectivity, or what he calls onto-typology, in *Typography: Mimesis, Philosophy, Politics*.
29 On the relation between Judaism and myth, see "The Jewish People Do Not Dream" (with Philippe Lacoue-Labarthe), *Stanford Literary Review* 6(2) (1989): 191–209 and 8(1–2) (1991): 39–55.
30 See also "Communism, the Word" in *The Idea of Communism*, ed. Costas Douzinas and Slavoj Žižek, 145–54.
31 As we said in our Introduction, this is what interests Nancy in *The Speculative Remark*.

Chapter 4 Politics

1 Cited in RP 114 from Marx's *Critique of Hegel's Philosophy of Right*, §279. In O'Malley's translation, the passage reads: "In all states distinct from democracy the state, the law, the constitution is dominant without really governing, that is, materially permeating the content of the remaining non-political spheres. In democracy the constitution, the law, the state, so far as it is political constitution, is itself only a

self-determination of the people, and a determinate content of the people" (p. 30).

2   For a discussion of how this is the case in Heidegger's philosophy, see Lacoue-Labarthe, "Transcendence ends in politics," in *Typography: Mimesis, Philosophy, Politics*.

3   For a critical reading of Nancy and Lacoue-Labarthe on this point, see Critchley, "Re-tracing the Political: Politics and Community in the Work of Philippe Lacoue-Labarthe and Jean-Luc Nancy," in *The Political Subject of Violence*, 73–93. Critchley argues that far from experiencing depoliticization and uniformization, contemporary "democratic" societies experience increasing fragmentations and antagonisms and hence increasing political possibilities (82).

4   Nancy shows how the "monarch," who is said to be the embodiment of the indivisible unity of the State and of the concrete will of the people, represents a "tremendous contradiction" in Hegel's political philosophy and undoes the absolute unity of particularity and universality. See "The Jurisdiction of the Hegelian Monarch" in BP.

5   See again Critchley's "Re-tracing the Political."

6   Ibid., 86.

7   Nancy Fraser also levels a similar criticism, accusing Nancy and Lacoue-Labarthe of retreating into a "transcendental safehouse" and abandoning the "terrain of politics" to neoliberals. See "The French Derrideans: Politicizing Deconstruction or Deconstructing the Political?," *New German Critique* 33 (Fall 1984): 127–54. The problem with such criticisms is that they still work within the opposition between philosophy and politics, the transcendental and the empirical: they criticize Nancy and Lacoue-Labarthe for withdrawing to one side of the opposition and ask them to "find a passage back" to the other side. What is missed here is how the whole rhetoric of the "retreat" tries to undermine this opposition. In fact, the "political" is not so much "the transcendental" as opposed to empirical politics. Rather, it is something, a "relation" or "being-in-common," that underlies both and undoes all foundational discourse. For a discussion of Fraser's and Critchley's criticism with regard to the question of "relation," see Armstrong, *Reticulations: Jean-Luc Nancy and the Networks of the Political*, ch. 1. See also Readings, "The Deconstruction of Politics" in *Reading de Man Reading*.

8   "Re-tracing the Political," 85.

9   For a reading of this problem in Rousseau's *Social Contract*, see Norris, "Jean-Luc Nancy and the Myth of the Common," *Constellations* 7(2) (June 2000): 272–95.

10   Nancy's discussion of sovereignty is found most explicitly in "*Ex Nihilo Summum* (Of Sovereignty)" in CW.

11   Derrida provides a reading of this mystical foundation of authority in *Force of Law* and in "Declarations of Independence," *New Political Science* 7(1) (1986): 7–15.

12   Though we cannot go into the complex relations between Nancy's and Derrida's analysis of the structure of sovereignty here, the concept of sovereignty plays a central role in Derrida's late works. In *Rogues*, Derrida appeals to an "unconditional renunciation of sovereignty" (*Rogues* xiv), since only such a renunciation can provide the radical opening to what and who comes, without which there can be no justice, no hospitality, etc. For an excellent discussion of sovereignty in Derrida's later work, see Naas, *Derrida: From Now On*. On the relation between sovereignty and the theologico-political, see especially ch. 3.

13   On the difference between the subject and someone for Nancy, see SW 68–75.

14   Here Nancy might have in mind not so much Foucault's biopolitics as Agamben's "bare life." See *Homo Sacer: Sovereign Power and Bare Life*. See also Agamben's discussion of the *Muselmann* in *Remnants of Auschwitz*.

15   On the measuring of market value by opposition to absolute value, see BSP 73–5 and also "Vaille que vaille" in *La Pensée dérobée*, 149–54. In "The Kategorein of Excess," Nancy develops this "incommensurability in finitude" in terms of freedom and respect starting from the Kantian categorical imperative. See FT 133–51.

16   *Politics of Friendship*, 154.

17   *Force of Law*, 22. See also *Specters of Marx*, 23–8.

18   *Force of Law*, 16.

19   For a discussion of the relation between Nancy and Derrida on the topic of fraternity, see Gratton, *The State of Sovereignty*, ch. 6.

20   *Rogues*, 58.

21   Ibid., 59.

22   "Nothing but the World: An Interview with *Vacarme*," *Rethinking Marxism* 19(4) (2007): 525, trans. mod.

23   Ibid., 526, trans. mod.

24 We could also say that it was an event in the Derridean sense of the term: the opening of an "absolute future" or a "to-come," of an instant outside of the temporal succession of past, present, and future. However, Nancy is skeptical of the need to understand this breach in messianic terms, be it a messianism "without messianism" or "without Messiah" (TD 13). At the same time, he seems to follow Derrida in thinking the event in terms of the irruption and disruption of the present and the greeting of what or who comes.
25 *The Communist Hypothesis*, 52.
26 Ibid., 64.
27 On Badiou's concept of democracy, see his *Metapolitics*, ch. 5.
28 Nancy is alluding to Pascal's *Pensées*, §434.
29 Nancy is alluding to Book One, ch. 8, where Rousseau recognizes that the "civil state" is the proper and original state of the human being, since it is the civil state that "made him an intelligent being and man" (p. 27).
30 *Economic and Philosophical Manuscripts*, 91.
31 Marx, *Capital: A Critique of Political Economy, Volume I*, ch. I, section 1, 44–5.
32 Ibid., ch. III, section 1, 106.
33 Ibid., ch. I, section 3, §3, 69.
34 Ibid., ch. V, 182.
35 "Introducing Disagreement," *Angelaki* 9(3) (2004): 3–9, here 5.
36 Rancière, *Disagreement: Politics and Philosophy*, 23.
37 *Rogues*, 63.
38 See *Rogues*, §8.
39 See *The Gift of Death*, especially 67–71, 77–9 and 84–7.
40 See my "A *mêlée* without Sacrifice: Nancy's Ontology of Offering against Derrida's Politics of Sacrifice," *Philosophy Today* 50, SPEP Supplement (2006): 139–43.

Chapter 5 From Body to Art

1 This is also how Nancy reads Freud's posthumous fragments: "*psyche* is extended, knows nothing about it" (C 21, 95, 144).
2 Nancy says that we need a new, finite "transcendental aesthetics" for which the condition of possibility of experience would not be space and time as pure forms of sensibility, but "gravity": not an abstract form, but always a localized finite

here-and-now, and not a "pure form," since gravity always implies materiality (see GT 77 and FT 27).

3   On birth as coming-to-presence, see O'Byrne, *Natality and Finitude*, ch. 5.

4   See *The Fragmentary Demand*, 149–50.

5   This also means that, despite what we said above about the need for a *new* transcendental aesthetic, Nancy's thinking in fact undoes any "transcendental" aesthetics since it cannot be a question of circumscribing the conditions of possibility of experience. For transcendental philosophy, what is presented can only ever be something that is defined a priori as presentable, so that any presentation is held in check by the conditions delimiting in advance any possible presentation. For Nancy, the reality of experience "precedes all possibility. It is the impossible and real, the *impossibly real* experience of some thing" (BP 177). Hence experience (as the combination of sensibility and thought, of receptivity and spontaneity) is for Nancy grounded on the possibility that "thought/sensibility" welcome, register, or be passible to, the *shock* of the thing (see GT 69).

6   In "The Origin of the Work of Art," Heidegger does mention the weight of the stone, but it is in relation to the work of art, and in terms of what remains closed off within the work of art. Nancy might say that even there Heidegger does not think our access to the stone's impenetrability as such, that is, as non-access. See *Off the Beaten Track*, 24–5.

7   *The Evidence of Film*, 42.

8   On the relation between this interruption and the birth of art, see "Painting in the Grotto" in *The Muses*, especially M 73–4.

9   On the portrait, see "The Look of the Portrait" in *Multiple Arts: The Muses II*, 220–47.

10   *Critique of Pure Reason*, A141/B181.

11   *The Twilight of the Idols*, 18.

12   This is why Christian painting is possible: it does not aim at rendering the inaccessible beyond (God) present here and now, but paints the movement of "ab-sensing" or "dis-enclosing" described in chapter 2. See "Visitation: Of Christian Painting" in GI 108–38, especially 135.

13   For Nancy's discussion of mimesis, see "The Image: Mimesis, Methexis," *Theory@Buffalo* 11 (2007): 9–26.

14   In "Forbidden Representation," Nancy links this discussion of the image as ab-sense on the one hand and as pure blow on

the other to the Nazi camps. In "Image and Violence," he insists that the problem is one of learning to distinguish between two forms of violence or of intractability, and hence between two kinds of images: the violence of a truth that comes on the scene and, by disrupting the established order of knowledge, opens a space for sense or the pure violence of the blow that only imprints the marks of its own violence and closes off all possibility of sense-making. Both texts are found in GI.

15 Hegel, *Aesthetics: Lectures on Fine Art*, vol. I, 116.
16 Ibid., vol. II, 962–3.
17 Ibid., vol. I, 11.
18 Ibid., vol. II, 976; cited in M 43.
19 Ibid., 977; cited in M 43.
20 This girl appears at the beginning of the section on Revealed Religion in the *Phenomenology of Spirit*, §753 and is the topic of the eponymous essay by Nancy in *The Muses*.
21 "The Origin of the Work of Art" in *Off the Beaten Track*, 1. According to Nancy, Heidegger is more attentive to the plurality of the arts in *Ding und Raum* (1969). See M 108 n. 34.
22 "The Origin of the Work of Art," 16.
23 Ibid., 44–5.
24 See "Hölderlin and the Essence of Poetry" in *Elucidations of Hölderlin's Poetry*.
25 "The Origin of the Work of Art," 24.
26 *On the Way to Language*, 159.
27 *Athenaeum Fragment* no. 206. In *"Che cos'è la poesia?"* and *"Istrice 2: Ick bünn all hier,"* Derrida also mentions Schlegel's hedgehog in relation to Nancy and Lacoue-Labarthe's *The Literary Absolute* and opposes to the figure of the absolute fragment another hedgehog, and hence another understanding of the work of art or of the poem: "rolled up in a ball, prickly with spines, vulnerable and dangerous, calculating and ill-adapted (because it makes itself into a ball, sensing the danger on the autoroute, it exposes itself to an accident)" (*Points . . .* , 297).
28 Art is necessarily "there for apprehension by the senses, so that, in consequence, the specific characterization of the senses and of their corresponding material in which the work of art is objectified must provide the grounds for the division of the individual arts" (*Aesthetics*, vol. II, 621).
29 Ibid. On the division of the senses, see Hegel's *Philosophy of Mind* (Part III of the *Encyclopedia of the Philosophical Sciences*

[1830]), Section One: Subjective Spirit, A. Anthropology §401. Sight and hearing are theoretical senses: they leave their object "untouched" or unchanged. Because of this independence, they can be understood as the most noble of the senses. But they are incomplete because they apprehend only the "ideal" side of bodies and not their concrete totality. Smelling and tasting, on the other hand, are concrete senses; they receive bodily particles from the body itself. Yet they only grasp the body in the process of its division, or volatization, and not as concrete totality. Touch is the most concrete sense since it apprehends the unchanging reality of the body as a whole.

30   *Aesthetics*, vol. II, 623.

31   On the relation between the senses and sense, see *Listening*, especially 2. We could perhaps say that for Nancy, touch is the essence or principle of the senses, the condition of possibility of all sensing. In fact, Derrida will say that touch is a *quasi-transcendental* sense. "Quasi" because at the same time as it makes all the senses possible, it necessarily includes, as we already mentioned, a moment of interruption, obscurity, or untouchability, which limits each sense's or each sensation's appropriation of what is sensed (see OT 275).

32   This quote is found in a text written to accompany the exhibition of Parisian painter François Martin's *Le semainier* (literally, a weekly calendar). Here is Nancy's description of the work: "The work was presented in fifty-two panels composed of six sheets of drawing paper, each of which bore a different painting or drawing. For a year, François Martin had made himself paint one sheet of paper a day in addition to his usual work. Every Sunday, he mounted the six sheets of the past week on panels" (BP 341 n.).

33   In relation to this interpellation, Nancy mentions Baudelaire's *Correspondances*. See M 23 and SW 130.

34   See "Les arts se font les uns contre les autres" in *Art, regard, écoute*, 157–66.

Conclusion

1   See Baugh, *French Hegel*, 6.

2   See Nancy's mention of the helpfulness of the concept of being-in-common for social workers in "Interview with Jean-Luc Nancy: The Commerce of Plural Thinking" in *Jean-Luc Nancy and Plural Thinking*, 234.

Bibliography

Primary works

L'Adoration. Déconstruction du christianisme, 2. Paris: Galilée, 2010.

"Les arts se font les uns contre les autres." In Béatrice Bloch et al. *Art, regard, écoute. La perception à l'œuvre*. Paris: Presses universitaires de Vincennes, 2000.

Being Singular Plural, trans. Robert D. Richardson and Anne E. O'Byrne. Stanford: Stanford University Press, 2000.

"The Being-With of the Being-There," trans. Marie-Eve Morin. *Continental Philosophy Review* 41(1) (2008): 1–15.

"Between Story and Truth," trans. Franson Manjali. *The Little Magazine* 2(4) "The Wall" (July/Aug 2001). www.littlemag.com/jul-aug01/nancy.html

The Birth to Presence, trans. Brian Holmes et al. Stanford: Stanford University Press, 1993.

"Chromatic Atheology." *Journal of Visual Culture* 4(1) (April 2005): 116–28.

"Church, State, Resistance." *Journal of Law and Society* 34(1) (March 2007): 3–13. Reprinted in *Political Theologies: Public Religions in a Post-Secular World*, ed. Hent de Vries and Lawrence E. Sullivan. New York: Fordham University Press, 2006.

"Communism, the Word." In *The Idea of Communism*, ed. Costas Douzinas and Slavoj Žižek. London: Verso, 2010.

"La Comparution/The Compearance: From the Existence of Communism to the Community of Existence," trans. Tracy B. Strong. *Political Theory* 20(3) (August 1992): 371–98.

"The Confronted Community," trans. Amanda Macdonald. *Post-Colonial Studies* 6(1) (2003): 23–36.

"Consecration and Massacre," trans. Amanda Macdonald. *Post-Colonial Studies* 6(1) (2003): 47–50.

Corpus, trans. Richard A. Rand. New York: Fordham University Press, 2008.

The Creation of the World or *Globalization*, trans. François Raffoul and David Pettigrew. Albany: SUNY Press, 2007.

The Discourse of the Syncope: Logodaedalus, trans. Saul Anton. Stanford: Stanford University Press, 2007.

Dis-Enclosure: The Deconstruction of Christianity, trans. Bettina Bergo, Gabriel Malenfant, and Michael B. Smith. New York: Fordham University Press, 2008.

"*Dum scribo*," trans. Ian McLeod. *Literary Review* 3(2) (1978): 6–20.

L'évidence du film/The Evidence of Film: Abbas Kiarostami. Bruxelles: Yves Gevaert, 2001.

The Experience of Freedom, trans. Bridget McDonald. Stanford: Stanford University Press, 1993.

The Fall of Sleep, trans. Charlotte Mandell. New York: Fordham University Press, 2009.

A Finite Thinking, ed. Simon Sparks. Stanford: Stanford University Press, 2003.

God, Justice, Love, Beauty: Four Little Dialogues, trans. Sarah Clift. New York: Fordham University Press, 2011.

The Gravity of Thought, trans. François Raffoul and Gregory Recco. New York: Humanities Press, 1997.

The Ground of the Image, trans. Jeff Fort. New York: Fordham University Press, 2005.

Hegel: The Restlessness of the Negative, trans. Jason Smith and Steven Miller. Minneapolis: Minnesota University Press, 2002.

L' "il y a" du rapport sexuel. Paris: Galilée, 2001.

"The Image: Mimesis, Methexis," trans. Ron Estes and Jean-Christophe Cloutier. *Theory@Buffalo* 11 (2007): 9–26.

The Inoperative Community, ed. Peter Connor. Minneapolis: University of Minnesota Press, 1991.

"The Insufficiency of 'Values' and the Necessity of 'Sense.'" *Journal for Cultural Research* 9(4) (2005): 437–41.

"Introduction." In *Who Comes After the Subject?*, ed. Eduardo Cavada, Peter Connor, and Jean-Luc Nancy. New York: Routledge, 1991.

"The Jewish People Do Not Dream" (with Philippe Lacoue-Labarthe), trans. Brian Holmes. *Stanford Literary Review* 6(2) (1989): 191–209 and 8(1–2) (1991): 39–55.

"Larvatus pro Deo," trans. Daniel A. Brewer. *Glyph* 2 (1977): 14–36.

Listening, trans. Charlotte Mandell. New York: Fordham University Press, 2007.

The Literary Absolute: The Theory of Literature in German Romanticism (with Philippe Lacoue-Labarthe), trans. Philip Barnard and Cheryl Lester. Albany: SUNY Press, 1988.

Multiple Arts: The Muses II, ed. Simon Sparks. Stanford: Stanford University Press, 2006.

"Mundus est fabula," trans. D. Brewer. *Modern Language Notes* 93(4) (1978): 635–53.

The Muses, trans. Peggy Kamuf. Stanford: Stanford University Press, 1997.

"The Nazi Myth" (with Philippe Lacoue-Labarthe), trans. Brian Holmes. *Critical Inquiry* 16(2) (Winter 1990): 291–312.

"Nietzsche's Thesis on Teleology." In *Looking After Nietzsche*, ed. Laurence A. Rickels. Albany: SUNY Press, 1990.

Noli Me Tangere: On the Raising of the Body, trans. Sarah Clift, Pascale-Anne Brault, and Michael Naas. New York: Fordham University Press, 2008.

"Of Being in Common." In *Community at Loose Ends*, ed. The Miami Theory Collective. Minneapolis: University of Minnesota Press, 1991.

On the Commerce of Thinking: Of Books and Bookstores, trans. David Wills. New York: Fordham University Press, 2009.

"On the Meanings of Democracy." *Theoria: A Journal of Social and Political Theory* 53(111) (December 2006): 1–5.

La pensée dérobée. Paris: Galilée, 2001.

Philosophical Chronicles, trans. Franson Manjali. Stanford: Stanford University Press, 2008.

Retreating the Political (with Philippe Lacoue-Labarthe), ed. Simon Sparks. New York: Routledge, 1997.

The Sense of the World, trans. Jeffrey S. Librett. Minneapolis: University of Minnesota Press, 1997.

"Sharing Voices." In *Transforming the Hermeneutic Context: From Nietzsche to Nancy*, ed. Gayle L. Ormiston and Alan D. Schrift. Albany: SUNY Press, 1990.

"The So-Called/Self-Saying People." In *Translation, Biopolitics, Colonial Difference*, ed. Naoki Sakai and Jon Solomon. Hong Kong: Hong Kong University Press, 2006.

The Speculative Remark (One of Hegel's Bons Mots), trans. Céline Surprenant. Stanford: Stanford University Press, 2001.

The Title of the Letter: A Reading of Lacan (with Philippe Lacoue-Labarthe), trans. François Raffoul and David Pettigrew. Albany: SUNY Press, 1992.

The Truth of Democracy, trans. Pascale-Anne Brault and Michael Naas. New York: Fordham University Press, 2010.

"The War of Monotheism," trans. Amanda Macdonald. *Post-Colonial Studies* 6(1) (2003): 37–46.

Selected interviews

"An Interview with Jean-Luc Nancy." In Michel Gaillot, *Multiple Meaning: Techno, An Artistic and Political Laboratory of the Present.* Paris: Editions Dis Voir, 1998.

"Nothing but the World: An Interview with *Vacarme.*" *Rethinking Marxism* 19(4) (2007): 521–35.

"On Derrida: A Conversation with Sergio Benvenuto," trans. Marcel Lieberman. *Journal of European Psychoanalysis* 19(2) (2004). www.psychomedia.it/jep/number19/benvenuto.htm

"Our World: An Interview." *Angelaki: Journal of the Theoretical Humanities* 8(2) (2003): 43–54.

"Philosophy as Chance: An Interview with Jean-Luc Nancy" (with Lorenzo Fabbri), trans. Pascale-Anne Brault and Michael Naas. *Critical Inquiry* 33(2) (Winter 2007): 427–40.

"The Question of the Common and the Responsibility of the Universal." A dialogue with Artem Magun and Oxana Timofeeva. *What Is to Be Done? A Newspaper for Engaged Creativity* 9 (2005). www.chtodelat.org

Secondary sources

General introductions, collections, or special issues on Nancy's work

Gratton, Peter and Morin, Marie-Eve (eds). *Jean-Luc Nancy and Plural Thinking: Expositions of World, Ontology, Politics, and Sense.* Albany: SUNY Press, 2012. Contains, among others, essays on speculative realism, the plurality of the arts, globalization and Christianity, justice and the Bosnian war, as well as an interview with Nancy.

James, Ian. *The Fragmentary Demand: An Introduction to the Philosophy of Jean-Luc Nancy*. Stanford: Stanford University Press, 2006. Contains chapters on subjectivity (including the early works on Lacan and Kant), community (including the works around the retreat of the political), space, the body, and art.

Kamuf, Peggy. *On the Work of Jean-Luc Nancy*. Special Issue of *Paragraph* 16(2) (July 1993). Contains a shorter version of Derrida's *Le toucher* as well as essays on Nancy's early work on community, freedom, transcendence, and the body.

Michaelsen, Scott J. and Johnson, David E. (eds). *At the Heart: Of Jean-Luc Nancy*. Special Issue of *The New Centennial Review* 2(3) (2002). Focuses on Nancy's heart transplant and notions of selfhood, alterity, intrusion, technology, and power.

Sheppard, Darren, Sparks, Simon, and Thomas, Colin (eds). *The Sense of Philosophy: On Jean-Luc Nancy*. New York: Routledge, 1996. Contains, among others, essays on community, finitude, violence, and sacrifice.

Books, articles, collections of essays, and special issues on specific topics

On ontology, world, and the singular plural

Brogan, Walter. "The Parting of Being: On Creation and Sharing in Nancy's Political Ontology." *Research in Phenomenology* 40(3) (2010): 295–308.

Librett, Jeffrey S. "The Practice of the World: Jean-Luc Nancy's Liminal Cosmology between Theory and History." *International Studies in Philosophy* 28(1) (1996): 29–44.

Watkin, Christopher. "A Different Alterity: Jean-Luc Nancy's 'Singular Plural.'" *Paragraph* 30 (July 2007): 50–64.

On Nancy and Heidegger

Benjamin, Andrew. "Having to Exist." *Angelaki: Journal of the Theoretical Humanities* 5(3) (2000): 51–6.

Critchley, Simon. "With Being-With? Notes on Jean-Luc Nancy's Rewriting of *Being and Time*." In *Ethics – Politics – Subjectivity*. London and New York: Verso, 1999.

George, Theodore. "From the Life of a People to the Death of Others: On Jean-Luc Nancy's Unworking of Heidegger's." *International Studies in Philosophy* 40(1) (2008): 65–77.

Roney, Patrick. "Evil and the Experience of Freedom: Nancy on Schelling and Heidegger." *Research in Phenomenology* 39(3) (2009): 374–400.

On Christianity

Devisch, Ignaas, ten Kate, Laurens, van Rooden, Aukje, and Alexandrova, Alena (eds). *Re-treating Religion: Deconstructing Christianity with Jean-Luc Nancy*. New York: Fordham University Press, 2011. Contains essays on deconstruction, creation, myth, prayer, incarnation, art, and the body. Also contains a substantial preamble by Nancy and a concluding interview.

Morin, Marie-Eve. "Towards a Divine Atheism: Jean-Luc Nancy's Deconstruction of Monotheism and the Passage of the Last God." *Symposium: The Canadian Journal for Continental Philosophy* 15(1) (Spring 2011): 29–49.

Schrijvers, Joeri. "What Comes after Christianity? Jean-Luc Nancy's Deconstruction of Christianity." *Research in Phenomenology* 39(2) (2009): 266–91.

Van Peperstraten, Frans. "Displacement or Composition? Lyotard and Nancy on the 'trait d'union' between Judaism and Christianity." *International Journal for Philosophy of Religion* 65(1) (Feb. 2009): 29–46.

Watkin, Christopher. "Neither/Nor: Jean-Luc Nancy's Deconstruction of Christianity." *Research in Phenomenology* 37(1) (2007): 136–43.

On touch

Barker, Stephen. "Threshold (pro-)positions: Touch, *Techné*, Technics." *Derrida Today* 2(1) (May 2009): 44–65.

Derrida, Jacques. *On Touching – Jean-Luc Nancy*, trans. Christine Irizarry. Stanford: Stanford University Press, 2005.

Lambert, Gregg. "Decrypting 'The Christian Thinking of the Flesh, Tacitly, the Caress, in a Word, the Christian Body' in *Le Toucher – Jean-Luc Nancy*." *Sophia: International Journal for Philosophy of*

Religion, Metaphysical Theology and Ethics 47(3) (Nov. 2008): 293–310.

McQuillan, Martin. "Toucher I: (The Problem with Self-Touching)." *Derrida Today* 1(2) (Nov. 2008): 201–11.

McQuillan, Martin. "Toucher II: Keep Your Hands to Yourself, Jean-Luc Nancy." *Derrida Today* 2(1) (May 2009): 84–108. Issues 1.2 and 2.1 of *Derrida Today* are devoted to Derrida's *On Touching*.

Naas, Michael. "In and Out of Touch: Derrida's *Le toucher, Jean-Luc Nancy* (Galilée, 2000)." *Research in Phenomenology* 31 (2001): 258–65.

On the body

Garrido, Juan Manuel. "Jean-Luc Nancy's Concept of the Body." *Epoche: A Journal for the History of Philosophy* 14(1) (Fall 2009): 189–211.

O'Byrne, Anne. *Natality and Finitude*. Bloomington: Indiana University Press, 2010.

Shapiro, Gary. "Jean-Luc Nancy and the Corpus of Philosophy." In *Thinking Bodies*, ed. Juliet Flower MacCannell and Laura Zakarin. Stanford: Stanford University Press, 1994.

Sorial, Sarah. "Heidegger, Jean-Luc Nancy, and the Question of Dasein's Embodiment: An Ethics of Touch and Spacing." *Philosophy Today* 48(2) (Summer 2004): 216–30.

Spivak, Gayatri Chakravorty. "Response to Jean-Luc Nancy." In *Thinking Bodies*, ed. Juliet Flower MacCannell and Laura Zakarin. Stanford: Stanford University Press, 1994.

On community

Bernasconi, Robert. "On Deconstructing Nostalgia for Community within the West: The Debate between Nancy and Blanchot." *Research in Phenomenology* 23 (1993): 3–21.

Coward, Martin (ed.). "Being-with: Jean-Luc Nancy and the Question of Community." Special Issue of *Journal for Cultural Research* 9(4) (2005). Contains essays on myth, the Hegelian monarch, and Carl Schmitt.

Deppman, Jed. "Jean-Luc Nancy, Myth, and Literature." *Qui Parle* 10(2) (1992): 11–32.

Devisch, Ignaas. "The Sense of Being(-)With Jean-Luc Nancy." *Culture Machine* 8 (2006). www.culturemachine.net/index.php/ cm/article/view/36/44

James, Ian. "Naming the Nothing: Nancy and Blanchot on Community." *Culture, Theory and Critique* 51(2) (2010): 171–87.

Morin, Marie-Eve. "Putting Community under Erasure: The Dialogue between Jacques Derrida and Jean-Luc Nancy on the Plurality of Singularities." *Culture Machine* 8 (2006). www. culturemachine.net/index.php/cm/article/view/37/45

Norris, Andrew. "Jean-Luc Nancy and the Myth of the Common." *Constellations: An International Journal of Critical and Democratic Theory* 7(2) (June 2000): 272–95.

On politics, totalitarianism, and sovereignty

Armstrong, Philip. *Reticulations: Jean-Luc Nancy and the Networks of the Political*. Minneapolis: University of Minnesota Press, 2009.

Critchley, Simon. "Re-tracing the Political: Politics and Community in the Work of Philippe Lacoue-Labarthe and Jean-Luc Nancy." In *The Political Subject of Violence*, ed. David Campbell and Michael Dillon. Manchester: Manchester University Press, 1999.

Fraser, Nancy. "The French Derrideans: Politicizing Deconstruction or Deconstructing the Political?," *New German Critique* 33 (Fall 1984): 127–54.

Gratton, Peter. *The State of Sovereignty: Lessons from the Political Fictions of Modernity*. Albany: SUNY Press, 2012.

Hutchens, Benjamin. *Jean-Luc Nancy and the Future of Philosophy*. Montreal: McGill-Queens/Acumen, 2005.

Ingram, David. "The Retreat of the Political in the Modern Age: Jean-Luc Nancy on Totalitarianism and Community." *Research in Phenomenology* 18 (1998): 93–124.

Morin, Marie-Eve. "A Mêlée without Sacrifice: Nancy's Ontology of Offering against Derrida's Politics of Sacrifice." *Philosophy Today* 50, SPEP Supplement (2006): 139–43.

Readings, Bill. "The Deconstruction of Politics." In *Reading de Man Reading*, ed. Lindsay Waters and Wlad Godzich. Minneapolis: University of Minnesota Press, 1989. Response to Fraser's article above.

Wagner, Andreas. "Jean-Luc Nancy: A Negative Politics?" *Philosophy and Social Criticism* 32(1) (Jan. 2006): 89–109.

On art

Heikkila, Martta. *At the Limits of Presentation: Coming-into-Presence and Its Aesthetic Relevance in Jean-Luc Nancy's Philosophy*. Helsinki: University Printing House, 2007.

Kaplan, Louis and Ricco, John Paul. *Regarding Jean-Luc Nancy*. Special Issue of *Journal of Visual Culture* 9(1) (2010). Contains articles on the image as well as on film, photography, and drawing.

Ross, Alison. "'Art' in Nancy's 'First Philosophy': The Artwork and the Praxis of Sense Making." *Research in Phenomenology* 38(1) (2008): 18–40.

On writing and finitude

Luszczynska, Ana. "Nancy and Derrida: On Ethics and the Same (Infinitely Different) Constitutive Events of Being." *Philosophy and Social Criticism* 35(7) (2009): 801–21.

On exscription

Morin, Marie-Eve. "Thinking Things: Heidegger, Sartre, Nancy." *Sartre Studies International* 15(2) (Winter 2009): 35–53.

On Bataille and dialectics

Devisch, Ignaas. "The Disclosure of a Metaphysical Horizon, or How to Escape Dialectics." *South African Journal of Philosophy* 29(1) (2010): 17–27.

On justice and law

Hutchens, Benjamin (ed.). *Jean-Luc Nancy: Justice, Legality and World*. London: Continuum, 2012.

Other works cited

Agamben, Giorgio. *The Coming Community*, trans. Michael Hardt. Minneapolis: University of Minnesota Press, 1993.

Agamben, Giorgio. *Homo Sacer: Sovereign Power and Bare Life*, trans. Daniel Heller-Roazen. Stanford: Stanford University Press, 1998.

Agamben, Giorgio. *Remnants of Auschwitz*, trans. Daniel Heller-Roazen. New York: Zone Books, 1999.

Badiou, Alain. *The Communist Hypothesis*, trans. David Macey and Steve Corcoran. New York: Verso, 2010.

Badiou, Alain. *Metapolitics*, trans. Jason Barker. London: Verso, 2005.

Baugh, Bruce. *French Hegel: From Surrealism to Postmodernism*. New York: Routledge, 2003.

Birault, Henri. *De l'être, du divin et des dieux*. Paris: Éditions du Cerf, 2005.

Blanchot, Maurice. *The Unavowable Community*, trans. Pierre Joris. Barrytown: Station Hill Press, 1988.

Blanchot, Maurice. *The Infinite Conversation*, trans. Susan Hanson. Minneapolis: University of Minnesota Press, 1993.

Botting, Fred and Wilson, Scott (eds). *The Bataille Reader*. Oxford: Blackwell, 1997.

Derrida, Jacques. *Writing and Difference*, trans. Alan Bass. Chicago: The University of Chicago Press, 1978.

Derrida, Jacques. *Dissemination*, trans. Barbara Johnson. Chicago: The University of Chicago Press, 1981.

Derrida, Jacques. *Margins of Philosophy*, trans. Alan Bass. Chicago: The University of Chicago Press, 1982.

Derrida, Jacques. *Positions*, trans. Alan Bass. Chicago: The University of Chicago Press, 1982.

Derrida, Jacques. "Declarations of Independence," trans. Tom Keenan and Tom Pepper. *New Political Science* 7(1) (1986): 7–15.

Derrida, Jacques. *Limited Inc.*, trans. Samuel Weber et al. Evanston: Northwestern University Press, 1988.

Derrida, Jacques. "Force of Law: The 'Mystical Foundation of Authority.'" In *Deconstruction and the Possibility of Justice*, ed. David Gray Carlson, Drucilla Cornell, and Michel Rosenfeld. New York: Routledge, 1992.

Derrida, Jacques. *Given Time: I. Counterfeit Money*, trans. Peggy Kamuf. Chicago: The University of Chicago Press, 1994.

Derrida, Jacques. *Specters of Marx: The State of the Debt, the Work of Mourning, and the New International*, trans. Peggy Kamuf. New York: Routledge, 1994.

Derrida, Jacques. *The Gift of Death*, trans. David Wills. Chicago: The University of Chicago Press, 1995.

Derrida, Jacques. *Points . . . Interviews, 1974–1994*, ed. Elizabeth Weber. Stanford: Stanford University Press, 1995.

Derrida, Jacques. *Of Grammatology*, trans. Gayatri Chakravorty Spivak. Baltimore: The Johns Hopkins University Press, 1997.

Derrida, Jacques. *Politics of Friendship*, trans. George Collins. New York: Verso, 1997.

Derrida, Jacques. "Faith and Knowledge," trans. Samuel Weber. In *Religion*, ed. Jacques Derrida and Gianni Vattimo. Stanford: Stanford University Press, 1998.

Derrida, Jacques. *Rogues: Two Essays on Reason*, trans. Pascale-Anne Brault and Michael Naas. Stanford: Stanford University Press, 2005.

Derrida, Jacques. *Psyche: Inventions of the Other, Volume II*, ed. Peggy Kamuf and Elizabeth Rottenberg. Stanford: Stanford University Press, 2008.

Derrida, Jacques. *Voice and Phenomenon: Introduction to the Problem of the Sign in Husserl's Phenomenology*, trans. Leonard Lawlor. Evanston: Northwestern University Press, 2010.

Descartes, René. *Meditations on First Philosophy*, trans. Donald A. Cress. Indianapolis: Hackett, 1993.

Foucault, Michel. *The Order of Things: An Archaeology of the Human Sciences*. New York: Vintage Books, 1970.

Gasché, Rudolphe. *The Tain of the Mirror: Derrida and the Philosophy of Reflection*. Cambridge: Harvard University Press, 1988.

Greisch, Jean. "The Eschatology of Being and the God of Time in Heidegger." *International Journal of Philosophical Studies* 4(1) (1996): 17–42.

Guibal, Francis and Martin, Jean-Clet (eds). *Sens en tous sens, autour des travaux de Jean-Luc Nancy*. Paris: Galilée, 2004.

Hegel, G. W. F. *Philosophy of Mind: Encyclopedia of the Philosophical Sciences, Part III*, trans. William Wallace and A. V. Miller. Oxford: Oxford University Press, 1971.

Hegel, G. W. F. *Phenomenology of Spirit*, trans. A. V. Miller. Oxford: Oxford University Press, 1979.

Hegel, G. W. F. *Aesthetics: Lectures on Fine Art*, in two volumes, trans. T. M. Knox. Oxford: Oxford University Press, 1998.

Heidegger, Martin. *Being and Time*, trans. John Macquarrie and Edward Robinson. New York: Harper & Row, 1962.

Heidegger, Martin. *On the Way to Language*, trans. Peter D. Hertz. New York: Harper & Row, 1971.

Heidegger, Martin. *On Time and Being*, trans. Joan Stambaugh. New York: Harper & Row, 1972.

Heidegger, Martin. *Elucidations of Hölderlin's Poetry*, trans. Keith Hoeller. Amherst, NY: Humanity Books, 2000.

Heidegger, Martin. *Introduction to Metaphysics*, trans. Gregory Fried and Richard Polt. New Haven: Yale University Press, 2000.

Heidegger, Martin. *Contributions to Philosophy (From Enowning)*, trans. Parvis Emad and Kenneth Maly. Bloomington and Indianapolis: Indiana University Press, 2001.

Heidegger, Martin. *Identity and Difference*, trans. Joan Stambaugh. Chicago: The University of Chicago Press, 2002.

Heidegger, Martin. *Off the Beaten Tracks*, ed. and trans. Julian Young and Kenneth Haynes. Cambridge: Cambridge University Press, 2002.

Hill, Leslie. *Blanchot, Extreme Contemporary*. London: Routledge, 1997.

Kant, Immanuel. *Critique of Pure Reason*, trans. Werner S. Pluhar. Indianapolis: Hackett Publishing, 1996.

Lacoue-Labarthe, Philippe. *Heidegger, Art and Politics: The Fiction of the Political*, trans. Chris Turner. Malden, MA: Blackwell, 1990.

Lacoue-Labarthe, Philippe. *Typography: Mimesis, Philosophy, Politics*, trans. Christopher Fynsk. Stanford: Stanford University Press, 1998.

Lacoue-Labarthe, Philippe. *Heidegger and the Politics of Poetry*, trans. Jeff Fort. Evanston: University of Illinois Press, 2007.

Levinas, Emmanuel. *Totality and Infinity: An Essay on Exteriority*, trans. Alfonso Lingis. Pittsburgh: Duquesne University Press, 1969.

Levinas, Emmanuel. *Collected Philosophical Papers*, trans. Alfonso Lingis. Dordrecht: Martinus Nijhoff, 1987.

Levinas, Emmanuel. *God, Death, and Time*, trans. Bettina Bergo. Stanford: Stanford University Press, 2000.

Macdonald, Amanda. "Working Up, Working Out, Working Through: Translator's Notes on the Dimensions of Jean-Luc Nancy's Thought." *Postcolonial Studies* 6(1) (2003): 11–21.

Marx, Karl. *Economic and Philosophical Manuscripts of 1844*, trans. Martin Milligan. Moscow: Progress Publishers, 1974.

Marx, Karl. *Critique of Hegel's Philosophy of Right*, trans. Joseph O'Malley. Cambridge: Cambridge University Press, 1977.

Marx, Karl. *Capital: A Critique of Political Economy, Volume I*, trans. Samuel Moore and Edward Aveling. Moscow: Progress Publishers, 1986.

Naas, Michael. *Derrida: From Now On*. New York: Fordham University Press, 2008.

Nietzsche, Friedrich. *Twilight of the Idols and The Antichrist*, trans. Thomas Common. Mineola, NY: Courier Dover Publications, 2004.

Pascal, Blaise. *Pensées*, trans. W. F. Trotter. New York: E. P. Dutton, 1958.

Rancière, Jacques. *Disagreement: Politics and Philosophy*, trans. Julie Rose. Minneapolis: University of Minnesota Press, 1998.

Rancière, Jacques. "Introducing Disagreement." *Angelaki: Journal of the Theoretical Humanities* 9(3) (Dec. 2004): 3–9.

Richman, Michele. *Reading Georges Bataille: Beyond the Gift*. Baltimore: Johns Hopkins University Press, 1982.

Rousseau, Jean-Jacques. *On the Social Contract*, trans. Donald A. Cress. Indianapolis: Hackett Publishing, 1988.

Schrift, Alan D. *Twentieth-Century French Philosophy: Key Themes and Thinkers*. Malden, MA: Blackwell, 2006.

Stambaugh, Joan. *The Finitude of Being*. Albany: SUNY Press, 1992.

Tönnies, Ferdinand. *Community and Society*, trans. José Harris. Cambridge: Cambridge University Press, 2001.

Waters, Lindsay and Godzich, Wlad. *Reading de Man Reading*. Minneapolis: University of Minnesota Press, 1989.

Index